Markus Bayer, Oliver Schwarz, Toralf Stark (eds.)
Democratic Citizenship in Flux

Markus Bayer (Dr.) works as a senior researcher at the Bonn International Center for Conversion (BICC). He holds a Ph. D. in Political Science from the University of Duisburg-Essen. He is specialised in the fields of resistance studies, democratic transitions, peace and conflict studies, arms control and militarization.

Oliver Schwarz (Dr.) is a lecturer and researcher at the Institute of Political Science at the University of Duisburg-Essen. His research interests include the European integration and its effects on the member states, the EU enlargement and the external relations of the European Union.

Toralf Stark (Dr.) works as a researcher at the professorship for Comparative Politics at the Institute of Political Science at the University of Duisburg-Essen. His research focuses on the following areas: political culture and political attitudes, understanding of democracy and political participation.

Markus Bayer, Oliver Schwarz, Toralf Stark (eds.)

Democratic Citizenship in Flux

Conceptions of Citizenship in the Light of Political and Social Fragmentation

[transcript]

Bibliographic information published by the Deutsche Nationalbibliothek

The Deutsche Nationalbibliothek lists this publication in the Deutsche National-bibliografie; detailed bibliographic data are available in the Internet at http://dnb.d-nb.de

© 2021 transcript Verlag, Bielefeld

Cover layout: Maria Arndt, Bielefeld

Print-ISBN 978-3-8376-4949-9
PDF-ISBN 978-3-8394-4949-3
https://doi.org/10.14361/9783839449493

Contents

Citizenship in flux: Introduction and a conceptual approach

Markus Bayer, Oliver Schwarz and Toralf Stark

1. Introduction

The history of this edited volume is probably different from those of others. It dates back to 2012 when some early career researchers at the University of Duisburg-Essen dared the endeavour to bring together the expertise of Political Science and Sociology to study the foundations and consequences of the erosion of traditional models of legitimacy.[1] Such forms of collaboration between different disciplines of social sciences are still rare – even or especially at bigger faculties like ours in Duisburg. For most of the authors and editors that have been involved, this project was an important milestone for their career and an inspiring academic experience. The outcome, the edited volume »Legitimitätspraxis« (Practices of legitimacy) published by Springer VS in 2016, has been downloaded over 11.000. (Aug. 2020) times and can be regarded as an important contribution to the scientific debate on the concept of legitimacy (Lemke et al. 2016).

Some four years later, we decided that it is time for a revival. In times of Brexit, increasing worldwide migration movements and rising nationalism (not only) in Europe, we decided to deal with the important topic of »democratic citizenship« as the current debates on this concept are obviously »in flux«. However, we opted for some changes in the concept of this edited volume: First, we deemed it beyond argument that visibility is of great importance to young academics, the main target group of our call. Thus, we decided to publish an English edited volume in Open Access (OA). OA is not only a possibility to increase visibility and readership but also a form of publication that provides open access to knowledge to everyone beyond academic paywalls.

---

1   For more information, see: https://www.uni-due.de/legitimitaet/

In other words, it contributes to the democratisation of our knowledge and findings. The next innovation concerned the publishing procedure: A double-blind peer review, meaning that every contribution is evaluated independently and anonymously by two peer reviewers, currently represents the state of the art in terms of academic quality control and is therefore widely used in the academic community. Furthermore, publishing double-blind reviewed articles represents major achievements for young scholars. However, as such a procedure is not very common for edited volumes, this volume here is one of the few that implements such a rigorous form of quality control. Finally, we decided to extend the circle of contributors beyond researchers at the University of Duisburg-Essen with the aim to stimulate academic cooperation and the exchange between young researchers from different universities.

2.   Citizenship and democracy

Given its historical origin, the connection between citizenship and democracy is not surprising. The term citizenship was first used in ancient Greece. Since then, the meaning of citizenship was essentially contested and is in constant flux till today (Isin 2009). When Aristotle was confronted with the task of defining »citizen« at the beginning of Book III of his Politics, he described it as »a man who shares in the administration of judiciary and in the holding of office« (cf. Johnson 1984: 74). According to this, citizens must actively participate in judiciary and government. Therefore, it is not enough to simply enjoy the right to seek office, but citizens must actually hold it. Still, this is a very narrow conception of citizenship. Moreover, it is not an accurate description of democratic involvement in today's modern societies. Today, the possibilities for participation range from elections, participation in political parties or citizens' initiatives to joining demonstrations and political protest.

While political affiliation in the form of citizenship in ancient Greece was the exception and limited to the city-state and the able-bodied free men, nowadays it represents the norm and describes a relationship between the citizen and a nation state »in which the two are bound together by reciprocal rights and obligations« (Heywood 1994: 155). In that sense, the Aristotelian view on citizenship gives us a baseline to start from: to understand citizenship as a form of social relationship. However, as Bellamy (2008: 2) argues, citizenship is a special form of a social relationship, namely one between an individual and a state or a society. Firstly, it differs from everyday social relationships like friendships and family ties in as far as it is genuinely political. Beyond this, it also diverges from other forms of political affiliation, such as subjecthood in monarchies or dictatorships since it consists of *civil and political rights* – especially participation in the political process – which are not guaranteed in non-democracies. According to Marshall, citizenship thereby represents a »status bestowed on those who are full members of a community« with all bearers of the status being »equal with respect to the rights and duties with which the status is endowed« (Marshall 1950: 28). Although Marshall admits that there is no »universal principle that determines what those rights and duties shall be« (1950: 29), he concludes from his historical analysis in England that these rights and duties can be located in three different spheres. Individual *civil rights*, such as the freedom of the person, including freedom of speech, opinion and religion, and the right to own property, were granted by the state from the 18th century onwards. These individual civil rights were complemented by *political rights*, like the freedom of association and the right to vote in the 19th century and, eventually, by *social rights, for example the right to economic welfare and social security* in the 20th century (Turner 1986: 8).

Marshall's conception was criticised for being evolutionistic since it understands the development of citizenship rights as a historical progress towards full citizenship. Furthermore, with its focus on the process of granting a formal status and corresponding rights by the state, Marshall's theory therefore can be labelled as one-dimensional (Giddens 1982: 108). It has also been criticised for being unable to grasp the difference between passive (mere bearer of rights) and active citizen (Turner 1989; 1997) and for ignoring »second-class« citizen such as women or homosexuals (Walby 1994; Turner 2009), thereby disguising or omitting existing inequalities. Additionally, Mouffe (1992: 29) rightly argues that Marshall's definition of citizenship as »a set of rights that we hold against many others« is bound to a certain understanding of democracy, namely a liberal one. Authors from communitarian and republican traditions therefore often argued that citizenship is not only a legal status granted by the state, but also linked to an identity as citizen. This identity is thought to be bound to a set of democratic values which are quintessential for a democratic polity (Almond/Verba 1963; 1980).

Therefore, more advanced conceptions of citizenship tend to go beyond the narrow definition of citizenship, focussing on the legal status and the social, political and civil rights which go along with it and also address aspects of belonging (identity) and participation (Bellamy 2008). Furthermore, most authors accommodate that citizenship is not a static institution, but constantly »[mediates] rights between the subjects of politics and the polity to which these subjects belong« (Isin/Nyers 2014: 1). To grasp the increasing fluidity and manifoldness of different (non-)citizen statuses and the diversity of rights associated with them, scholars began to understand citizenship in terms of a social process, social practices or »enacted processes« which provided some stability and endurance to the concept and, at »the same time opened to reinvention and contingent rearticulations« (Nyers 2017: 118). This theoretical shift was largely influenced by the work of Bourdieu (1993) and his concepts of habitus, field and social capital.

3.   Status, habitus and practice

This very brief overview already illustrates that citizenship and in particular democratic citizenship is necessarily a concept in constant flux since the notion of a) democracy and b) the perception of who should be entitled to citizenship changes over time. Therefore, democratic citizenship is a political concept per se and as such always a matter of constant contestation. For a working definition we are building upon the aforementioned classical conception of citizenship, understanding it as a legal status which differentiates members and non-members of a polity. This requires some supplementary notes: First of all, we think it is important to mention the Janus face of citizenship: While it represents a mechanism of inclusion and an entitlement to certain rights on the one hand, it is at the same time also a mechanism of exclusion and discrimination on the other. Furthermore, in face of roughly 200 nation states worldwide, the nation state is currently clearly the main polity in terms of citizenship arrangements. However, in times of multilateralism and global governance, it is not the only political authority. We therefore want to follow Insin's tripartition of citizenship, which complements the notion of legal status with the aspects of acts and habitus of citizenship (2008; 2009).

Being intrigued by the various peculiarities of non-citizens in form of the foreigner, the migrant, the illegal alien, the wanderer, refugee, or émigré, Insin assumes non-citizens can perform »acts of citizenship« to claim certain rights they are formally not entitled to (2009: 383). This understanding brings in all the aforementioned subjects and thus overcomes the narrow focus limiting citizenship to citizens: Non-citizens can also claim rights, perform duties or perceive themselves as citizens.

Insin assumes that citizenship also comprises a certain habitus – a term borrowed from Bourdieu – which indicates habits that have been formed over a relatively long period to such an extent that they are taken for granted and repeated without much thinking or questioning. Participate in elections would be such a routine action explained by a habitus of citizenship. Together with acts of citizenship, it is the active part of citizenship which Turner (1997) demanded. Thus, a democratic habitus can be understood as a mediating element between the formal status and the singular act of citizenship. As outlined in Figure 1 below and we assume that democratic citizenship is coined by a status as citizen and a respective habitus. Furthermore, we assume that this status is not only granted top-down but also claimed bottom-up.

Figure 1: Ideal types of (democratic) citizenship

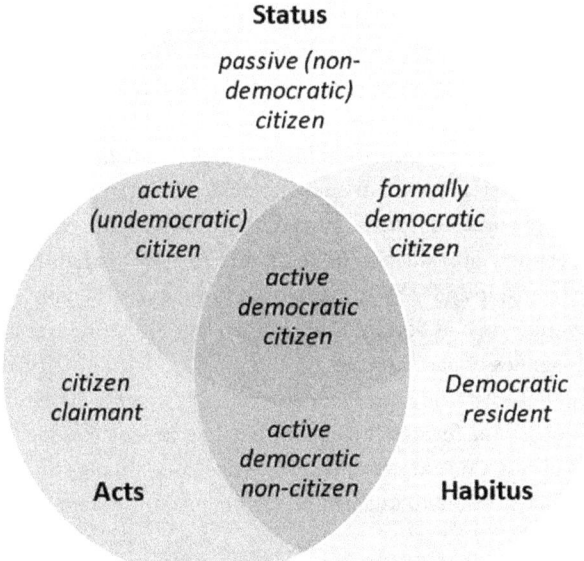

Source: Author's own compilation.

We presume seven different ideal types of democratic citizens that can be derived from the different combinations of status, habitus and actions. First, we can distinguish three clear-cut types:

- The *passive (non-democratic) citizen* who is entitled to civil, social and political rights by his status as a citizen of a democratic state. However, (s)he neither develops a democratic habitus to participate formally nor does (s)he participates in any informal practices to develop, deepen or defend democratic participation.
- Contrary, the *democratic resident* developed a democratic habitus. Without a citizen status, however, (s)he is formally not allowed to (fully) participate in the country of residence. (S)he does not attempt to change the situation.
- The *citizen claimant* differs with regard to the last aspect. (S)he has not developed a democratic habitus (yet), but is eager to achieve the status of citizenship including the respective rights that come along with it.

In addition, there are four additional mixed types:

- The *active democratic citizens*, building the core of our concept, enjoys the formal status of being a citizen and has developed a democratic habitus. Additionally, deeply rooted democratic values are driving the active democratic citizen to resort to non-formal civil acts to deepen and defend democracy.
- The *active democratic non-citizen* exhibits a democratic habitus and participates democratically without enjoying the formal status of citizenship.
- The *formally democratic citizen*, in contrast, possesses the citizen status in his/her country of residence. (S)he developed a certain habitus of democratic citizenship and is likely to take part in the routine actions of political participation such as voting. However, her/his actions do not go beyond formal avenues of participation.
- Last, but not least, the *active (undemocratic) citizen* enjoys all the rights that come along with formal citizenship but has never developed a democratic habitus. Contrary to his/her passive counterpart, however, (s)he uses his/her freedom to undermine the democratic system.

4.   Political and social fragmentation

The purpose of this edited volume is not to rewrite or update the concept of citizenship. Rather, we aim to (re)explore the challenges to democratic citizenship in times of worldwide political and social fragmentation. The term

»fragmentation« is used in a number of areas and academic disciplines, such as political science, sociology, economics, history and law. However, it was the international lawyer Jenks (1953: 403) who initially referred to two phenomena of fragmentation and its consequences: First, there is no general legislative body on the international level. Second, in the absence of such a world legislature, »law-making treaties are tending to develop in a number of historical, functional and regional groups which are separate from each other and whose mutual relationships are in some respects analogous to those of separate systems of municipal law.« About 60 years later, the International Law Commission (2006: 10) concluded: »There is little to be added to that analysis today.« Although the phenomenon of fragmentation has been a key concept in international legal scholarship for the past decades, scholars have struggled to agree on how to define the phenomenon in a way that accurately captures their concerns (Megiddo 2018: 118).

As Peters points out, the term »fragmentation« is used to denote both a process and a result. In fact, fragmentation is often used to capture such a vast array of phenomena that all of international law's development in the past century seems to be enveloped in it (2016: 1012). Increasingly, scholars of international relations and international economics also refer to the concept of fragmentation (Benvenisti/Downs 2007; Zürn/Faude 2013). Some of these authors conceptualise fragmentation in a broader socio-cultural sense, namely as the opposite of globalisation (Clark 1997; Sur 1997; Menzel 1998). However, fragmentation is not necessarily a negative development. Following this view, Biermann et al. (2009) differentiate between three types of fragmentation: synergistic fragmentation, cooperative fragmentation and conflictive fragmentation. By illustrating these concepts in the field of global climate governance, they show that different types of fragmentation are likely to have different degrees of performance. While cooperative forms of fragmentation may entail both significant costs and benefits, only the absence of coordination may lead to additional undesirable outcomes.

In the previous section, citizenship was defined as a special form of a social relationship between an individual and a state or a society. By and large, citizenship is enormously affected by the fragmentation of the three entities that make up democratic citizenship: the state, the society and the individuum. For centuries, democratic citizenship has been a distinct characteristic of the nation state only. However, the forces of political fragmentation have transformed modern statehood tremendously. The European integration process has deeply affected the relationship between member states and their citizens. Today, concepts of local, national and the EU citizenship exist side by side within the European Union. Consequently, this development has made democratic citizenship in the EU a multi-layered phenomenon (van Waarden/Seubert 2018: 5). On the other hand, the content of state sovereignty and the modes of government are not only transforming in Western Europe (Krasner 1999; Sørensen 2004). Worldwide, the paradigm of governance has shed a new perspective on democratic citizenship (Carter 2001; Kostakopou-lou 2008). During the last decades, international migration has increasingly challenged the notion of citizenship as an exclusive national concept. So far, current realities – like the growing numbers of citizens with multiple iden-tities and citizen statuses or the globalisation of citizenship – have been re-flected in concepts such as cosmopolitan (Hutchings/Dannreuther 1999), glo-bal (O'Byrne), transnational (Bauböck 1994) or transborder citizenship (Glick Schiller/Fouron 2001: 25).

Processes of fragmentation are also affecting individuals and their social communities around the world. Societies are becoming more and more com-plex, dynamic, and diverse every day (Touraine 2003). Public organisations, companies and individuals are experiencing that current challenges cannot be resolved in the same manner as they were in the past. Some argue that a »glo-bal risk society« (Beck 2000) has emerged and new forms of non-hierarchical relationships between state and non-state actors play a growing role. These new relationships reshape the social contract between the state and its citi-zens and provide space for new global power structures. Extra-parliamentary popular resistance, refusing to adhere to the politics of the count on the one hand and populist movements disclosing their distrust against political elites on the other, challenge the existing relations between representational demo-cracy and its citizens. The »neurotic citizen« (Isin 2004) emerges, who governs itself to responses to anxieties and uncertainties. In addition, the growing so-cial mobilisation of individuals and intensified international migration have produced new spaces of democracy (Pugh 2009). Recently, several countries have been witnessing an era of political polarisation, thus indicating a possi-ble crisis of representational democracy (Brennan 2017; Levitsky/Ziblatt 2018; Mounk 2018). This raises fundamental questions about the very essence of citizenship and gave the impulse to this edited volume.

5.   Structure and rationale of the volume

This volume analyses democratic citizenship in flux. It reflects on recent conceptions of citizenship in the light of political and social fragmentation. The volume aims to bring together insights from different disciplines, such as political science, sociology, law and history. However, the predominant represented discipline remains political science. Nevertheless, the choice of authors of the chapters responds to the aim to ensure a twofold overall balance: First, a balance between different methodological approaches. As such, a one-sided perspective on citizenship generates a limited set of insights only. We therefore strived for a diversification of research methods used in the contributions to our volume. Authors use both qualitative and quantitative approaches, which are both complementary to each other when studying democratic citizenship. Second, there is a balance between female and male scientists. Arguably the most important measure to promote gender equality in science is an open door for female scientists at all levels. Consequently, 50 percent of the authors involved in this volume are female.

The chapters in this volume cover a variety of recent developments like the emergence of a transnational citizenship within the European Union, asylum and migration, the rise of populism, increasing polarisation and the challenging of representative democracy in Western Europe. These issues are examined in the context of different formations of status, habitus and actions of democratic citizenship.

The volume consists of three major parts. The *first part* investigates democratic citizenship in the European Union and starts with a historical

and institutionalist perspective to outline the evolution of modern citizenship rights. This contribution by Christian Tischmeyer focuses in particular on the historical observation that citizenship has served as a method of exclusion for the modern nation state. Tischmeyer argues that citizenship and biopolitical selectivity are inimically tied up with notions of collective identity and chauvinistic nationalism. His chapter concludes with a reflection on how to situate the institutional rationales of democratic citizenship within nation states between the extreme points of safeguarding against discrimination, versus an exclusive set of state-granted privileges, perfectly suited for discrimination on nationalistic grounds.

This institutionalist approach to citizenship is followed by a quantitative empirical analysis of citizenship in a supranational organization, namely the EU. In his chapter, Oliver Schwarz analyses the public perception of EU citizenship in its local setting and thereby tackles the problem of multiple and competing forms of citizenship on different levels. His main point of interest is to explore the extent to which EU citizens' knowledge about their rights is accompanied by a positive public perception of European Union citizenship. For this purpose, the chapter first explores the development of EU citizenship and the relationship between citizenship and democracy in a European context. Then, the chapter presents findings of a face-to-face survey of 425 local residents in Duisburg, Germany. On the basis of the analysis, he finally formulates specific policy recommendations about how to vitalise the link between local citizens and the EU.

In a similar way, Aukje van Loon addresses the EU and the question to what extent the national citizen can influence his or her government position within the superior supranational entity. Using the case of the introduction of a European financial transaction tax, she applies a societal approach to governmental preference formation and analyses a broad range of stakeholders potentially affected by the introduction of such a tax (sectoral interest associations, trade unions, voters and NGOs). Her qualitative analysis concludes that the German government clearly followed dominant domestic ideas during the European debate.

Concluding the first part, Kathrin Behrens deals with the concept of formal citizenship in its legal dimension through a constitutional analysis of 27 European member states. She discusses the inclusion and exclusion of people in societal subsystems and the relevance of constitutional regulation of insiders and outsiders based on the systems theory. By analysing constitutional documents, her chapter shows that formalised membership via constitutionally organised citizenship to a state does not follow uniform trends in all its facets. Formal inclusion and exclusion are two dimensions that go hand in hand. Citizenship seems to be a fluid, dynamic political construction that is surprisingly only minutely finalised in constitutions. The impression suggests itself that citizenship is a very dynamic mechanism of inclusion and exclusion, which is why constitutions serve as too stable constructs to capture this important aspect of modern societies in its formal-legal dimension.

The *second part* of the book deals with the nexus between citizenship and migration. In the first chapter of this part, Feyza Yildirim Sungur, together with Oliver Schwarz, focuses in her analysis on the implications of dual citizenship in the context of political participation opportunities in more than one country, namely dual citizenship for Turkish citizens living in Germany. Their analysis focuses particularly on the German migration and integration policy and the diaspora engagement policy of Turkey. The main argument is that transnational political involvement of Turkish migrants in Germany is shaped by Germany's late-coming self-definition as a country of immigration and by Turkey's recent progressive diaspora policy. Based on the study of the participation in German and Turkish polls, the authors conclude: Dual citizenship seems to be beneficial for the increase of the political participation of people with a Turkish migration background in Germany.

Thorsten Schlee's chapter deals with the differential inclusion of the asylum seekers and refugees in Germany. Schlee exemplifies the concept of differential inclusion in current changes in German asylum and immigration law and thereby further disaggregates citizenship on the national level. Based on case studies in German labour and public order administrations, the chapter demonstrates that despite processes of Europeanisation, the German labour market remains nationally bounded and regulated. The growing efforts in migration and integration management follow a logic of optimising the processes of the population. This kind of bio-political rationality aims at economic benefits rather than democratic legitimation.

The chapter concludes with the contribution of Lea Rzadtki, who introduces a critical citizen's perspective. Based on a constructivist grounded theory exploration of immigrant rights activism in Hamburg, it aims at closing gaps in the conceptualization of non-citizens' struggles over citizenship. By relying on insights from feminist, post-colonial and black theories, the chapters conclusions are twofold: First, in many groups, non-citizens struggle together with citizens, creating new dimensions in conceptualizing citizenship. Second, the general debate is rather focused on disruptive activities on the one hand and pro-refugee volunteering on the other hand, while the multitude of everyday politics within activist groups is not captured.

The *third and final part* of the book discusses individual perceptions of citizenship and how these effects the democratic constitution of modern societies. Carsten Wegscheider and Rula Nezi examine European citizens' notions of national and EU citizenship and their political and societal implications. In their analysis, they use data from the European Values Study covering 20 member states of the European Union. Their empirical results confirm the importance of political identity in supporting restrictions on the conditions for acquiring citizenship. While political identity determines the support or rejection of national and European restrictions on citizenship, social liberal values and anti-immigration attitudes are also very important factors. Furthermore, the results suggest that both notions of European citizenship are comparatively more inclusive to their national counterparts, although the degree of inclusiveness is based on the distinction between the ethnic and civic dichotomy.

Last but not least, Merve Schmitz-Vardar explores socio-psychological determinants of individual critical-liberal desire for democracy in 20 member states of the European Union. The data for her analysis stem also from the European Social Survey. The aim of her chapter is to answer the question how including and excluding ideas of identity, trust and belonging affect the democratic value orientation of European citizens. Based on a series of OLS regressions and on the theoretical foundations of social identity theory, social threat theory and group-based enmity, the results show that nationalism does not favour democratic value orientation on its own. Particularly when analysing the interplay of resentment towards immigrants, trust in supposed foreign groups and democratic value orientation, it becomes clear that, depending on the national context, these can benefit each other. Here, other marginalised groups are often used as a pretext for hostility towards others.

We, the editors, have dispensed with the usual practice of closing this volume with an additional summary of the main findings. We believe that each contribution stands for itself and speaks for itself.

6.   Acknowledgements

The whole endeavour would not have been possible without the help of many different people. First, we would like to thank Prof. Dr. Michael Kaeding, the Vice Dean for Research and Early Career Scientists of the Faculty for Social Sciences of the University of Duisburg-Essen. He supported our project right from the start and helped to provide it with the necessary funding for the publication. Further, we are indebted to Katrin Falkenstein-Feldhoff, appointee for OA at our university library, who did not only provide further funds to cover the OA fees but also helped with her immense knowledge. We are also indebted to the team of our publisher transcript, especially Anne Sauerland and Johanna Tönsing, who were extremely supportive in every step of the process. Furthermore, we would like to thank Ingetraud Fischer and Julia Nachtigall, who helped us to navigate the jungle of administration and accounting, thus making it possible to avoid several bureaucratic pitfalls on the way. Of course, we owe thanks to the authors for their contributions and taking this journey with us. We, the three editors, contributed to chapters but also reviewed the chapters with a number of external reviewers, namely Dr. Petra Ahrens (Tampere University), Dr. Felix Bethke (Peace Research Institute Frankfurt), Dr. Simone Castellani (University Institute of Lisbon), Dr. Dannica Fleuß (Helmut Schmidt University), Dr. Martin Gross (Ludwig Maximilian University of Munich), Dr. Sebastian Heidebrecht (University of Vienna), Sven Hilgers (University of Hagen), Dr. Ulf Kemper (University of Münster), Dr. Elitsa Kortenska (University of Leiden), Dr. Daniel Lambach (Goethe University Frankfurt), Dr. Christoph Mohamad-Klotzbach (University of Würzburg), Dr. Marek Neuman (University of Groningen), Dr. Norma Osterberg-Kaufmann (Humboldt University of Berlin), Dr. Christine Unrau (Centre for Global Cooperation Research), Prof. Dr. Wim van Meurs (Radboud University), Dr. Daniel Witte (University of Bonn), Dr. Taylan Yildiz (NRW School of Governance) and Prof. Dr. Pieter Zwaan (Radboud University). Additionally, we have to thank Jan Schilling from the Technical University Dortmund who helped to improve every contribution with his careful language editing. After all, we owe much to Carla Cingil who helped us tremendously in getting the chapters finally organised.

References

Almond, Gabriel A./Verba, Sidney (1963): The Civic Culture. Political Attitudes and Democracy in Five Nations, Princeton: SAGE Publications.

Almond, Gabriel A./Verba, Sidney (1980): The Civil Culture Revisited, Boston/Toronto: Little Brown.

Bauböck, Rainer (1994): Transnational Citizenship. Membership and Rights in International Migration, Cheltenham/Northhampton: Edward Elgar Publishing.

Beck, Ullrich (2000): What is Globalization? Cambridge: Polity Press.

Bellamy, Richard (2008): Citizenship: A Very Short Introduction. Vol. 192. New York: Oxford University Press.

Benvenisti, Eyal/Downs, George W. (2007): The Empire's New Clothes: Political Economy and the Fragmentation of International Law. Stanford Law Review 2. 595-632.

Biermann, Frank/Pattberg, Philipp/van Asselt, Harro/Zelli, Fariborz (2009): The Fragmentation of Global Governance Architectures: A Framework for Analysis. Global Environmental Politics 4, 14-40. https://doi:10.1162/glep.2009.9.4.14

Bourdieu, Pierre (1993): Sociology in Question. London: Sage.

Brennan, Jason (2017): Against Democracy. Princeton University Press.

Carter, April (2001): The Political Theory of Global Citizenship, New York: Routledge.

Clark, Ian (1997): Globalization and Fragmentation, Oxford: Oxford University Press.

Giddens, Anthony. (1982): A Reply to my Critics. Theory, Culture & Society 1.2: 107-113.

Glick Schiller, Nina/Fouron, Georges Eugene (2001): Georges Woke Up Laughing. Long-Distance Nationalism and the Search for Home, Durham/London: Duke University Press.

Heywood, Andrew (1994): Political Ideas and Concepts. An Introduction, New York: St. Martin's Press.

Hutchings, Roland/Dannreuther, Kimberley (eds.) (1999): Cosmopolitan Citizenship, New York: St. Martin's Press.

International Law Commission (2006): Fragmentation of International Law: Difficulties Arising from the Diversification and Expansion of International Law, Geneva: United Nations.

Isin, Engin F. (2004): The Neurotic Citizen. Citizenship Studies 3: 217-235.

Isin, Engin F. (2008): Theorizing Acts of Citizenship, In: Engin F. Isin/Greg M. Nielsen (eds.), Acts of Citizenship, London: Palgrave Macmillan, 15-43.

Isin, Engin F. (2009): Citizenship in Flux: The Figure of the Activist Citizen. Subjectivity 29: 367-388.

Isin, Engin F./Nyers, Peter (2014): Globalizing Citizenship Studies, In: Engin F. Isin/Nyers, Peter (eds.), Routledge Handbook of Global Citizenship Studies, London/New York: Routledge, 1-11.

Jenks, C. Wilfried (1953): The Conflict of Law-Making Treaties. British Yearbook of International Law 30: 401-453.

Johnson, Curtis (1984): Who Is Aristotle's Citizen? Phronesis 1: 73-90. https://doi:10.1163/156852884X00193

Kostakopoulou, Dora (2008): The Future Governance of Citizenship. Cambridge University Press.

Krasner, Stephen D. (1999): Sovereignty. Organised Hypocrisy, Princeton: Princeton University Press.

Lemke, Matthias/Schwarz, Oliver/Stark Toralf/Weissenbach, Kristina (eds.) (2016): Legitimitätspraxis. Politikwissenschaftliche und soziologische Perspektiven. Wiesbaden: Springer VS.

Levitsky, Steven/Ziblatt, Daniel (2018): How Democracies Die. What History Reveals About Our Future, New York: Penguin Random House.

Marshall, Thomas H. (1950): Citizenship and Social Class and Other Essays, Cambridge: University Press.

Megiddo, Tamar (2018): Beyond Fragmentation: On International Laws Integrationist Force. Yale Journal of International Law 1. 115-147.

Menzel, Ulrich (1998): Globalisierung versus Fragmentierung, Frankfurt: Suhrkamp.

Mouffe, Chantal (1992): Citizenship and Political Identity. The Identity in Question 61: 28-32.

Mounk, Yascha (2018): The People vs. Democracy. Why Our Freedom Is in Danger and How to Save It, Cambridge/London: Harvard University Press.

Nyers, Peter (2017): Citizenship and an International Political Sociology, In: Xavier Guillaume/Pinar Bilgin (eds.), Routledge Handbook of International Political Sociology, London/New York: Routledge, 115-124.

Peters, Anne (2016): Fragmentation and Constitutionalism, In: Anne Orford/Florian Hoffmann/Martin Clark (eds.), The Oxford Handbook of the Theory of International Law, Oxford University Press: Oxford, 1011-1031.

Pugh, Jonathan (2009): What Are the Consequences of the ›Spatial Turn‹ for How We Understand Politics Today? A Proposed Research Agenda. Progress in Human Geography 5: 579-586. https://doi:10.1177/030913250 8099795

Sørensen, Georg (2004): The Transformation of the State. Beyond the Myth of Retreat, Basingstoke: Palgrave Macmillan.

Sur, Serge (1997): The State between Fragmentation and Globalization. European Journal of International Law 3: 421-434. https://doi:10.1093/oxfordjo urnals.ejil.a015591

Touraine, Alain (2003): Sociology Without Societies. Current Sociology 2: 123-131. https://doi:10.1177/0011392103051200S

Turner, Bryan S. (2009): T. H. Marshall, Social Rights and the English National Identity. Citizenship Studies 1: 65-73. https://doi:10.1080/13621020802586 750

Turner, Bryan S. (1997): Citizenship Studies: A General Theory. Citizenship Studies 1: 5-18. https://doi:10.1080/13621029708420644

Turner, Bryan S. (1989): Outline of a Theory of Citizenship. Sociology 2. 189-217. https://doi:10.1177/0038038590024002002

Turner, Bryan S. (1986): Personhood and Citizenship. Theory, Culture & Society 3.1: 1-16. https://doi:10.1177/0263276486003001002

van Waarden, Frans/Seubert, Sandra (2018): Introduction: Being a Citizen in Europe, In: Sandra Seubert/Marcel Hoogenboom/Trudie Knijn/Sybe de Vries/Frans (eds.), Moving Beyond Barriers. Prospects for EU Citizenship, Cheltenham/Northhampton: Edward Elgar Publishing, 3-25.

Walby, Sylvia (1994): Is Citizenship Gendered? Sociology 2: 379-395. https://doi:10.1177/0038038594028002002

Zürn, Michael/Faude, Benjamin (2013): On Fragmentation, Differentiation, and Coordination, In: Global Environmental Politics 3: 119-130.

Exclusive citizenship as basis for chauvinistic nationalism
A historical institutionalist perspective on the ruling rationales of liberal regimes

Christian Tischmeyer

1. Introduction

»[I]f you believe you're a citizen of the world, you're a *citizen of nowhere*. You don't understand what the very word ›citizenship‹ means« (May 2016). With the speech this quote is taken from (I became aware of it through the eponymous book by Marsili/Milanese 2018), then recent British Prime Minister May denounces »too many people in positions of power«, whom she finds too cosmopolitan, for a lack of national identification. She blames unpatriotic elites to collaborate with foreigners, employing EU and other supra-national organisations for their egoistic schemes to avoid contributing to British society. Thereby they are betraying »the spirit of citizenship« and consequently the ordinary Brit. May promises to end this situation by strengthening government intervention. She portrays state agency, equal citizenship and collective national identity as mutually dependent.

May's speech mirrors the fashionable ›my country first‹ rhetoric and increasing awareness of continuous migration and global connectivity, posited against national interest. As she is Prime Minister of *the* European, liberal democracy, I consider her statement a very pointed illustration of the discourse I want to analyse. Are we witnessing a turning point in the political discourse on citizenship, a renunciation of an inclusive, liberal understanding, in favour of an exclusive, nationalistic one?

Seen from a historical perspective, the answer is *no*. When looking at genesis and development of modern citizenship, it becomes clear that citizenship has always been exclusionary. The problem with this is mainly one of claim versus reality. The inclusion of a defined group through exclusion of everybody else may be considered the basic function of all groups which organise beyond face-to-face level (Barth 1970). However, this does not sit well with the emancipatory claims of liberal constitutions. Especially identitarian exaltations of citizenship (creating unity among citizens by denigrating others) contradict an inclusive and liberating self-conception of modern societies, which is said to find its expression in the status of democratic citizenship (Linz/Stepan 1996: 28; Menke 2015: 35; Przeworski 1995: 34). So, in this paper, I want to explicate the connection between those two elements of citizenship. How does the potential for liberation and emancipation relate to the instrument of exclusion?

The historical-institutional analysis shows that the contradiction between inclusive claim and exclusionary reality is only superficial. Tracing the historical development of modern citizenship clarifies its function for modern political systems (cf. Menke 2015: 11; Migdal 2001). From this perspective, citizenship is an administrative status, a political institution of unmediated, modern state rule. In this light, the current debate on legal inclusion and its political implications is a continuation of one of the foundational discussions on constitutional regimes in general, and democracies in particular (Linz/Stepan 1996: 28).

I will argue that the formal status of citizen allows for nationalistic exaltation of citizenship as primary identity. May's initial quote invokes the idea of citizenship as fateful belonging to a nation. In his chapter, Schlee (2020) points out how non-citizens are subjected to biopolitical selectivity. But as citizens are much more vital for political institutions, one should expect them to be accordingly more targeted by such biopolitical rationales (cf. Menke's 2015: 287-95 reading of Foucault). Through my institutional analysis, I intend to show to what extent exclusion is inherent to the dominating rationales of liberal democracies. To do so, I will sketch the evolution of modern citizenship rights. In the first part, I will briefly elaborate on my approach, to then argue for the function citizenship fulfils in electoral regimes. This will connect to the general rationales of liberal rule, some of which shall be outlined using critical theory of Foucault and Marx. Afterwards, I will position nationalism within these logics, leading to the final discussion of aspects of self-discipline within liberal institutions. I argue that the biopolitical selectivity applied to non-citizens shapes the institution of citizenship insofar as it supports nationalistic chauvinism.

Before going into the analysis, I will make a final remark on the theoretical position that I will take, in reference to Isin's (2009) concept of citizenship, which has a guiding function for this volume. To analyse the political design of citizenship in liberal mass-democracies, I will focus on the legal, or administrative, status of full citizenship.

2.   A historically grounded perspective

What is citizenship? In his influential lecture, Marshall (1950: 8) understands citizenship as »full membership of a community«[1]. Przeworski (1995: 43) also takes this point of departure and adds that »[m]odern citizenship entails a bundle of predictable and enforceable rights and obligations for every member of the political community«. Going one step further, Linz and Stepan (1996: 28) infer the political institution of the state in defining who is citizen. Almost in line with the initial quote by May, they argue: »Without a state, there can be no citizenship; without citizenship, there can be no democracy« (Linz/Stepan 1996: 28). Empirical operationalisation of citizenship points into this direction as well. Despite a variety of existing approaches, Pammett (2016: 1-2) finds the three elements, »rights, identity and participation« as crucial dimensions of citizenship. All three specify the relationship between the designated individual (citizen) and the political community. While partially going beyond, all aspects centre on the legal status[2]. In summary, it seems uncontroversial that citizenship denotes the relationship of full membership that certain persons (citizens) have in the political community. In modernity, this community is framed by the state – typically called the nation. It is a status of accumulated, specifiable rights which entail both negative protection from and participati-

---

1   Marshall (1950: 10) separates three dimensions of citizenship along a historical »evolution« of the concept through »civil, political and social« rights. While it is clear that notions of rights have expanded throughout the centuries, one can defer political and social rights from the same basic ideas as civil rights – they are at least compatible, if not already inherent (cf. Menke 2015: 222-25). Marshall (1950: 14) also suggests to follow the separation of »three elements of citizenship« not too rigorously.

2   For example, they elaborate that identity means the »citizens‹ orientations and attitudes as members of a political community« (Pammett 2016: 2), both towards official position-holders within the state apparatus and their fellow citizens. Thus, it presents the overarching frame of that relationship

on rights within a state. Thus, citizenship is most meaningful in an electoral regime.

As mentioned in the introduction, Isin's (2009) idea of citizenship is distinct from my theoretical position. To him, citizenship is a much broader concept; anybody who claims rights in any community (thereby making statements how one relates to members and non-members of that group) is engaging in citizenship. While this is useful in other investigations on citizenship, e.g. how non-citizens can overcome their principal exclusion (cf. Rzadtki's 2020 chapter in this volume), I will use the concept narrowly, denoting the relation that full members have towards the modern state.

A »historical institutionalist« approach (following Migdal 2001: 246-55) can trace the origin of political practices, specifically the development of their underlying rationales (cf. Tischmeyer 2018: 8-9). In this way, it is similar to a Marxist notion of critique (cf. Menke 2015: 11; 170-171). Especially the historical institutionalist approach is based on the premise that political regimes are shaped by specific histories which still frame present politics. Institutions, broadly understood as continuous structuring patterns of routine behaviour, are the very link between historical developments and individual behaviour (Giddens 1985: 11-12; Migdal 2001: 246). While already pragmatic decisions of individual actors lead to the routinisation of relations, it is especially organisations that purposefully pursue routine interaction in order to lower costs of continuous relations. As expectations are specified and options narrowed down, behaviour is increasingly predictable; order is installed. Thus, processes of institutionalisation are intimately linked to the establishment of continuous power relations (Giddens 1985: 11-12); even when not directly backed by sanctions. At the very least, institutions serve as guidelines how to imagine a *normal* course of action and what to imagine at all (Migdal 2001: 246). While individual preferences how to act are massively shaped by institutions, human actions determine institutions vice versa (Giddens 1985: 11-12; Migdal 2001: 246).

I take citizenship as a fundamental political institution of liberal, electoral regimes. This institution was created through bourgeois revolutions (cf. Menke 2015), namely in USA and France, and adapted in later constitutions following these examples. Such institutions have a functional and a cultural side (Migdal 2001: 255-62). By focussing on the former, I aim to show the consequences on the latter. As has been mentioned introductorily, citizenship is charged with dimensions of identity. Concomitant to this, the history of achieving citizenship rights is also idealised. However, uncritically applauding past revolutions and constitutions means to outright deny the authoritative positing of a specific order – especially the ignorance towards alternative options. This idealisation also has a certain kind of ›solemn‹ element to it. After all, as even critics acknowledge (Marx 1976 [1843]: 356), bourgeois constitutions do present crucial steps towards liberation from earlier, more despotic regimes. However, as historians (Mann 1993), theoreticians of the state (Giddens 1985, Migdal 2001), and political philosophers (Foucault 2008; Menke 2015) agree, citizenship rights were gradually granted by the ones in power – albeit under pressure ›from below‹. To understand citizenship rights in their historical continuity means to see them as functional adaptations to the ruling rationales of modernising regimes.

3.   Citizenship as political institution, functional to state rule

To ground citizenship in historical perspective, one has to be aware that liberal democracies are systems of rule. The claim to authority is no weaker than in autocracies, it is just different in its specifics. In this part, I will outline some of these rationales, considering three interrelated aspects. I will structure the chapter roughly along the historical development of statehood during the formative period of institutions of modern rule, i.e. rule in liberal mass-democracies. Doing this, I will consider influential criticisms of capitalistic societies of mass-production and increasing mass-consumption by Marx and Lenin. I will devote special attention to Foucault's concept of biopolitics. Following Menke (2015: 287-95), Marx and Foucault present very different critiques of liberal regimes. Marx' critique is based on the de facto inequality of formally equal members of society, and consequently class-based exploitation. On the other hand, Foucault's critique targets the institutions of rule, specifically how domination is installed through self-discipline when interacting with or participating within authoritative institutions. I seek to combine those two critiques.

In the process of political modernisation to unmediated, central state rule, the populace was no longer just the object of rulers, but emerging to demand participation. Modernising regimes successfully channelled the political voices of the masses into national representative institutions (Mann 1993: 252; Marsili/Milanese 2018: 48). Its staffing was decided on in public elections, with suffrage continuously expanding, until it comprised the vast majority of the population (Hobsbawm 2000: 83; Marshall 1950: 20). This is only consistent with the move to direct rule. Historical accounts show that representative institutions have already been critical to pre-modern regimes to foster compliance within the groups they depended upon (Giddens 1985; Mann 1993). As modern states depend on mass-compliance, broad segments of the population are now integrated into the representation mechanisms.

As Giddens (1985: 206) puts it, rights were granted as concessions to compensate for deeper intrusion of the state into societal life. As the Ancient Régime first incorporated the grand bourgeoisie, property guarantees were codified before the protection of liberty (Mann 1993: 247-52). Gradually those protection and participation rights were expanded in substance and reach to compose the contemporary ›bundle‹ of citizenship rights (cf. Marshall 1950). In line with continuous extension of suffrage, universal civil liberties might also be seen as gradually inflated rights of the grand bourgeoisie (Williams 1984: 126). From this perspective, mass-democracy can be regarded rather as quantitative expansion of the citizen group than the new quality of a constitutional state.

Menke (2015) also sees the seminal codification of property rights as precedent for all modern rights, including citizenship rights. These subjective rights are framed as »natural or pre-political« (Menke 2015: 210; my translation). He recapitulates John Locke, who frames property as continuation of the free will of the individual. Hence, any regulation of property is understood as intrusion into the personal sphere (Menke 2015: 213). As Foucault (2008) argues, this aversion to directly intervene into individual affairs, however, did not mean that political authorities reduced their activities. On the contrary, under the banner of a lean or »frugal« state, government activity was ever increasing. According to Foucault, this is because liberal government concerns itself with the welfare of the people. This general orientation, as well as the more specific rationales applied by political actors to that end, are what he calls biopolitics. At the same time stands the realisation that government cannot directly produce societal wealth, but has to rely on the market to drive its production.

Thus, a *successful* government effectively creates the conditions under which the population thrives – measured by a range of pre-determined indicators. This means to enable the individuals who compose the population to utilise the granted freedoms (e.g. those of the market, but also political freedoms of discussion and expression; Foucault 2008: 63). In practice, however, this enablement requires to respond to all kinds of threats to the foundational freedom of liberal regimes. Foucault (2008: 66) deduces that in liberalism,

»individuals are constantly exposed to danger, or rather, they are conditioned to experience their situation, their life, their present, and their future as containing danger«. Thus, liberal government not only becomes immensely active, but also engages in a paradox (or dialectical) relationship to freedom. It attempts to enable individual freedom by limiting the general decision space (Foucault 2008: 64)[3]. In other words, it is generally acknowledged that free agency may well constitute a threat to the freedom of others. Therefore, to become a subject in (or of) a liberal order means to waive political agency[4].

Marx (1976 [1843]) also criticises the authoritative positing of a specific order in and through liberalism. To him (Marx 1976 [1843]: 366), the very process of the declaration of rights is opposed to collective political action. He considers it baffling that at the very moment of successful collective political (bourgeois) revolution, the principle of individual, private enclosure is solemnly endorsed. Even more so, the revolution is declared to serve this very individualistic aim. The reason is a decision to establish the societal model of the bourgeois state as absolute[5]. The bourgeoisie de-politicises the preconditions of their rule by denying that those are consciously set conditions (Marx 1976 [1843]: 354). This does not only mean to avoid political regulation of the bases of their power – property, education etc.[6] – but also to pronounce difference instead of community within non-national characteristics, e.g. religion (Marx 1976 [1843]: 356). Only in this fashion may the national state establish itself as the general or common characteristic, while all other dimensions of social life are regarded as individual traits. To Marx, the result of this is a societal development shaped by commodification and estrangement.

Summarising the two critiques, both qualify idealistic claims of bourgeois emancipation, but Foucault and Marx offer different readings of the limits of

---

3   One of Foucault's (2008) examples are policies to protect the domestic economy from free trade via tariffs, so that it can develop ›freely‹.

4   While I put this here in definite, abstract terms, Foucault (2008: 313) clarifies that there is a constant process of weighing different interests at play – a process known as politics.

5   Menke (2015: 8-10) finds this too simple and delivers a ›critique of rights‹ based on real-existing liberal regimes‹ ignorance towards the continuous process of codifying rights out of acclaimed ›natural‹ or non-legal matter. While very rich in theoretical references, his argument emphasises the dialectics of freedom mentioned in the paragraph above, with reference to Foucault (2008: 64).

6   Thereby, bourgeois regimes rely on private governance of such goods, however critical they are deemed for the effective exercise of citizenship, as Przeworski (1995: 43) argues.

citizenship in liberal regimes. Foucault analyses that and how the subject of liberalism is dominated by the political order. Marx, on the other hand, states that the order is designed in order to allow for ›pre-political‹ privilege of property and education to manifest. Rights are stylised as personal possessions, because they have been designed as additional asset of the bourgeoisie. In order to sustain this class rule, nationality is posited as *the* dividing line between people (of e.g. same class or religion; Marx 1976 [1843]: 354). To clarify matters, in this context Marx criticises national entitlement, not citizenship – seeing that in his days only a minority of nationals were citizens. I will clarify the connection of nationality and citizenship subsequently.

4. Equal citizens, unequal humans

The concessions to an empowered mass as described above have one major implication: the citizenship status becomes much more meaningful (Noiriel 1994: 83, 306; Torpey 2000: 121). Simply put, in electoral polities the question arises: Who is part of the citizenry? Who possesses the citizenship rights to participate in the state's decision-making? The nation is the abstract answer to this question. In this chapter, I will first deliver a terminological clarification of the term nation and then relate it to citizenship. I will outline the exclusive and often violent history of establishing citizenship in the modern nation-state before pointing out its relevance for contemporary democracies.

The historical context of nationalism – promoting a nation – also lies in expanded state activity and the consequent political modernisation (Tischmeyer 2018: Chapter 4). Through unmediated rule, inhabitants needed to comply directly with central state institutions via taxation, military service, and later schooling (Giddens 1985; Mann 1993). Being in need of mass-compliance without comprehensive local knowledge, rulers promoted the political culture of nationalism.

Nations are, borrowing Anderson's (1991 [1983]) famous term, »imagined communities«. That means they are too large for any member to know all co-members. Thus, their characteristics are also never completely known, and consequently object of continuous political struggle (Migdal 2001: 14-15, 259f). Being in the best position to do so, state rulers promote their interpretation of national culture. Through national narratives, the display of symbols, public holidays etc. (Anderson 1991), they attempt to make the nation a lived experience, to embed a diversity of cultural experiences in one over-arching framework of a common, national culture (Migdal 2001). Nationality is aimed to be a primary and »natural« source of identification (Giddens 1985: 221; cf. also Marx 1976 [1843]: 354), so that those in government of the state can use it to mobilise for their own ends. However, due to the political nature of who and what best represents national interests, governments are often challenged by other nationalistic actors, promoting their own ideas, typically presented with chauvinism, i.e. degrading the non-national.

Infamously, Schmitt (1996 [1923]: 14-15) argued that in order to ensure de-mocratic equality of nationals, all real-existing democracies relied on the ex-clusion of those groups of the population who were perceived to ultimately not fit in. Analyses of historical cases support this controversial author's claim. Mann (2005) suggests that exclusive settler democracies acted significantly more violent than their authoritarian equivalents against local – non-citizen – populations. In addition to this, the frequent mass-deportations in 20th century Europe since the Balkan Wars had been commonly welcomed by lea-ding politicians of democracies as a means to achieve the desired ›congruence of nation and state‹ (cf. Schwartz 2013). Finally, already the earliest modern nationalisms in revolutionary USA and France were immediately followed by widespread persecution of non-republicans, or aristocrats respectively – the rhetoric about human rights notwithstanding (Schwartz 2013: 10). In prac-tice, privileging part of the population with citizen entitlements meant to subject other parts to severe violations of their human rights, through expul-sion, forced labour, or even ethnic cleansing. Establishing modern citizenship rested on active, partially massively violent exclusion – at least in the past.

Now, to what extent does this relate to the rationales of citizenship, whe-reas not, e.g. of the nation? In historical practice, these two ideas are not distinct, but rather inseparable aspects of the same political modernisation leading to the democratic nation-state. According to Schnabel-Schüle (2004: 55-56) citizen was originally used to signify a carrier of rights, while nationals denote those of common origin. However, from the later 19th century on-wards, the concepts of citizen and national were meant to coincide (Schnabel-Schüle 2004: 56-57). Also Noiriel (1994: 73-75) and Torpey (2000: 107-110) argue that in modernity these two aspects are not clearly separable. In the modern nation-state, the rights and obligations of citizenship are an expression of na-tional in- and exclusion. Torpey's (2000) investigation of modern citizenship centres on identity papers – since there simply is no other way to know a per-son's nationality. This trivial recognition points out, how nationality typically has been a top-down ascription by state administrations. In the United States, for example, »those held to be unworthy of admission into citizenship« comprised »a variety of groups regarded as impure, unclean, idiotic, non-white, or incapable of understanding the principles of republicanism« (Torpey 2000: 102). Identification papers are not a casual side-effect of modern states, but imperative for the protection of one's rights, e.g. as visible during First World War, when imprisonment was the normal way to treat nationals of enemy states. As soon as most of a country's inhabitants receive the status of citizens, the separation of nationality and citizenship becomes meaningless[7]. Thus, the above-mentioned human rights violations can be equally attributed to both nationalisation – designing one national culture out of a diverse population – as well as liberal emancipation – privileging citizens over ›foreigners‹.

And this is why, for modernity, I find Isin's (2009: 376) terminological separation invalid, which states that nationality is tied to origin (or ethnicity), while citizenship is tied to claiming rights. This means to deny the common, top-down practices of *granting* rights. While these typically were concessions from governments being confronted with demands by their populations, this process must not be confused with casting idealistic notions of liberal emancipation into political reality.

How exactly is this history of exclusive citizenship present in contemporary democracies? Przeworski (1995: 43), in discussing the challenges of »new democracies«, makes the point that »[c]itizenship can be universally exercised only when« certain, e.g. »social and economic perquisites« are met (cf. also Pammett 2014: 2). Hence, early liberal regimes set a ›property qualification‹ on citizenship, granting full participatory privileges only to those who were (economically) able to fulfil their obligations (Przeworski 1995: 43). Now, in the era of almost universal citizenship, political inequality results from states not promoting citizenship in all classes and throughout the whole country.

Viewed from this perspective, today's situation seems civil and inclusive, at least in established democracies. Lenin (1957 [1916]) famously argued that economically powerful nations bribe ›their‹ masses at the expense of workers abroad, in order to keep the exploitative system running. In this line of argument, liberal constitutions offer privileges for those parts of the population considered more critical to the functioning of the global economic system.

---

7   This is not to deny discrimination between formally equal citizens. However, in principal, this discrimination *cannot* be based on nationality, as this quality of a person is invisible (cf. Torpey 2000).

However, this domestic social pacification is consciously built on the inequality of others. While this initially affected most of the populations of the ›democracies‹, non-propertied men, women, and non-whites were gradually included (cf. Williams 1984: 126). After incorporating most of a state's permanent population into the political regime, most disadvantaged are those subjected to a state's control without being considered as citizens. Today, this applies mainly to refugees (Noiriel 1994: 83-86), but also resident non-citizens in general. Even if granted protection, they always depend on the voluntary, hence precarious benevolence of the state[8]. Since the claim to full political privilege in the form of legal rights is no longer based on minority qualities like property plus masculinity, citizenship is effectively based on nationality. While the ideational bases of citizenship and nationality used to be separated (as also Isin 2009 points out), in modernity they denote a practically inseparable compound – full membership in the political community plus organisation called the nation-state. The imagined community of the nation finds its legal expression in full citizenship rights.

5.   Citizenship as disciplining institution

While the above argument delineates how the principal distinction between privileged citizens and precarious non-citizens has been set up, this chapter will discuss some effects that its exclusivity has on both the institution of citizenship and the citizens. Linking to the critiques presented above, the participatory element of democratic citizenship has to be qualified. The voices of the masses are channelled into representative institutions, while the (material and social) bases of effective participation are depoliticised. Instead, politics is concerned with regulating the biosocial qualities of the population, attempting to shape the conditions conducive to society's welfare (Foucault 2008). However, this is accompanied by the heightened awareness to the dangers such liberties bring. Being a citizen in a liberal society does not only mean to succumb to a ruling order. Participation under these conditions entails self-

---

8   As Depelchin (2008: 28) points out, it is common only in cases of such underprivileged people to speak about violations of human rights. Contrary to the full entitlement expressed by citizenship, human rights are minimum criteria for underprivileged inhabitants of a state. Marx (1976 [1843]: 363) also sees human rights as the negative bourgeois rights of individualist separation. Human rights are individual and negative, whereas citizenship rights are political and participatory.

discipline to adhere to the ruling rationales as codified within political institutions. Subsequently, I will elaborate on this aspect of self-discipline.

The attempt to discipline certain groups within the citizenry was part of
the speech delivered by Theresa May, as quoted initially. As Menke (2015:74-
82) states, self-discipline has been part and parcel of liberal thought from the
start. He refers to Thomas Hobbes' idea to relinquish some ›natural liberty‹ in
order to receive security. Hobbes argues that the official religious confession
of a person may, or even has to be, subordinate to the common good of civil
peace, while (only) the inner creed remains free. Thus, in order to be free, one
has to behave in a certain way. A common contemporary manifestation is the
duty of citizens to stick to designated participation channels. Citizens who,
for example, fail to transform their political opinion into a vote can be easily
disregarded. Teenagers, who deliberately refuse to go to school as they feel
their future is ultimately challenged, are being denounced as absentees. Not
sticking to institutionalised ways of action means being exposed to sanctions.
In liberal democracies, these reach from comparatively benign ones, like being
misunderstood or ignored, up to being banned from certain institutions, or
even criminalised (e.g. for civil disobedience)[9].

Building on the logic of self-discipline, Foucault (2008: 226) argues that
under the biopolitical rationales of liberal societies, every member of society
is seen as »entrepreneur of himself«. Competition becomes a main regulating rationale in all spheres of society (Foucault: 148-149), and human capital
investment is seen as the main driver of market success (Foucault: 230-32).
Consequently, the »migrant is an investor. He is an entrepreneur of himself who incurs expenses by investing to obtain some kind of improvement«
(Foucault 2008: 230). In order to stimulate that entrepreneurial spirit, go-

---

9   This coarse argument can do with two qualifications. First, my assessment of institutio-
     nally prescribed action and individual deviance is very one-sided. In reality, those ac-
     ting within institutions do shape them, if only by reproducing original rationales, but
     more commonly by gradually shifting the recommended courses of action. Additio-
     nally, as Isin (2009: 382) argues, institutions can be changed by those acting explicitly
     outside of them. Second and relatedly, liberal regimes may be especially accommo-
     dative to such ›unconventional participation‹ in that, for instance, greater importance
     is attached to freedom of expression than to regulatory law. Nonetheless, instituti-
     ons equipped with authority do sanction what they consider to be deviant behaviour.
     Then, the decision whether to sanction rests on the political distinctions between civil
     disobedience and crime, or unconventional as opposed to deviant behavior.

vernments (and other political actors) design institutions that are being re-sponsive to such individual effort.

Ong (2006) analyses the situation in East Asia's special economic zones where states, in competition for transnational investment, bargain with rights of the workforce to supply the right combination of highly trained experts and exploitable ›migrant‹ workers. This behaviour clearly shows the nature of citizenship as accumulated »bundle« of rights (Przeworski 1995: 43), which may be disaggregated and separately granted or withheld, depending on cost-benefit calculations of state administrations.

While Ong's examples are non-democracies, her argument can be trans-ferred to the West. Administrations inside the EU also differentiate between desired non-citizens and foreigners who are tolerated at best, as Schlee's chapter in this volume shows. Inter alia, the handling of working permits and residency status show highly unequal treatment, depending on the rationales of the receiving society. To signify that the migrant is not a full member of society, she or he is lacking in legal status. The way out of mere toleration is open only for those who perform well along the standards set for immigrants. As Schlee (2020; in this volume) analyses, in Germany this means language proficiency, specific job skills, and acceptance of some diffuse social norms. Consequently, it can be stated that even liberal democracies resort to a regime of differential inclusion of non-citizens. In other words, only ›good‹ foreigners may become equal citizens.

Coming to my final and main argument, this has certain effects on the natural(ised) population[10]. Under the demand of a flexible workforce, citi-zens compete with migrants (who are perceived as economic chance-seekers). Additionally, migration is problematized, as certain immigrants are said to endanger society (criminals, terrorists, welfare cheaters etc.; cf. Götz 2011: 146). This leads to the logic of selectivity, as societies should neither accept everybody, nor anybody: immigrants need to prove their value for societies. Borders are defined as instruments enabling this selection. An efficient bor-der regime promises control and knowledge (and even truth, as can be seen by the ›threat‹ Sans-Papiers are posing). Again, this connects to the dangers

---

10   Maybe it is necessary to spell out that my argument does not depend on how one defi-nes national belonging (e.g. communitarian vs. libertarian). The relevant institutional logics are based solely on the dichotomous status of citizens vis-à-vis non-citizens – irrelevant of individuals receiving this status through birth, naturalisation or other cir-cumstances.

inherent to freedom, the fear of losing control as one becomes more aware of global connectivity. It is a small step for an anxious workforce, stimulated by nationalistic chauvinism, to demand that chance-seeking migrants not only fit labour market and administrative demands, but also offer a ›cultural fit‹.

Bassam Tibi (2017), one of the seminal voices in the German debate promoting a ›guiding culture‹ (*Leitkultur*)[11] when dealing esp. with Muslim immigrants, provides an illustrative argument to this cultural fit. His point of departure is that governments should regulate migration, i.e. decide on the demand for foreigners (Tibi 2017). While explicitly rejecting any ethno-nationalistic or religious interpretation of national culture, and making rather general and probably widely accepted suggestions[12], he nonetheless proposes a set of values which only non-citizens have to abide to, in order to be granted a mere chance of becoming full members of society. It becomes clear that citizens are in a privileged position compared to non-citizens. Tibi's points are an illustration of what has been stated about national culture; who ever attempts to describe such a culture is actually attempting to define it (Götz 2011: 81). And due to their agenda setting, legislative and implementation powers, governments are in the best position to do so – in fact, Tibi explicitly calls for government action.

Governments postulate nationalism for their own ends, but cannot stay on top of the forces they unleash. This perception of national distinctiveness, economic competition and outside dangers supports aggressive, chauvinistic nationalism – especially in combination with the shortcomings of capitalistic (commodification, estrangement) and national integration (limits of participation). Hence, the ruling rationales of liberal societies depend on and thereby reproduce the separation between citizen and non-citizen, and consequently the exclusion of non-citizens. Interestingly, this refers back to how rationales of the creation of nations were theorised by Carl Schmitt (1996 [1923]) the borders of the nation are defined by those who are considered equals.

---

11   Cf. Götz (2011: 14; 145-47) for an ideational contextualisation of the *Leitkultur* debate.
12   His European ›guiding culture‹ includes: 1. primacy of reason over religious dogma, 2. individual as opposed to group rights (esp. freedom of religion), 3. secular democracy and 4. pluralism including tolerance as basis for a rational way of dealing with cultural difference (Tibi 2017).

6.   Conclusion

This paper understood citizenship as a functional adaptation to the ruling rationales of liberal regimes. Citizenship has been defined as a status of accumulated specifiable rights, meaningful mainly in relation to a democratic nation-state. Having historically started as a privilege for a few, citizenship now offers protection and participation rights for most inhabitants within liberal democracies. The flip side of the coin, however, is that this citizenship overlaps with categories of national belonging.

While nationalism is also supposed to be functional for state rule, it enables challengers of both government and state on this very ground. Chauvinistic nationalism is not only a function of nationalistic challengers, but already inherent to the institution of citizenship. The structural inequality between citizens and non-citizens is a legal signifier for national distinctiveness and the formal basis for processes of socio-cultural (de-)grading. Liberal subjects are trained to see themselves in constant competition and exposed to dangers resulting from the freedom of others. At the same time, political participation rights of citizens are limited by two domination rationales. For one, freedom of expression is subject to self-discipline, as the voices of the masses are channelled into representative institutions. Secondly, the material and social bases of actual participation are de-politicised.

To what extent, then, is the institution of citizenship »in flux«? While Marshall (1950) seminally described the qualitative expansion of the concept in early modernity, historical accounts (e.g. Mann 1993) describe the quantitative enlargement of the citizen group. However, the general pattern remained unchanged. While some are privileged, most do not benefit from the protection and participation rights thus codified. Acknowledging that identity papers are a sine-qua-non to those ends, the effects of this legal exclusion must not be underestimated. Citizenship has been designed to serve as an exclusion instrument – although awareness of this is low when social change is little problematized. In this chapter, I explicated how the emancipatory and the exclusionary aspects of citizenship are related. To this extend, nationalistic interpretations of liberal institutions, as they are being put on the agenda by right-wing populists more recently, do not present a departure or re-definition.

Admittedly, the approach in the abstract way I applied it here is rather coarse and I shall discuss some consequences of my theoretical choices in brief. Specifically, I narrowed down the concept of citizenship to a formal institution in relation to the modern nation-state, more specifically liberal democracies. Focussing on ruling rationales embedded in institutions, I ignored how those very institutions develop and may transform through the actions ›under their roof‹ – and even explicitly outside their boundaries (exactly Isin's 2009 focus). Hence, alternative concepts take citizenship as a continuum. Notably, Isin (2009) understands it as a kind of audacious behaviour by anybody claiming political agency, even where it is officially and explicitly proscribed. However, to be effective in political practice, such efforts have to be met with acquiescence, at least. As historical cases show, democracies do not necessarily welcome ›unconventional‹ participation either. Hence, I deliberately chose my approach to highlight major rationales shaping the institution of citizenship and allowing for identitarian interpretation.

Still, democratic states of law usually not only acknowledge the validity of human rights, they offer certain juridical and constitutional safeguards against arbitrary administrative decisions, also for non-citizens. As already mentioned, Marx (1976 [1843]) also struggled to understand the duality of emancipation and exclusion in liberal regimes. In a recent analysis, Isin (2009: 369) states that citizenship always entails both domination and empowerment. While democratic citizenship is virtually synonymous to the subjects' eligibility to question and potentially alter a state's political institutions, this ability rests on the entitlement of some, typically granted in a top-down fashion. So, what does follow from my critical approach to citizenship? I think the core insight is to acknowledge that the status of citizen is mainly a one-sided dependency of the citizen on the state. Real existing, representative democracy is characterised by restrained institutional influence, even of citizens. Thus, a reform of the citizenship regime would benefit both non-citizens and citizens.

As we can conclude that citizenship is insufficient to safeguard protection and participation, what other bases can be thought of to secure rights beyond nationality? Are other institutions able to provide such safeguards? The transnational discourse on human rights seems very fitting here, as it scales up the narrow notion of state-sanctioned individual privileges. The legitimacy and capabilities to enforce such rights, however, is simply non-existing. To enable such competencies beyond the nation-state would not only require fundamental restructuring of political authority, but their desirability is also questionable (as this simply means to shift principal and to date unresolved issues onto a different level). The most feasible solution then, appears to lie in smaller, legal adaptations of citizenship within the nation-state framework.

These could allow for more acknowledgement of the continued reality of migration. There are examples, in which certain electoral rights are based on residency rather than nationality (e.g. in Germany the *Ausländerbeiräte*). Such ›best practices‹ may be expanded and disseminated by international and supranational (EU) organisations. This, however, could provide only a very unreliable solution, given the severity of a precarious, permanent non-citizen status.

References

Anderson, Benedict (1991): Imagined Communities. Reflections on the Origin and Spread of Nationalism. Reviewed and Extended Edition. London and New York: Verso.

Barth, Fredrik (1970): Ethnic Groups and Boundaries. The Social Organization of Culture Difference. Fifth Printing. Bergen: Universitets Forlaget.

Depelchin, Jacques (2008): The History of Mass Violence Since Colonial Times. Trying to Understand the Roots of a Mindset, in: Henning Melber (ed.), Revisiting the Heart of Darkness. Explorations into Genocide and other Forms of Mass Violence. 60 Years after the UN Convention. Uppsala: Dag Hammarskjöld Centre, 13-31.

Foucault, Michel (2008): The Birth of Biopolitics. Lectures at the Collège de France, 1978-1979. London: Palgrave Macmillan.

Giddens, Anthony (1985): The Nation-State and Violence. A Contemporary Critique of Historical Materialism, Volume 2 of 3. Cambridge and Oxford: Polity Press.

Götz, Irene (2011): Deutsche Identitäten. Die Wiederentdeckung des Nationalen nach 1989. Köln: Böhlau.

Hobsbawm, Eric (2000): Nations and Nationalism since 1780. Programme, Myth, Reality. Canto. Reprint of 2nd Edition of 1992. Cambridge: University Press.

Isin, Engin (2009): Citizenship in Flux: The Figure of the Activist Citizen. Subjectivity 29: 367-388. https://doi:10.1057/sub.2009.25

Lenin, Wladimir Iljitsch (1957): Der Imperialismus und die Spaltung des Sozialismus. Published in December 1916, in: Wladimir Iljitsch Lenin, Werke, Vol.23, Berlin: Dietz Verlag, 102-118. https://www.marxists.org/d eutsch/archiv/lenin/1916/10/spaltung.html

Linz, Juan/Alfred Stepan (1996): Problems of Democratic Transition and Consolidation: Southern Europe, South America, and Post-Communist Europe. Baltimore: Johns Hopkins University Press.

Mann, Michael (1993): The Sources of Social Power. Volume 2: The Rise of Classes and Nation-States, 1790-1914. 2nd Edition. Cambridge: University Press.

Mann, Michael. (2005): The Dark Side of Democracy. Explaining Ethnic Cleansing. New York: Cambridge University Press.

Marshall, Thomas (1950): Citizenship and Social Class. And other Essays. Cambridge: University Press.

Marsili, Lorenzo/Milanese, Niccolo (2018): Citizens of Nowhere. How Europe Can Be Saved from Itself. Chicago: University Press.

Marx, Karl (1976 [1843]): Zur Judenfrage.. In Karl Marx/Friedrich, Friedrich: Werke. Band 1. Berlin: Dietz Verlag, 347-377.

May, Theresa (2016): Keynote Speech at Tory Conference in Full. Published at independent.co.uk on 5 Oct. 2016 https://www.independent.co.uk/news/uk/politics/theresa-may-speech-tory-conference-2016-in-full-transcript-a7346171.html

Menke, Cristoph (2015): Kritik der Rechte. Berlin: Suhrkamp.

Migdal, Joel (2001): State in Society. Studying How States and Societies Transform and Constitute One Another. Cambridge Studies in Comparative Politics. Cambridge: University Press.

Noiriel, Gérard (1994): Die Tyrannei des Nationalen. Sozialgeschichte des Asylrechts in Europa. 1. Auflage, Lüneburg: Zu Klampen.

Ong, Aihwa (2006): Neoliberalism as Exception. Mutations in Citizenship and Sovereignty. Reprint. Durham/London: Duke University Press.

Pammett, Jon (ed.) (2016): ISSP 2014 – Citizenship II: Questionnaire development report. Ottawa. https://search.gesis.org/research_data/ZA6670

Przeworski, Adam (1995): Sustainable Democracy. Cambridge: University Press.

Rzadtki, Lea (2020): Activist Citizens Challenging Dichotomies, in: Markus Bayer/Oliver Schwarz/Toralf Stark (eds.), Democratic Citizenship in Flux. Conceptions of Citizenship in the Light of Political and Social Fragmentation, Bielefeld: transcript, 153-171.

Schlee, Thorsten (2020): Borders of Citizenship? Biopolitics and Differential Inclusion in Local Fields of Labor and Asylum, in: Markus Bayer/Oliver Schwarz/Toralf Stark (eds.), Democratic Citizenship in flux. Conceptions of Citizenship in the Light of Political and Social Fragmentation, Bielefeld: transcript, 108-130.

Schmitt, Carl (1996 [1923]): Die geistesgeschichtliche Lage des heutigen Parlamentarismus. 8th Edition. Berlin: Duncker& Humblot.

Schnabel-Schüle, Helga (2004): Wer gehört dazu? Zugehörigkeitsrechte und die Inklusion von Fremden in politische Räume. in: Andreas Gestrich/Lutz Raphael (eds.), Inklusion/Exklusion. Studien zu Fremdheit und Armut von der Antike bis zur Gegenwart, 51-61. Bern: Peter Lang D.

Schwartz, Michael (2013): Ethnische »Säuberungen« in der Moderne. Globale Wechselwirkungen nationalistischer und rassistischer Gewaltpolitik im 19. und 20. Jahrhundert. Oldenbourg/München: De Gruyter.

Tibi, Bassam (2017): Leitkultur als Integrationskonzept – revisited. Zwei missglückte deutsche Debatten 2000-2017. Bundeszentrale für politische Bildung, Dossier »Islamismus« (08.09.2017). https://www.bpb.de/politik/extremismus/islamismus/255521/leitkultur-als-integrationskonzept-revisited

Tischmeyer, Christian (2018): The Strong Nation-State and Violence. UAR Graduate Centre for Development Studies -Working Paper on Global Governance and Development Studies 16. https://www.uni-due.de/imperia/md/images/inef/uar-working-paper-tischmeyer.pdf

Torpey, John (2000): The Invention of the Passport. Surveillance, Citizenship, and the State. Cambridge: University Press.

Williams, Raymond (1984): The Long Revolution. Reprint. Harmondsworth: Penguin.

Public perception of European Union citizenship at the local level

Oliver Schwarz

1. Introduction

European Union (EU) citizenship and the rights included in it are one of the major cornerstones of the European integration process. The creation of EU citizenship goes back to the Maastricht Treaty, which entered into force on 1 November 1993. Since then, every national citizen of a member state is also a citizen of the Union. The ultimate goal of this initiative was to encourage a sense of identification with and belonging to the European Union and thereby foster a common European identity. While certain rights, like the right of free movement and residence, are firmly anchored in European primary law and have undergone considerable developments in secondary legislation during the last decades, a significant gap remains between the content of the legal norms of EU citizenship and the civic realities of everyday life. This phenomenon is well known. Every three years since 1993, the European Commission reports on the progress towards effective EU citizenship. The Standard Eurobarometer, published twice a year, regularly examines people's perception of EU citizenship. In addition, two specific Eurobarometer surveys were carried out in view of the 2017 EU citizenship report. Academic literature has stressed the importance of knowledge for a positive perception of the EU (Gabel 1998; Hooghe/Marks 2005). It is expected that the more familiar people get with European institutions and politics and the better knowledge they have about EU policies, the stronger becomes their identification with the European Union. However, what is missing is a local perspective on this cognitive path between knowledge about and perception of EU citizenship. Therefore, the aim of this chapter is to examine the extent to which EU citizens' knowledge about their rights is accompanied by a positive perception of European Union citizenship. For this purpose, the chapter first explores the development of EU citizenship

and the relationship between citizenship and democracy on the European level. Then the chapter presents findings of a face-to-face survey of 425 local
residents in Duisburg, Germany. Finally, the analysis of these findings will be
used to formulate concrete policy recommendations about how to vitalise the
link between local citizens and the EU.

2.   From »market citizenship« to »Union citizenship«

The concept of EU citizenship has been evolving highly dynamically over
the past six decades of European integration. Since the foundation of the
European Coal and Steel Community (ECSC) in the 1950s, the rights of the
»market citizen« (Ipsen/Nicolaysen 1964: 340) have been gradually extended
by the subsequent treaties and secondary legislation. Already in 1957, the
Treaty of Rome, establishing the European Economic Community (EEC),
explicitly mentioned the people in addition to the member states in its
preamble. This was the very first sign that European integration not only
directly affected the member states but also each individual citizen. As a
result, market citizens, namely workers, businessmen and consumers, where
the first beneficiaries of the internal market with the establishment of the
four European freedoms (capital, goods, people and services). These four
freedoms, formally contained in the treaties, were dynamically developed by
the European Court of Justice (ECJ) and shaped the relationship of individual
citizens with the community, based on the core norm of non-discrimination.

However, the 1980s witnessed a renewed interest in the issue of European
identity and, as a result, the concept of citizenship started to develop as a
boost to the political legitimacy of European integration (Isin/Wood 1999). In
1984, the European Parliament adopted a Draft Treaty establishing the European Union, whose Article 3 recommended the formal establishment of a
»citizenship of the Union«. Only one year later, the Adonnino report proposed
the development of »special rights of citizens« (Adonnio 1985: 7), in particular
local electoral rights and voting rights in European Parliament elections in
the according member state of residence. Nevertheless, the European Parliament's draft proposal was not accepted by the member states and the Adonnio
report did not show a direct result.

A crucial catalyst in the development of EU citizenship was the often underestimated Single European Act (SEA) in 1986 (Warleigh 1998: 116). The SEA
provided important innovations which prepared the ground for the ratifica-

tion of the Maastricht Treaty in 1992. With entry into force of the Treaty of the European Union (TEU) on 1 November 1993, the EU legally established the institution of Union citizenship stating that »every person holding the nationality of a Member State is a citizen of the Union« (Article 8(1) TEU). One of the Treaty's main objectives was »to strengthen the protection of the rights and interests of the nationals of its Member States through the creation of a citizenship of the Union« (Article B TEU). To reach this objective, the Maastricht Treaty added three additional rights to the existing free movement and residence rights of the classic market citizen: the right to vote and to stand as a candidate both in municipal and European Parliament elections,, the right of consular or diplomatic protection by member state authorities when travelling abroad and the right to petition the European Parliament or to apply to the Ombudsman. As a result, the Treaty of Maastricht legally established a political relation between the EU and its citizens which goes beyond the legal and economical relation of market citizenship.

As Kostakopoulou (2013: 24) points out, the potential of EU citizenship to strengthen citizens' rights and enhance democratic practices at all levels of governance was not sufficiently appreciated by policy makers and academics at the time. Initially, even the ECJ adopted a cautious approach. This resistance changed in 1998 with the *Martínez Sala* case where the ECJ gave a big impetus to the concept of European citizenship. In that case, the refusal of the authorities to grant an economically inactive Spanish citizen who lived in Germany certain social benefits was dismissed by the ECJ. The next important step was the *Grzelczyk* case in 2001, where the ECJ was asked whether a French student could claim social assistance benefits in Belgium (Cornelissen 2009). These two decisions could be interpreted as the ECJ developing a general right to non-discrimination for EU citizens, independent of the performance of any economic activity.

The Treaty of Amsterdam in 1997 did not substantially modify the concept of Union citizenship introduced by Maastricht. Only some additional rights were included, such as the right to write directly to any of the institutions or bodies of the EU, the right to be replied to in any official language represented in the Treaty or the right of access to any of the documents of the European institutions and bodies. However, in Article 8(1) TEU it clarified that »citizenship of the Union shall complement and not replace national citizenship«. According to Barber (2002: 1), this provision is »an expression of both European ambition and Member State conservatism«. It was rooted in the so-called Edinburgh Agreement, which was made in the aftermath of the negative Danish referendum of the Maastricht Treaty. In that agreement, the Council (1992: 53) underlined that provisions of the Treaty »do not in any way take the place of national citizenship. The question whether an individual possesses the nationality of a Member State will be settled solely by reference to the national law of the Member State concerned.« By making national citizenship a prerequisite for European citizenship, it is plausible to say that the EU did not create a system of double citizenship, but a system of dual citizenship (Saputelli 2018: 263). Double citizenship is characterised by the fact that a citizen can hold two (or more) citizenships which are independent and separated from each other and are not linked as in the European citizenship. For more discussion on the concept of dual citizenship, see Yildirim Sungur's and Schwarz' contribution to this volume (2020).

The next important boost to EU citizenship was the proclamation of the Charter of Fundamental Rights of the European Union in 2000. Although it did not become legally binding until the entry into force of the Lisbon Treaty in 2009, the document underlined the EU's ambition »to adopt its own Bill of Rights« (de Búrca 2013: 172). The Charter contains inalienable rights, principles and values that all EU citizens are entitled to and all European actors must comply with when implementing European law. In this sense, the text has brought a new impetus to the EU's human rights framework (von Bogdandy: 2000). The Charter contains a preamble and 54 articles divided into VII chapters and some general rules. Chapter V lays down the rights attached to the status of EU citizenship. These rights include the right to vote and stand as a candidate at the elections to the European Parliament and at municipal elections, the right to good administration, the right to petition at the European Parliament, the freedom of movement and residence and the diplomatic and consular protection.

Scholars have praised the Charter for establishing »a direct link between the European institutions and citizenship« (Balaguer 2013: 233). In parallel, the Charter has attained considerable recognition through European jurisprudence (Sarmiento 2013). In 2011, the *Zambrano* case attracted wide attention (van Eijken/de Vries 2011; Hailbronner/Iglesias Sánchez 2011). This case dealt with the issue whether a residence permit should be given to two Colombian citizens who were parents of two Belgian children. The ECJ affirmed that such derivative rights exist for parents from third countries if EU member states have previously granted citizenship to their children. Moreover, in her opinion, the ECJ's Advocate General Eleanor Sharpston called for a reconsideration of the bonds between the EU citizen and the EU. This could only be implemented through a more extensive protection of human rights and fundamental rights for EU citizens. The ECJ (2011) followed by deciding that Member States could no longer deprive Union citizens of the »genuine enjoyment of the substance of the rights conferred by virtue of their status as citizens of the Union«.

3.   European Union citizenship at the local level

Today, EU citizenship can best be described as a kind of federal citizenship (van den Brink 2019: 33). A federal citizen possesses »membership in two political communities within the same state« (Carens 2000: 164). She or he is a member of the federation as a whole as well as of one of the federation's constituent states. EU citizens, according to today's Article 20 TFEU, enjoy this kind of federal membership as well: »every person holding the nationality of a Member State shall be a citizen of the Union«. As a result, EU citizenship, like other forms of federal citizenship, is characterised by a horizontal and a vertical dimension. The horizontal dimension allows the federal citizen to move and reside freely within the EU and not to be discriminated on grounds of national citizenship. The vertical dimension represents the core of EU citizenship as it represents a direct link between the Union and its citizens.

As outlined in the introductory chapter of this volume (Bayer et al. 2020: 7-22), there are generally three different aspects of citizenship: one focusing on the legal status granted by a political community, one relating a certain identity to a community and one highlighting social practice of democratic participation. Concerning status, van den Brink (2019: 33) resumes that »EU citizenship may indeed look rather meagre when considering solely its vertical dimension«. But how about practice and identity? The turnouts of the elections to the European Parliament indicate that the public does not see its EU citizenship as its most important status. This immediately leads to the even more puzzling question: Are Europeans really passive (non-democratic) citizens? One factor that may explain passivity in terms of participation is the extent to which individuals know their legal rights. Public knowledge of rights has been a subject of a number of empirical enquiries over the last decade (Denvir/Balmer/Pleasence 2013). Delli Carpini and Keeter (1996: 1), for instance, state that »Democracy functions best when its citizens are politically informed.«

The importance of political knowledge for the development of support for a European community was confirmed by Inglehart (1970). However, the author acknowledged cognitive mobilization and education as a necessary condition only but not as a sufficient one: »One must become aware of it before one can develop a sense of commitment« (Inglehart 1970: 47). This argument was empirically supported by Díez Medrano and Gutiérrez (2012) who measured the degree of cognitive mobilisation by evaluating the consumption of international news in newspapers. The authors' results were confirmed by Scharkow and Vogelsang (2009). Furthermore, there is evidence from research on EU support that possessing knowledge of European institutions affects support for EU authority in areas involving cross-border political issues (Clark/Hellwig 2012). Faas (2007) nuances these results. In a comparison study, he shows that a positive relationship of citizens towards the EU can only be expected in countries with strong European agendas and where Europe is conceptualised as an inclusive multi-ethnic concept. This view is confirmed by Thorpe (2008), whose work shows that social groups who stand little or nothing to gain from identifying with Europe are highly unlikely to do so.

Verhaegen, Hooghe and Dejaeghere (2015) also nuance the relationship between knowledge about Europe and identity. In a comparative analysis among adolescents in 21 EU member states, they show that knowledge about the EU has a significant but still limited effect on European identity.

The European Union argues similarly. In its programme *Europe for Citizens* (2007-2013), the EU argues that promoting knowledge about European citizenship rights will lead to the strengthening and safeguarding of the integration process (European Commission 2011: 4). 2013, the year that marked the twentieth anniversary of the entry into force of the Maastricht Treaty, was even designated as the »European Year of Citizens« by the European Commission. This initiative aimed at promoting the visibility and accessibility of EU citizenship. The European Year of Citizens also formed one of the main rationales for the research activities behind this chapter. »20 years of European citizenship. Progress and challenges« was a one-year project (September 2013 – September 2014) funded by the Stiftung Mercator. The project's main goal was to gather information on the knowledge of Duisburg inhabitants about their rights as citizens of the EU and to ask them about their opinions and ideas in regard to the future of the EU. Specifically, the project pursued a three-pronged strategy: (1) implementation of a comparative survey in selected districts of Duisburg, (2) analysis of the survey results and (3) presentation of the survey outcomes to the public through dialogue forums. All activities of the project were part of the academic course »Practical application of research methods« at the Institute of Political Science at the University of Duisburg-Essen. The project was carried out in close cooperation with the Office of Elections, European Affairs and Information Logistics of the City of Duisburg.[1]

This chapter summarises the main findings of the project outlined above. Accordingly, the rest of this chapter is organised as follows: In section 4, an overview of the survey is given. Section 5 presents the survey results. Lastly, section 6 offers concluding remarks and practical recommendations about how to vitalise EU citizenship on a local level.

4.   Survey overview

The questionnaire of the survey contained 39 questions which were grouped into seven sections from A to G. Section A contained 2 filter questions to select only respondents who live in Duisburg and have EU citizenship. Section B entailed three questions to consider whether respondents are aware of their status as a citizen of the EU. Section C covered 9 questions related to the EU citizens' rights of participation in local and European elections. Sections D entailed 9 questions about the right of free movement within the EU. Section E (four questions) aimed to gather information on the respondents' perception of the EU. Section F (5 questions) asked for demographic details such as gender, age, income and professional status. Finally, section G contained seven questions for the interviewers on the credibility of the respondent and the quality of the obtained information. The questionnaire contained a mixture of closed and open questions. The formal survey was conducted by students based on the guidance of the lecturer. The interviews were conducted in October/December 2013 and April 2014. In the end, 425 questionnaires were usable. All interviews were conducted face-to-face and on the street in central locations of Duisburg and other parts of the city. The average interview duration was intended to be no longer than 20 minutes. Interviewers aimed to achieve a reasonably representative sample by age and gender. A comparison of the survey data with the demographics of the city of Duisburg is provided in Table 1 below.

---

1   For more information, please visit the project's website at www.uni-due.de/unionsbuerger/

Table 1: Demographic profile of respondents

		Survey (n = 425) n	Percentage	Duisburg population Percentage
Gender	Female	178	41.5	49
	Male	251	58.5	51
Age	<18	23	5.4	16.6
	18-24	106	24.9	8.4
	25-64	238	56	54.2
	≥65	56	13.6	20.8

Source: Data obtained from the city of Duisburg (Stadt Duisburg 2018).

5.   Survey findings

The results of the survey are not representative. Thus, the collected information is best thought of as representing a picture of opinion and mood in the seven months from October 2013 and April 2014 in Duisburg. Nevertheless, the findings can contribute to an increased understanding of public perception of EU citizenship on the local level. The results that follow pertain to selected questions of the survey questionnaire and in this way represent a part of the survey and the statistical analysis that was carried out.

5.1.   Familiarity with the term »citizen of the European Union«

The first section of the questionnaire was concerned with the familiarity of the respondents with the term »citizen of the European Union«. Asked »Are you familiar with the term ›citizen of the European Union‹?«, the respondents were able to ascertain their knowledge in the range from »Yes, and I know what it means«, to »Yes, I have heard about it, but I am not sure what it means« and »No, I have never heard the term ›citizen of the European Union‹«. Almost three-quarters of the respondents (74.5 %) said they were familiar with the concept of EU citizenship. However, awareness of the term does not necessarily mean that it is also understood in terms of content. More than 42 % of the respondents said they had heard the term before, but could not say exactly what it stands for. About a third of the respondents (31.9 %) was familiar with the concept of EU citizenship and knew its meaning. Nearly 26 % of the respondents were unacquainted with the concept of EU citizenship and had never heard of it.

Figure 1: Are you familiar with the term »citizen of the European Union«?

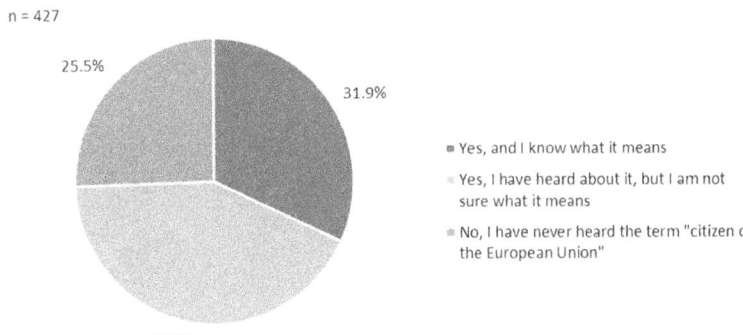

n = 427

25.5%

31.9%

- Yes, and I know what it means
- Yes, I have heard about it, but I am not sure what it means
- No, I have never heard the term "citizen of the European Union"

42.6%

Source: Own compilation.

5.2.   Perception of EU citizenship

The respondents' perception of EU citizenship was obtained by asking them »What does EU citizenship mean to you? What do you associate with it?« To code the answers to this open question, a coding system was used on the same lines as the one used by the European Commission (2012: 35). This system had six categories: »Sense of belonging to the EU«, »Common values and common history«, »Additional rights«, »Participating in community/civic life«, »Participating in political life« and »Other«. To more than 30 % of the respondents, EU citizenship meant a sense of belonging to the European Union. Slightly fewer respondents associated EU citizenship with common values and a common history (29.5 %). The item »Additional rights« came in at third place as a response to this question. This was followed by »Participating in political life« with 9.9 % and »Participating in community/civic life« with 9.2 % of the answers. It should be highlighted that only a minor proportion of the respondents (4.8 %) had a negative perception on EU citizenship which was coded as »Other«.

Figure 2: What does EU citizenship mean to you? What do you associate with it?

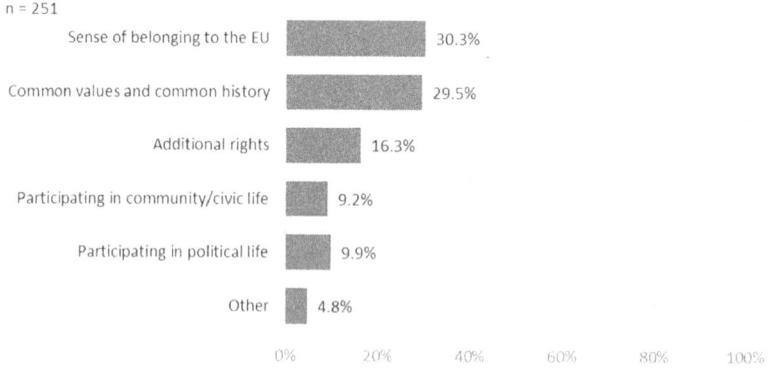

Source: Own compilation.

5.3. Awareness of EU citizens' rights

The next part of the questionnaire was designed to test the respondents' awareness of some of the most important rights they hold as EU citizens. To this end, the students carrying out the survey explained to the respondents that since 1993 all citizens of the EU member states are »citizens of the European Union«. Five statements describing EU rights were then read out and the respondents were asked which of these rights an EU citizen has. When asked about the possibility of residing in another EU country, the vast majority of all respondents indicated that they knew they were entitled to this right. The right of free movement was familiar to 91.4 % of the respondents. Around eight in ten respondents also knew that an EU citizen, when abroad, has the right to seek help from an embassy of any other EU member state if the own country does not have an embassy in the according country. In total, 85.2 % of the respondents were aware of this right to seek help from other EU embassies. The right to participate in an EU Citizens' Initiative was also known to most of the respondents. With over 70 % of the respondents, a clear majority knew about this right. The opportunity to participate in local elections when EU citizens reside in another EU member state is an important opportunity to participate in the political decision-making process and influence local politics. However, less than half of the respondents (43.5 %) were informed that they have the right to vote or even stand as a candidate in local elections in another EU country while they residing there. The last question in regard to the rights of EU citizens was the only question that constituted a right which is not given to EU citizens. There is no right to participate in national general elections as an EU citizen if you live in the concerned country. The majority of respondents were aware that participation in national elections is not an EU citizen's right. 72.1 % of respondents in Duisburg knew that they are not entitled to this right.

Figure 3: In your opinion, which rights does a citizen of the Union have?

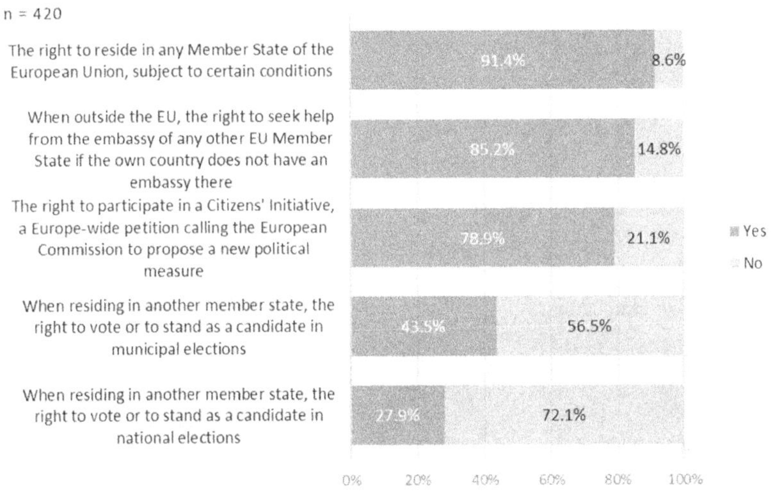

n = 420

Source: Own compilation.

5.4.   Knowing what to do when rights are not respected

Being asked »How well-informed do you feel about what you can do if your rights as an EU citizen are not respected?«, respondents could rate their subjectively perceived level of information on a scale from »very well informed« to »fairly well informed«, »not very well informed« or »not informed at all«. Only 6.4 % of the respondents said that they felt very well informed. After all, just under a fifth of those surveyed sample (19.9 %) stated that they feel fairly well-informed, so that the sum for the positive values was only about one quarter of the sample (26.3 %). Conversely, this means that nearly three-quarters of respondents (73.7 %) had no or no good level of information. Almost half of the respondents (49.2 %) said they were not very well informed, while almost a quarter (24.1 %) did not feel informed at all.

Figure 4: How well do you feel informed about what you can do when your rights as an EU citizen are not respected?

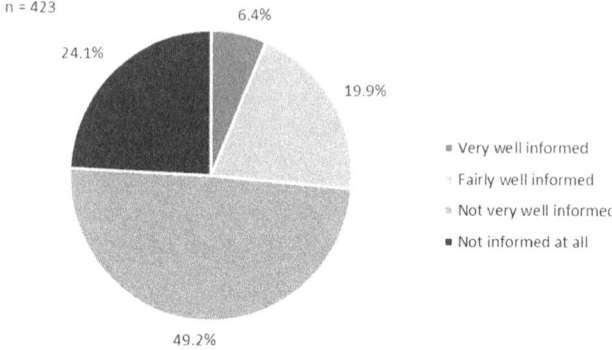

Source: Own compilation.

6. Conclusion

This chapter has presented the results of a survey on the public perception of European Union citizenship on a local level. For this purpose, firstly, the development of EU citizenship and the relationship between citizenship and democracy was explored in a European context. Then an overview on the survey questions and a summary of selected results were given. In a nutshell, the vast majority of respondents said they were familiar with the term ›citizen of the European Union‹ (74.5 %). Respondents were most familiar with their right of free movement: 91.4 % were aware that an EU citizen has the right to reside in any member state of the EU. 85.2 % knew that, when outside the EU, a European citizen has the right to ask for help at embassies of other EU Member States if her or his country does not have an embassy there. More than three-quarters of the respondents (78.9 %) were also aware of the right to participate in a Citizens' Initiative. The least known right was the right to vote or to stand as a candidate in municipal elections: Just over half of the respondents (56.5 %) correctly identified this right. In addition, a sizeable number of respondents (27.9 %) incorrectly thought that a non-national citizen of the EU living in their country has the right to vote or stand as a candidate in national elections. Just over one quarter of the respondents (26.3 %) said they feel informed (either »very well informed« or »fairly well informed«) about what they can do when their rights as an EU citizen are not respected. Finally, to more than 30 % of the respondents, EU citizenship meant a sense of belonging to the EU. Almost the same number of respondents associated EU citizenship with common values and a common history (29.5 %).

Although the results of the survey are not representative, they nonetheless demonstrate that Duisburg citizens are very well aware of their status as EU citizens and have developed a sense of belonging to the EU. Interestingly, the differences between the socio-demographic categories on the sense of European citizenship are limited. However, the concrete knowledge on certain rights varies considerably between the generations. Younger respondents and students in particular know their rights better than the older or less educated respondents. In addition, respondents who place themselves at the top of the social scale are better informed than those who place themselves at the bottom of the social scale. It is therefore encouraging that a huge majority of respondents, regardless of their socio-demographic background, wants to know more about their EU citizenship rights and about what to do if their rights are not respected. As outlined above, the survey was conducted in the years 2013 and 2014. Since then, some important developments have taken place. More than 9 million Europeans have already spoken up through the European Citizens' Initiative. As of 2020, new rules on the European Citizens' Initiative will apply. These rules should make the European Citizens' Initiative more accessible, less burdensome and easier to use for organisers and supporters and therewith »facilitate the participation of as many citizens as possible in the democratic decision-making process of the Union« (Publications Office 2019: 55). In addition, throughout the EU, people have engaged themselves in pro-European grassroots movements like »Pulse of Europe« or »Stand Up for Europe«. Last but not least, two European elections have taken place. The turnout for the European elections in 2019 was the highest since 1979. A total of 50.6 % of EU citizens voted in the elections this year. In the previous European elections five years ago, the turnout was only 42.6 % (Schwarz/Stark 2019).

To conclude, EU citizenship as a legal, practical and habitual form of membership plays a distinct role in the European Union. However, in times with populist and Eurosceptic forces on the rise, there is an urgent need to foster the citizens' trust in the European integration project and remove all remaining obstacles standing in the way of the citizens' enjoyment of their rights (ECAS 2017). Brexit is an exemplary showcase that the construction of democratic citizenship on a European level is not only still in flux but that changes are reversible (Schwarz 2017). The EU citizenship report 2017 lists numerous practical proposals to improve the value of EU citizenship (European Commission 2017). Some of these proposals have been implemented yet while others have not. It is therefore key that the new Commission under Ursula von der Leyen takes further steps to deepen the democratic life in the EU. These steps should revolve around the following key issues:

1. In many cases, member states are the best channel to inform citizens about their rights as citizens of the EU. Accordingly, member states should be further encouraged and financially supported to adopt a more proactive approach in raising awareness about the EU and its activities. Europe Direct Information Centres (EDIC) represent one of the main channels of information for EU citizens. The latest funding period was launched on 1 January 2018 and will run for three years (Nokes 2018). Unfortunately, the last Commission under Jean-Claude Juncker has decided to shut down a considerable number of EDICs. In Germany, the network has been cut down from 54 to 41 EDICs. North Rhine-Westphalia, the most populated federal state in Germany, was particularly effected: Only five of eleven EDICs were allowed to continue their work (Aachen, Duisburg, Essen, Gütersloh and Steinfurt), while only one new centre was opened in Düsseldorf (Europa-Union Deutschland 2018). This approach is short-sighted at best and should be reversed as soon as possible.

2. The elections to the European Parliament are the most visible expression of democratic EU citizenship. However, the European Parliament still suffers from problems of democratic representativeness due to the diversity of national electoral rules (Costa 2016: 53). European elections remain second-order elections (Träger/Anders 2020). Accordingly, the European dimension of EU elections should be strengthened. The introduction of transnational lists has repeatedly been proposed as one way to make Euro-

pean elections even more European and more democratic (Anastassopoulos 1998; Duff/Pukelsheim/Oelbermann 2009; Duff 2011, 2012). The latest attempt to allow transnational lists at European elections was made by the European Parliament rapporteurs Danuta Maria Hübner and Pedro Silva Pereira (2018). The proposal mentioned keeping 46 of the 79 seats vacated by the United Kingdom for a transnational list. The additional seats would have been redistributed to under-represented member states in the Parliament. In February 2018, the European Parliament unfortunately rejected the idea of a transnational list for the 2019 European elections, though MEPs agreed to change the composition of the Parliament in light of Brexit (Schwarz 2020). This decision is regrettable and should be re-examined.

3. The 2014 European elections could be characterised as the first ever »Europeanised elections«, because with the introduction of the *Spitzenkandidaten* system, a truly European political space and a Europe-wide public debate emerged (Koller 2017: 169). Unfortunately, in July 2019, none of the *Spitzenkandidaten*, including the EPP's Manfred Weber and the S&D's Frans Timmermans, was elected as the next President of the European Commission. Instead, the German defence minister was the choice of the European Council and the European Parliament. This is a huge setback in the constitutional development of the European Union and a massive disappointment of thousands of European voters. Although some have argued that the *Spitzenkandidaten* process is »even more dead than the parrot in the Monty Python sketch« (Legutko 2019), it is worth to work on a democratic reform of the election process. Therefore, it is a good sign that the political guidelines for the next European Commission acknowledge the need »to rebuild trust and confidence« and Ursula von der Leyen has proposed herself as a broker for the discussions between the European Parliament and the European Council (von der Leyen 2019: 20).

Last but not least, there is one underlying condition for any EU citizen to truly assert her or his democratic right: the primacy of the rule of law. The current EU lacks adequate mechanisms to monitor and deal effectively with violations of the rule of law in its member states. Recent democratic backsliding in Hungary, Poland and Romania has underlined this. As a matter of fact, the EU faces a »Copenhagen dilemma« (Reding 2013) and its long inaction poses a serious and alarming threat to the credibility of the European integration project as a whole. The central assumption of this chapter is that a truly democratic EU citizenship cannot emerge without serious attention to democracy and the rule of law across all EU member states. Therefore, it is an urgent matter that the next European Commission and Parliament credibly protect and enforce the rule of law and democracy as a backbone of the EU.

References

Adonnino, Pietro (1985): A Peoples Europe. Reports from the Ad Hoc Committee. Luxembourg: Office for Official Publications of the European Communities.

Anastassopoulos, Georgios (1998): Report on a Proposal for an Electoral Procedure Incorporating Common Principles for the Election of Members of the European Parliament. Strasbourg: European Parliament.

Balaguer, Francisco (2013): European Identity, Citizenship and the Model of Integration. In: Alessandra Silveira/Mariana Canotilho/Pedro Madeira Froufe (eds.), Citizenship and Solidarity in the European Union: From the Charter of Fundamental Rights to the Crisis, the State of the Art, Brussels: Peter Lang, 219-234.

Barber, Nicholas W. (2002): Citizenship, Nationalism and the European Union. European Law Review 27: 241-259.

Bayer, Markus/Schwarz, Oliver/Stark, Toralf (2020): Democratic Citizenship in Flux. Introduction and a Conceptual Approach, In: Markus Bayer/Oliver Schwarz/Toralf Stark (eds.), Democratic Citizenship in Flux. Conceptions of Citizenship in the Light of Political and Social Fragmentation, Bielefeld: transcript, 7-22.

Carens, Joseph H. (2000): Culture, Citizenship, and Community. A Contextual Exploration of Justice as Evenhandedness. Oxford: Oxford University Press.

Clark, Nicholas/Hellwig, Timothy (2012): Information Effects and Mass support for EU Policy Control. European Union Politics 4: 535-557. https://doi:10.1177/1465116512441506

Cornelissen, Rob (2009): 50 Years of European Social Security Coordination. European Journal of Social Security 11: 9-45. https://doi:10.1177/138826270901100102

Costa, Olivier (2016): The History of European Electoral Reform and the Electoral Act 1976. Issues of Democratisation and Political Legitimacy. Luxembourg: Publications Office of the European Union.

Council of the European Union (1992): Conclusions of the Presidency. Edinburgh, December 12. https://www.consilium.europa.eu/media/20492/199 2_december_-_edinburgh__eng_.pdf

De Búrca, Grainne (2013): After the EU Charter of Fundamental Rights: The Court of Justice as a Human Rights Adjudicator? Maastricht Journal of European and Comparative Law 20: 173-176. https://doi:10.1177/1023263X1 302000202

Delli Carpini, Michael X./Keeter, Scott (1997): What Americans Know About Politics and Why It Matters, New Haven: Yale University Press.

Denvir, Catrina/Balmer, Nigel J./Pleasence, Pascoe (2013): When Legal Rights are Not a Reality: Do Individuals Know Their Rights and How Can we Tell? Journal of Social Welfare and Family Law 35: 139-160. https://doi:10.1080/ 09649069.2013.774764

Díez Medrano, Juan/Gutiérrez, Paula (2001): Nested Identities: National and European Identity in Spain. Ethnic and Racial Studies 5: 753-778. https:// doi:10.1080/01419870120063963

Duff, Andrew (2011): Report on a Proposal for a Modification of the Act Concerning the Election of the Members of the European Parliament by Direct Universal Suffrage of 20 September 1976. Strasbourg: European Parliament.

Duff, Andrew (2012): Second Report on a Proposal for a Modification of the Act Concerning the Election of the Members of the European Parliament by Direct Universal Suffrage of 20 September 1976, Strasbourg: European Parliament. https://www.europarl.europa.eu/sides/getDoc.do?pubRef=// EP//NONSGML+REPORT+A7-2012-0027+0+DOC+PDF+V0//EN

Duff, Andrew/Pukelsheim, Friedrich/Oelbermann, Kai-Friederike (2009): The Electoral Reform of the European Parliament: Composition, Procedure and Legitimacy, Luxembourg: Publications Office of the European Union.

European Citizen Action Service (ECAS) (2016): 24 Years of EU Citizenship: Removing the Obstacles to Full Potential, Brussels.

European Citizen Action Service (ECAS) (2017): Brexit and Loss of EU Citizenship: Cases, Options, Perceptions, Brussels.

European Court of Justice (ECJ) (2011): Murat Dereci and Others v Bundesministerium für Inneres (Case C-256/11), https://eur-lex.europa.eu/legal-content/EN/TXT/HTML/?uri=CELEX:62011CJ0256&from=EN

Europa-Union Deutschland (2018): Europa-Union kritisiert Abbau von Europe Direct Informationszentren, https://www.europa-union-nrw.de/

meldungen/nrwnews/europa-union-kritisiert-abbau-von-europe-direct-informationszentren/

European Commission (2011): Europe for Citizens Programme 2007-2013. Programme Guide. Brussels: Directorate-General for Communication.

European Commission (2017): EU Citizenship Report 2017. Strengthening Citizens' Rights in a Union of Democratic Change. Luxembourg: Publications Office of the European Union.

Faas, Daniel (2007): Youth, Europe and the Nation: The Political Knowledge, Interests and Identities of the New Generation of European Youth. Journal of Youth Studies 2: 161-181. https://doi:10.1080/13676260601120161

Gabel, Matthew (1998): Public Support for European Integration: An Empirical Test of Five Theories. Journal of Politics 2: 333-354. https://doi:10.2307/26 47912

Hailbronner, Michaela/Iglesias Sánchez, Sara (2011): The European Court of Justice and Citizenship of the European Union: New Developments Towards a Truly Fundamental Status. Vienna Journal on International Constitutional Law 5: 498-537.

Hooghe, Liesbet/Marks, Gary (2005): Calculation, Community and Cues: Public Opinion on European Integration. European Union Politics 4: 419-443. https://doi:10.1177/1465116505057816

Hübner, Danuta Maria/Pereira, Pedro Silva (2018): Report on the Composition of the European Parliament, Strasbourg: European Parliament.

Inglehart, Ronald (1970): Cognitive Mobilization and European Identity. Comparative Politics 1: 45-70. https://doi:10.2307/421501

Ipsen, Hans Peter/Nicolaysen, Gert (1964): Haager Kongreß für Europarecht und Bericht über die aktuelle Entwicklung des Gemeinschaftsrechts. Neue Juristische Wochenschrift 17: 339-344.

Isin, Engin F./Wood, Patricia K. (1999): Citizenship and Identity, London: SAGE.

Koller, Boglárka (2017): European and National Agendas in the 2014 EP Elections in Hungary. In: Ruxandra Boicu/Silvia Branea/Adriana Ştefănel (eds.), Political Communication and European Parliamentary Elections in Times of Crisis. Perspectives from Central and Eastern Europe, London: Palgrave Macmillan, 167-183.

Kostakopoulou, Theodora (2013): What Fractures Political Unions? Failed Federations, Brexit and the Importance of Political Commitment. European Law Review 42: 339-352.

Legutko, Ryszard Antoni (2019): Conclusions of the European Council meeting of 20 and 21 June 2019, Strasbourg, www.europarl.europa.eu/doceo/document/CRE-9-2019-07-04-INT-3-019-0000_EN.html.

Nokes, Tom (2018): Launch of the New Europe Direct Generation, Eltis, https://www.eltis.org/discover/news/launch-new-europe-direct-generation

Publications Office of the European Union (2019): Regulation (EU) 2019/788 of the European Parliament and of the Council of 17 April 2019 on the European Citizens' Initiative, Luxembourg, 17 May, https://eur-lex.europa.eu/legal-content/EN/TXT/PDF/?uri=CELEX:32019R0788

Reding, Viviane (2013): Safeguarding the Rule of Law and Solving the »Copenhagen Dilemma«: Towards a New EU-Mechanism, Luxembourg: European Commission.

Saputelli, Gabriella (2018): Constitutional Design and Asymmetrical Federalism. In: Alain-G. Gagnon/Michael Burgess (eds.), Revisiting Unity and Diversity in Federal Countries. Changing Concepts, Reform Proposals and New Institutional Realities, Leiden: Brill, 259-276.

Sarmiento, Daniel (2013): Who's Afraid of the Charter? The Court of Justice, National Courts and the New Framework of Fundamental Rights Protection in Europe. Common Market Law Review 50: 1267-1304.

Scharkow, Michael/Vogelsang, Jens (2009): Effects of Domestic Media Use on European Integration. In: Communications 4: 73-91.

Schwarz, Oliver (2017): ... And Justice for All. Der Brexit als Chance für eine assoziierte Unionsbürgerschaft, Regierungsforschung.de, https://regierungsforschung.de/and-justice-for-all-der-brexit-als-chance-fuer-eine-assoziierte-unionsbuergerschaft/

Schwarz, Oliver (2020): The 2019 European Parliament Elections and Brexit: Business as Usual? In: Michael Kaeding/Manuel Müller/Julia Schmälter (eds.), Die Europawahl 2019. Ringen um die Zukunft Europas, Wiesbaden: Springer VS, 379-390.

Schwarz, Oliver/Stark, Toralf (2019): Europa hat gewählt. Politische Einstellungen und Wahlabsichten der Duisburger Bürgerinnen und Bürger bei der Europawahl 2019, Duisburg: Stadt Duisburg.

Stadt Duisburg (2018): Duisburger Quartalszahlen 2013-2014, Duisburg, https://www.duisburg.de/vv/medien/dez_i/Quartalszahlen_2013_2015.pdf

Thorpe, Chris (2008): The Distinguishing Function of European Identity: Attitudes Towards and Visions of Europe and the European Union among Young Scottish Adults, Perspectives on European Politics and Society 4: 499-513. https://doi:10.1080/15705850802416945

Träger, Hendrik/Anders, Lisa H. (2020): Die Europawahl 2019 – wieder eine second-order election? Eine Analyse der Wahlergebnisse in den 28 EU-Staaten. In: Michael Kaeding/Manuel Müller/Julia Schmälter (eds.), Die Europawahl 2019. Ringen um die Zukunft Europas, Wiesbaden: Springer VS, 315-326.

Van den Brink, Martijn (2019): EU Citizenship and (Fundamental) Rights: Empirical, Normative, and Conceptual Problems. European Law Journal 25: 21-36. https://doi:10.1111/eulj.12300

Van Eijken, Hanneke/de Vries, Sybe (2011): A New Route into the Promised Land? Being a European Citizen After Ruiz Zambrano. European Law Review 5: 704-721.

Venables, Tony (2016): Piecing together Europe's Citizenship. Searching for Cinderella, Baden-Baden: Nomos.

Verhaegen, Soetkin/Hooghe, Marc (2015): Does More Knowledge about the European Union Lead to a Stronger European Identity? A Comparative Analysis among Adolescents in 21 European Member States. Innovation 2: 127-146. https://doi:10.1080/13511610.2014.1000836

Von Bogdandy, Armin (2000): The European Union as a Human Rights Organization? Human Rights and the Core of the European Union. Common Market Law Review 37: 1307-1338

Von der Leyen, Ursula (2019): A Union That Strives for More. My Agenda for Europe, Brussels: European Commission.

Warleigh, Alex (1998): Frozen: Citizenship and European Unification. Critical Review of International Social and Political Philosophy 1: 113-151. https://doi:10.1080/13698239808403261

Yildirim-Sungur, Feyza/Schwarz, Oliver (2020): Citizenship Regimes and Diaspora Politics. The Case of Politically Involved Turkish Migrants in Germany. In: Markus Bayer/Oliver Schwarz/Toralf Stark (eds.), Democratic Citizenship in Flux. Conceptions of Citizenship in the Light of Political and Social Fragmentation, Bielefeld: transcript, 101-125.

Political contestation and domestic politics in EU financial regulation

Aukje van Loon

1. Introduction and puzzle

The Euro crisis revealed the incompleteness of the Economic and Monetary Union's (EMU) governance framework, prompting the promotion of multiple reform packages and proposals. This induced conflict between EU member states on the design of these reforms. Whereas contemporary literature has put member states' positions at centre stage (Degner/Leuffen 2019a; Schoeller 2018), the research gap on how and why European member *governments* advocate the adopted positions in reconstructing the EMU is still broad (Van Loon 2020). This chapter[1] builds on and contributes to this nascent literature by echoing that Euro crisis management has not resulted in the European Union (EU) being confronted with a democratic deficit at the national level, but has led to a strengthening of democratic citizenship and responsiveness at the level of domestic preference formation. In line with Valelly (2011), democratic citizenship is viewed as »membership in a political democracy«, with the nation-state as the »unit of analysis« and the role of government viewed as an »accountable representative performed by elected (...) officials« within the supranational order of the EU. With democracy's key component being »the continued responsiveness of the government to the preferences of the people« (Dahl 1971: 1), this chapter deals with mapping political contestation *within* one member state, Germany. It focuses specifically on domestic preference formation, where democratic citizenship is sought to have shaped the

1   The author is grateful for valuable assistance from André van Loon and helpful comments from the volume's editors and anonymous reviewers. Financial support from the RUB Research School PLUS (DFG GSC 98/3) is acknowledged.

government's position during negotiations of the European financial transaction tax (FTT) proposal. Democratic citizenship is viewed as encompassing a broad range of domestic stakeholders affected instantly by the crisis: sectoral interest associations, trade unions, voters and NGOs. It provides an answer to the research question: which of these domestic actors were more prevalent in shaping the German government's preference formation during the European FTT debate?

A comprehensive account of the German government's responsiveness is provided by applying the societal approach to governmental preference formation (Schirm 2011, 2013, 2018, 2020). This has been considerably conducive in directing attention to the role of two explanatory variables, domestic interests and ideas, in shaping the divergent positions of governments in the global financial and Euro crises. This study illustrates their role played in shaping the government's position, since cost-benefit analyses from sectoral interest associations and trade unions, and expectations from voters and NGOs towards tightening financial market regulation were of significance. Assuming that the German government's position reflects these societal dynamics, this contribution aims to account for (1) when these mattered, (2) how they interacted and (3) which of these prevailed in shaping the German government's FTT position.

The chapter's next section provides an overview of the post-crisis literature, reading a certain dissent between a decrease versus an increase in democratic citizenship and governments' responsiveness during EU reform negotiations in general, and the FTT in specific. This is followed by introducing the societal approach to governmental preference formation. A discussion of its development of domestic politics theories' core variants subsequently presents innovative elements and a formulation of core hypotheses. The proposed reform of the FTT Directive is briefly presented, leading to an in-depth case study of domestic preference formation, analysing the societal dynamics, interests and ideas to which the German government is assumed to be responsive. The chapter ends with a summary of the empirical results.

2.   European financial governance, democratic citizenship and governments' responsiveness

Contemporary post-crisis European financial governance literature deliberates reform initiatives to typically fall short of democratic legitimacy. Views that crisis management solutions were criteria of output rather than input legitimacy (Kreuder-Sonnen 2016) are prominent. This imbalance is derived from the Euro crisis, which generated a situation involving a substantive urgency, uncertainty of a threat and subsequently unknown consequences of decision-making (Boin et al. 2005). Having to act promptly and decisively, a specific »hour of the executive« (Lodge/Wegrich 2012: 1) and a subsequent democratic deficit seemed to be the result. Kreuder-Sonnen (2018: 962) states:

> »crises typically do imply a broader than usual menu of feasible policy options (...) as a critical threat to a referent community opens the way for policy-makers to employ extraordinary means to cope with the situation, because the sense of crisis induces public deference to claims of political necessity.«

The new European financial governance setting and dynamics regarding the relations between the national and supranational levels, and their reverberations for legitimacy and accountability in the EU, are echoed in recent literature. It is argued that post-crisis European financial governance has gained a stronger supranational character in empowering EU institutions, e.g. the European Commission, in the implementation and application of governance rules (Bauer/Becker 2014). Schmidt (2015) argues that these institutions' failure to achieve results during the Euro crisis, without much public input in reforms, has deteriorated democratic legitimacy. Conversely, the new inter-governmentalism literature argues that crisis management has inclined the Commission to partly depart from the Community method, empowering »de novo bodies« instead (Bickerton et al. 2015: 705). Although intergovernmental coordination within the European Council framework became more prominent during and after the crisis, Smeets and Beach (2019: 2) argue that its »informal and isolated character« marginalised member governments' control and »created more instead of less dependence on EU institutions.« These studies primarily encompass the increase of the EU's long-standing democratic deficit problem. Other literature illustrates the crisis' affirmative impact on explicit aspects of democracy. According to Kriesi (2018), the citizens' dissatisfaction with their countries' economic performance during the crisis led to the strengthening of democratic principles on the national level. The national economies' discontent nevertheless led to bailouts having an impact on citizens' support of democratic values (Cordero/Simón 2016). In sum, while some research illustrates crisis reactions having negatively affected European financial governance's democratic accountability, other academic discourse views crisis-induced actions on the national levels as indicators for an improvement of democratic principles.

This chapter aligns with the latter strand of literature, challenging the assertion that »when failure hits as in the Euro crisis, [...] all sources of legitimacy suddenly, simultaneously collapse« (Weiler 2012: 837). In fact, the Euro crisis may genuinely have enhanced the legitimacy of governments' position taking, particularly during the first phase of European integration, governmental preference formation (Degner/Leuffen 2019b). Pursuing the line of reasoning that the urgent, uncertain threatening crisis situation advanced political contestation, a so-called politicisation (De Wilde et al. 2016), it created a particular environment of democratic citizenship in flux. This mirrors a process leading away »from permissive consensus towards constraining dissensus«, while spilling »beyond interest group bargaining into the public sphere« (Hooghe/Marks 2009: 5). Considering that governments' responsiveness relates to decision-makers prioritising different domestic actors with wide-ranging issues, especially during a time of crisis, which actors' demands did they respond to and why?

Involving salient issues and unknown consequences, citizens were well-informed during these hard times, having concerns about their respective governments' positions in EU reform negotiations. When political contestation is intense, governments are expected to have a greater impulse to follow public opinion (Hobolt/Klemmensen 2008: 310). According to Culpepper (2012), the change from quiet to noisy politics induces (1) an increase of governments' responsiveness to citizens' demands, which simultaneously leads to (2) a decrease of interest groups' ability to shape a government's position. Hooghe and Marks (2009: 18) equally argue that »mass politics trump interest group politics when both come into play«. This contradicts traditional political economy literature, underlining the impact of interest group politics in domestic preference formation (Grossman/Helpman 1994). Additionally, it contrasts with liberal intergovernmentalism (Moravcsik 1993): domestically well-organised and well-endowed interest groups enjoy privileged institutional access to office-seeking/retaining governments, serving as conveyers in defending their demands. With established information channels and large expertise of the issue concerned, governments tend to be biased towards domestic interest groups. Kalaitzake (2017) and Kastner (2017) emphasise that financial interest associations secured their preferences by delaying and watering down the FTT proposal in most EU member states. These actors are considered more important in shaping governments' positions than national electorates. Sanders and Toka (2013: 22) argue the following:

> »[i]n sum, in determining their own stances towards the EU, political elites appear to place more weight on the views of the economically rich and powerful [interest groups] than they do on the views of their own constituents.«

Summing up, literature underlines the importance of both domestic sectoral associations and citizens' opinions as the crisis instantly affected both actor types, generating political contestation over revamping the EMU framework. Governments under scrutiny of a broad range of domestic stakeholders had strong incentives to align their positions according to these actors' demands. Thus, the puzzle of which domestic actors ultimately shaped the German government's FTT position and why is of importance.

3.   The societal approach to governmental preference formation

In analysing which domestic actors encompassing democratic citizenship, interest associations, trade unions, voters and NGOs, were more prevalent in shaping the German government's preference formation during the FTT debate, the societal approach to governmental preference formation is employed. This rests on domestic politics and liberal theories of IR and concentrates on endogenous domestic variables such as interest groups (Milner 1997; Moravcsik 1997) and ideas (Goldstein/Keohane 1993). Similar to these approaches, the assumption is that, in democratic political systems, office-seeking/retaining governments are likely to be responsive to domestic interest and ideas, prior to inter-state and international negotiations (Schirm 2013: 690). Contrary to these, instead of scholars' traditional employment of one or two variables exclusively, the imperative innovative elements of the societal approach are its inclusion of both variables, as well as its subsequent conceptualisation of hypotheses on the conditions for their prevalence vis-à-vis each other in shaping governments' positions. By addressing the question of when either interests or ideas matter in shaping governments' positions, it is a novel »complementary approach« (Schirm 2020: 5). In line with this, domestic interests are material considerations of German sectoral interest associations, whose short-term cost-benefit calculations tend to alter instantly in response to the proposed FTT due to subsequent potential changed market conditions. Domestic ideas are collective value-based expectations of German voters about the apt government's role in steering the economy. Rooted in the past, ideas cannot alter instantly in response to changed market conditions.

Two aspects are of relevance: (1) by refraining from a comparative analysis of divergent governments' FTT positions (Van Loon 2020), this study (2) contributes to research by analysing a broader range of stakeholders potentially affected by FTT introduction. The societal approach's relevant domestic actors sectoral interest associations are complemented by trade unions as sources for domestic interests, and voters are complemented by NGOs as domestic idea sources (Van Loon 2018). In an additional embracement of the societal approach, it is important to explain that the two explanatory variables can (1) concur and reinforce each other, or (2) differ and collide, and equally, (3) compete while shaping governments' positions (Schirm 2013: 690). This mutual complying or competing between and amongst the variables leads to a significant advancement of the to-date cogent aspect neglected by scholars applying domestic politics theories: to inquire into the circumstances for the prevalence of either interests or ideas. While the distinctive variable definitions serve the purpose of analysing when each prevails and why in shaping the German government's FTT position, three core hypotheses of the societal approach (Schirm 2020: 9) sum up the expectations on government's responsiveness during domestic preference formation. The first expects interest groups and trade unions to prevail in shaping the German government's FTT position: if tightening EU financial regulation directly affects specific German economic sectors and implies potential cost-benefit calculations, then domestic interests are more likely to prevail in shaping the government's position, because vocal lobbying efforts dominate preference formation. The second hypothesis outlines voters' and NGOs' predomination in the government's preference formation: if tightening EU financial regulation involves fundamental and salient long-term societal expectations on an apt government's role in steering the economy, then domestic ideas are more likely to prevail in shaping the government's position. These two hypotheses indicate that the explanatory variables can compete. In combination with the reinforcement/competing aspect, a third hypothesis accounts for their interplay: if tightening EU financial regulation raises both potential cost-benefit calculations for specific economic sectors and fundamental and salient long-term societal expectations on the apt government's role in steering the economy, the variables compete or reinforce each other in shaping the government's FTT position.

4.   Operationalisation

In testing German government's responsiveness towards domestic interests or ideas, or both, the empirical analysis applies a qualitative case study that relies on a document analysis tracing relevant interest and ideational-related indicators of the government's preference formation during the 2011-2013 FTT debate. This encompasses the time period of the proposed FTT Directive and the subsequent introduction of the enhanced cooperation mechanism. Document analysis is viewed as an adequate approach to a systematic in-depth investigation of a small-n study of German government's preference formation. As a key EU member state, Germany is chosen due to the substantive important role it played in accelerating the proposed FTT reform through the enhanced cooperation mechanism (Van Loon 2020).

The analysis examines whether the government's FTT position, expressed in statements of responsible elected politicians (finance minister and head of government), correlated with either (1) interest-related indicators articulated by sectoral interest associations' and trade union's demands in the form of position papers and representatives' statements, or to (2) ideational-related indicators such as voters' and NGOs' attitudes as indicated by public opinion polls and positions papers, or if in fact, (3) a correlation occurred between interest and ideational-related indicators. Concerning public opinion surveys, societal attitudes from the Eurobarometer are highlighted as well as two dyads of value-based ideas from the World Values Survey (WVS) on the role of the government in steering the economy: trust in government's regulation versus trust in market forces as well as individual responsibility versus collective solidarity (Schirm 2011: 50). Specialised media reports are applied to underline empirical evidence.

5.   The proposed European FTT

After the failure of the 2010 G20 Toronto Summit in reaching agreement on globally coordinated action to tax the financial sector, the President of the Commission, José Barroso, proposed a Directive in September 2011 to create a harmonised broad-based FTT in response to the global financial and Euro crises. To serve as an example of potential global implementation, the FTT was to be installed by member states. This tax was »to make the financial sector pay its fair share [and] to reduce competitive distortions in the single market, discourage risky trading activities and complement regulatory measures aimed at avoiding future crises« (European Commission 2011). Many member states contested the FTT mainly due to the risks of hindering growth and financial sector relocation. Once reaching the required unanimity to pass the proposal proved difficult, the most reluctant governments such as Sweden, the Netherlands and the UK were bypassed primarily by Germany, in requesting the Commission to introduce the enhanced cooperation mechanism (Van Loon 2020). This would permit those favourable FTT member states to participate in implementing the tax. The mechanism was supported by 11 EU member states[2] representing more than 90 % of Eurozone GDP and was approved by the European Parliament in December 2012 and the Council of the EU in January 2013.

Whereas earlier statements suggested FTT introduction by January 2014, the plan to have a legal basis was delayed until the end of 2014 with plans of implementation by 2016. Support has been waning since, with Estonia formally pulling out in 2016, Belgium blocking negotiations in 2017 (Barbière 2017), the Italian government revoking its wish to participate, and the UK's Brexit vote. FTT introduction still lingers in uncertainty. Statements of support mainly come from Germany, which is regularly putting the FTT on the ECOFIN agenda to advance the issue and renew the political commitment of the remaining member states.

6.   Domestic interests

German sectoral interest associations voiced distinct opposition to tightening financial regulation in form of the FTT. In a joint position paper, eight associations stated their doubts whether the tax could fulfill its objectives. Assuming it would negatively impact the financial sector as well as the economy as a whole, the general fear was that it would (1) have negative effects on companies and employees, (2) burden the economy, in particular in terms of credit supply, and (3) turn financial operations into poorly regulated markets – with consequences for market stability – if it were not introduced globally, or at least EU-wide (DIHK et al. 2011: 2). In the period to the Commission's

---

2   Austria, Belgium, Estonia, France, Germany, Greece, Italy, Portugal, Slovakia, Slovenia and Spain.

proposal for the FTT under enhanced cooperation, Germany's interest associations, the BDI, the BDB and the DIHK shared concerns over its negative
impact on Germany's real economy and private actors. The potential migration of financial institutions, banks and investment funds, to jurisdictions not
taxing transactions were main concerns, followed by the predicament of German enterprises borrowing money and expectations of stagnating growth and
employment. Goals of the FTT in making the financial sector contribute to the
cost of economic recovery but also the precautionary measure of potential future costs of crisis-ridden developments in the financial sector, and creating
disincentives for speculative trading, were viewed critically. In a 2011 public
hearing of the German parliament's finance committee, the ZK, the German
banking industry association, rejected these objectives and feared negative effects on the economy by stating that »[e]ven the EU Commission expects the
gross domestic product to suffer a loss of 1.76 percent with an EU-wide tax of
0.1 percent on equities (0.01 percent on derivatives)« (Deutscher Bundestag
2011). The FTT would not only affect financial institutions, but all purchasers
of financial products including small savers. The BDI, the German industry
association, additionally believed that the FTT would affect »those bearing
the cost of the EU estimated tax revenue of 57 billion euro (...) will be citizens
and the real economy« (Deutscher Bundestag 2011). A study commissioned by
Germany's equities institute estimated the burden on private households and
companies to amount between 5.0 and 7.3 billion Euro annually (DAI 2013: 5).
The BVI, the investment fund association, stated that »mainly long-term and
retirement savings« would suffer (Deutscher Bundestag 2011). This was reflected by the BDB, the association of German banks, stating that particularly the
German ›Mittelstand‹, the export industry as well as the citizens would suffer
significantly: »(t)he stupid one is the small investor in Germany, who cannot
move abroad« (Bankenverband 2013).

On the contrary, the DGB, the trade union confederation, welcomed the
Directive and advocated a broad-based FTT. Since the global financial and
Euro crises had resulted in rising unemployment, it was wary of the social
and political consequences with citizens having lost trust in the markets (DGB
2001la: 3). Its position was that although it was »financial market players that
were chiefly responsible for the biggest financial and economic crisis of the
past 80 years [yet] solely the taxpayers and workers (...) have borne the chief
burden of overcoming the crisis« (DGB 2013: 9). The misguided strategies of
the banks and growing inequality had triggered financial speculation, resulting in the primary problem of a lack of control over market actors, thus im-

plying the necessity of stronger governmental intervention. In February 2011, it called for political stability, economic prosperity and social security:

> »[f]inancial markets must not only be monitored, but also effectively regulated. (...) Those who cause the crisis must be asked to pay. That is why we need a financial transaction tax (...). Furthermore, all financial market products must be audited for their economic benefit (...). The same regulatory rules must apply for all financial market players« (DGB 2011a: 7).

Claus Matecki, DGB board member, stated the urgency of FTT implementation on the national level: »if the desired introduction of the tax on an international or European level does not seem feasible in the short term, Germany (...) must send a clear signal to the other EU member states« (DGB 2011b). The DGB proposed a »Marshall Plan for economic stimulus, investment and development« and suggested the FTT to generate revenue which would benefit employees, the environment, countries and the real economy (DGB 2013: 10).

7.   Domestic ideas

To illustrate the increased issue salience, the importance German citizens attached to the FTT reform proposal and its subsequent politicisation, media analyses from Kastner (2017) and Degner and Leuffen (2019b) confirm that public attention increased instantly, particularly during the years 2011 to 2013. Additionally, findings from the 2011 and 2012 Eurobarometer show that 79 % and 80 % of German respondents were in favour of »the introduction of a tax on financial transactions«. They were equally in favour of the principle of a tax on financial transactions, either on the global level or, failing that, on EU level initially (both 79 %) (Eurobarometer 2011, 15; 2012, T147). Concerning the question of an apt government's role in steering the economy and trust in government's regulation versus trust in market forces, as indicated by data from the 2013 WVS, 65.8 % of the respondents supported the statement »governments should take more responsibility« versus 33.8 % agreeing with »people should take more responsibility« (WVS 2013: V98). The indicators related to individual responsibility versus collective solidarity reveal that 76 % agreed that incomes should be made more equal as opposed to 22.7 % of the respondents who believed that large income divides are required (WVS 2013: V96). Beyond this, the fact that governments should tax the rich and subsidise the poor is considered an essential part of democracy by 68,9 % of the respondents (WVS 2013: V131).

The debate on the broad-based FTT was subject of a vocal campaign by German NGOs favouring it. Under the slogan »Steuer gegen Armut« (tax against poverty), tax campaigns focused mainly on the argument of tax justice and the attraction of potential revenue. The FTT could (1) serve to burden the costs of combatting the financial crisis primarily by the financial industry, not by the taxpayer, and furthermore, (2) the tax's progressive effect, primarily affecting high-income earners, would potentially reduce increasing inequalities in income distribution, thus serving as development aid in combatting national and international poverty. Referred to as a ›Robin Hood Tax‹ (Van Loon forthcoming), 32 signatories sparked this campaign by issuing an open letter to the newly elected German government. This emphasised the FTT advantages: (1) it decelerates and regulates financial transactions on financial markets, (2) it includes all speculation-relevant financial transactions, (3) short-term transactions are made less profitable, whereas medium and long-term investments face a low tax rate between 0.1 and 0.01 %, and (4) revenues are used for the implementation of the Millennium Development Goals (MDGs) and for development measures, the fight against poverty, and climate and environment protection (Alt 2011). Successful in gathering widespread public support, the campaign achieved a considerably broad membership in the first half of 2011 with trade unions (including the DGB) joining religious, development and environmental organisations in campaigning for the tightening of financial regulation. When prospects for a global and EU-wide transaction tax faded, strong support for the FTT via the enhanced cooperation mechanism commenced (Wahl 2014: 6). Campaign demands were issued in the form of a petition signed by 66,000 supporters within four weeks (Alt 2011). The German campaign leader, Peter Wahl, stated that »for civil society the process is a great success« due to the »Steuer gegen Armut« campaign, having established informal and formal permanent contacts with decision-makers and having mobilised public opinion by (1) organising public events to which decision-makers were invited, (2) organising formal petitions and collecting signatures, (3) writing letters, thereby (4) creating transparency and accountability of lobbying activities using traditional print media and the internet (Wahl 2014: 14-15).

8.   The german government's FTT position

The German government supported a broad-based FTT and when consensus on this was reached in 2010 (Tagesschau 2013), Germany was the main driver behind requesting the Commission to implement the enhanced cooperation mechanism (Bundesregierung 2014). In November 2011 Germany's finance minister, Wolfgang Schäuble, dismissed opposing arguments:

> »The objections made by some who claim it would mean a substantial drop in employment and in the economy generally seem to rest on exaggerated (...) projections and, more important, ignore the potential of such a tax to stabilize currency markets in a way to boost rather than damage the real economy« (Winnet et al. 2011).

By summing up the aims of the tax, Schäuble listed the following arguments: (1) the financial sector needs to contribute to the crisis' costs, (2) substantial tax revenue would be raised, and (3) financial markets' actions would be limited. The FTT's rationale was »not only a question of the economy and the budget but of democratic legitimacy«, and potentially raising 2 billion Euro a year for Germany, Schäuble stated »I'd prefer to have it in my budget but it's better to have it for climate change or development aid than to have nothing« (The Guardian 2011).

Without unanimous agreement, the German government accelerated the process by applying for FTT introduction through enhanced cooperation. At an ECOFIN meeting, Schäuble announced Germany's advancement with a smaller group of states (FAZ 2012) stating that even without this mechanism, it would »endeavour to achieve taxation in as many member states as possible within the framework of intergovernmental cooperation« (Bundesregierung 2012: 2). The German Chancellor Angela Merkel underlined the government's strong commitment, particularly after having gained support from the SPD and the Greens (Handelsblatt 2012):

> »We support the introduction of a financial transaction tax, because the people in our countries still have the impression (...) that the financial sector must make an appropriate contribution to managing the costs of the financial crisis, and the financial transaction tax will be levied precisely for this purpose« (Bundesregierung 2014).

In 2013, the FTT was included in the programme of the German grand coalition. By particularly stressing »[n]o financial market, no financial product, no
financial market player without supervision«, focus was on a broad-based FTT
within the EU framework of enhanced cooperation. This was to be implemented swiftly to strengthen the financial sector's participation in contributing to
the costs of the crisis by including all financial instruments: equities, bonds,
investment shares, foreign exchange transactions and derivative contracts. By
designing the tax, the government stated the importance to assess the tax's
impact on »pension instruments, small investors and the real economy (...)
while at the same time reducing unwanted forms of financial transactions«
(Koalitionsvertrag 2013: 46).

9. Conclusion

Through application of the societal approach to governmental preference formation, this chapter examined which domestic actors, forming democratic
citizenship as defined above, were more prevalent in shaping the German government's FTT position. By analysing a broad range of stakeholders potentially affected by FTT introduction, sectoral interest associations, trade unions,
voters and NGOs, this study illustrates that the government clearly followed
dominant domestic ideas. With the financial sector viewed as responsible for
causing the crisis and the FTT's objective for making them contribute to its
costs, sectoral interest associations had lost privileged weight in shaping the
German preference formation despite potential high cost-benefit calculations
and vocal lobbying against the FTT. Additionally, the increased issue salience
of financial regulation reform severely reduced government's representatives
to respond to sectoral interest associations' demands, resulting in these actors' inability to shape the position of the government.

This simultaneously created an opportunity for other domestic actors to
gain access to decision-makers, resulting in the government's responsiveness
to pro-reform demands from NGOs. The German FTT campaign established
good access opportunities and its intensive campaigning, including the support of most German voters and the trade unions' alignment of their concerns,
led to the government's endorsement of the FTT. Whereas both domestic interests and ideas were thus directly affected by a tightening of financial regulation, the former (sectoral interests associations and trade unions) compe-

ted, while the latter (voters and NGOs) reinforced each other in shaping the favourable government's position.

The urgent, threatening crisis situation resulted in a particular environment of democratic citizenship in flux, from rejecting the sectoral interest associations' political contestation to public sphere's advancement in favouring the FTT, leading to a genuine enhancement of democratic legitimacy of the German government's FTT's position taking.

References

Alt, Jörg (2011): Stellungnahme des Hauptpetenten aus Anlass der Öffentlichen Anhörung der Petition »Einführung einer Finanztransaktionssteuer« im Deutschen Bundestag. https://www.steuer-gegen-armut.org/fileadmin/Dateien/Kampagnen-Seite/Wer_wir_sind/Stellungnahmen/110207_Statement.pdf

Bankenverband (2013): Aktuelles Stichwort – Finanztransaktionssteuer – Wer zahlt? https://bankenverband.de/media/publikationen/aktuelles-stich_Mk56lu2.pdf

Barbière, Cécile (2017): Belgium Told to Get Off the Fence, Stop Blocking FTT, In: Euractiv, https://www.euractiv.com/section/economy-jobs/news/belgium-told-to-get-off-the-fence-stop-blocking-ftt/

Bauer, Michael W./Becker, Stefan (2014): The Unexpected Winner of the Crisis: The European Commission's Strengthened Role in Economic Governance. Journal of European Integration 36:3, 213-229. https://doi:10.1080/07036337.2014.885750

Bickerton, Christopher J./Hodson, Dermot/Puetter, Uwe (2014): The New Intergovernmentalism: European Integration in the Post-Maastricht Era. Journal of Common Market Studies 53:4, 703-722. https://doi:10.1111/jcms.12212

Boin, Arjen't/Hart, Paul/Stern, Eric/Sundelius, Bengt (2005): The Politics of Crisis Management. Public Leadership under Pressure. Cambridge: Cambridge University Press, 1-37.

Bundesregierung (2014): Finanztransaktionssteuer: Elf Mitgliedsstaaten gehen voran. 7 May 2014. https://www.bundesregierung.de/breg-de/aktuelles/elf-mitgliedstaaten-gehen-voran-420754

Bundesregierung (2012): Pakt für nachhaltiges Wachstum und Beschäftigung – Gemeinsames Papier der Bundesregierung und der Fraktionen

CDU/CSU, FDP, SPD und Bündnis 90/Die Grünen im Deutschen Bundestag, Pressemitteilung. https://archiv.bundesregierung.de/resource/blob/656922/744304/3d78b5c23bd0af2375ea935fe743dd90/2012-06-21-wachstum-pakt-data.pdf

Cordoro, Guillermo/Simón, Pablo (2016): Economic Crisis and Support for Democracy in Europe. West European Politics 39:2, 305-325. https://doi:10.1080/01402382.2015.1075767

Culpepper, Pepper D. (2012): Quiet Politics and Business Power. Corporate Control in Europe and Japan. Cambridge: Cambridge University Press.

Dahl, Robert A. (1971): Polyarchy: Participation and Opposition. New Haven: Yale University Press.

Deutsches Aktieninstitut (2013): Die Finanztransaktionssteuer – Ein Politischer Irrweg? Oliver Wyman, https://www.dai.de/files/dai_usercontent/dokumente/studien/190116%20Studie%20Mehr%20Aktionaere%20in%20Deutschland.pdf

De Wilde, Pieter/Leupold, Anna/Schmidtke, Henning (2016): Introduction: the Differentiated Politicisation of European Governance. West European Politics 39:1, 3-22. https://doi:10.1080/01402382.2015.1081505

Degner, Hanno/Leuffen, Dirk (2019a): Franco-German Cooperation and the Rescuing of the Eurozone. European Union Politics 20:1, 89-108. https://doi:10.1177/1465116518811076

Degner, Hanno/Leuffen, Dirk (2019b): Crisis and Responsiveness: Analysing German Preference Formation during the Eurozone Crisis. Political Studies Review. https://doi:10.1177/1478929919864902

Deutscher Bundestag (2011): Finanztransaktionssteuer unter Experten umstritten. https://www.bundestag.de/dokumente/textarchiv/2011/3670109 7_kw48_pa_finanzen-207024

Deutscher Gewerkschaftsbund (2011a): Europa neu justieren – Wachstum fördern, Beschäftigung sichern, Euro stabilisieren. 3 February 2011. https://www.dgb.de/++co++2b7d6dfa-2fb0-11e0-5ba7-00188b4dc422

Deutscher Gewerkschaftsbund (2011b): Finanztransaktionssteuer muss jetzt kommen. https://www.dgb.de/presse/++co++c7010542-9291-11e0-4695-00 188b4dc422

Deutscher Gewerkschaftsbund (2013): A Marschall Plan for Europe. https://www.dgb.de/++co++d92f2d46-5590-11e2-8327-00188b4dc422

Deutscher Industrie- und Handelskammertag (DIH)/Bundesverband der der deutschen Industrie/Zentralverband des deutschen Handwerks/Bundesvereinigung der deutschen Arbeitgeberverbände/Bundesverband

deutscher Banken/Gesamtverband der deutschen Versicherungswirt-
schaft/Handelsverband Deutschland der Einzelhandel/Bundesverband
Grosshandel, Aussenhandel, Dienstleistungen (BGA) (2011): Stellungnahme – Öffentliche Anhörung zur Finanztransaktionssteuer. https:
www.biv-kaelte.de/fileadmin/user_upload/mitglieder/Rechtsberatung/V
rbaende_Finanztransaktionssteuer.pdf

Eurobarometer (2011): Table of Results – Standard Eurobarometer 75 European Perceptions on the State of the Economy. https://ec.europa.eu/com
mfrontoffice/publicopinion/archives/eb/eb75/eb75_anx_en.pdf

Eurobarometer (2012): Table of Results – Standard Eurobarometer 77 Europeans, the European Union and the Crisis. https://ec.europa.eu/commfr
ontoffice/publicopinion/archives/eb/eb77/eb77_anx_en.pdf

European Commission (2011): Financial Transaction Tax: Making the Financial Sector Pay its Fair Share. Press Release. https://europa.eu/rapid/pres
s-release_IP-11-1085_en.htm?locale=en

Frankfurter Allgemeine (2012): Finanzminister-Treffen: Transaktionssteuer
kommt nicht in allen EU-Staaten. https://www.faz.net/aktuell/wirtscha
ft/finanzminister-treffen-transaktionssteuer-kommt-nicht-in-allen-eu-
staaten-11795448.html

Goldstein, Judith/Keohane, Robert O. (1993): Ideas and Foreign Policy: Beliefs,
Institutions and Political Change. Cornell: Cornell University Press.

Grossman, Gene M./Helpman, Elhanan (1994): Protection for Sale. The American Economic Review 84:4, 833-850

Handelsblatt (2012): ›SZ‹/EU: Finanztransaktionssteuer kann noch 2012 vere-
inbart werden. https://www.handelsblatt.com/dpa/economy-business-
und-finance-sz-eu-finanztransaktionssteuer-kann-noch-2012-vereinba
rt-werden/6742870.html?ticket=ST-7579869-26DwpFFugMSvJ1XnvTyz-
ap6

Hobolt, Sarah B./Klemmensen, Robert (2008): Government Responsiveness
and Political Competition in Comparative Perspective. Comparative Political Studies 41:3, 309-337. https://doi:10.1177/0010414006297169

Hooghe, Liesbet/Marks, Gary (2009): A Postfunctionalist Theory of European Integration: From Permissive Consensus to Constraining Dissensus.
British Journal of Political Science 39:1, 1-23. https://doi:10.1017/S0007123
408000409

Kalaitzake, Manolis (2017): Death by a Thousand Cuts? Financial Political Power and the Case of the European Financial Transaction Tax. New Political Economy 22:6, 709-726. https://doi:10.1080/13563467.2017.1311850

Kastner, Lisa (2017): Civil Society and Financial Regulation. Consumer Finance Protection and Taxation after the Financial Crisis. London: Routledge.

Koalitionsvertrag (2013): Deutschlands Zukunft gestalten. Koalitionsvertrag zwischen CDU, CSU und SPD, 18. Legislaturperiode. https://www.cdu.de/sites/default/files/media/dokumente/koalitionsvertrag.pdf

Kreuder-Sonnen, Christian (2016): Beyond Integration Theory. The (Anti-)Constitutional Dimension of European Crisis Governance. Journal of Common Market Studies 54:6, 1350-1366. https://doi:10.1111/jcms.12379

Kreuder-Sonnen, Christian (2018): Political Secrecy in Europe: Crisis Management and Crisis Exploitation. West European Politics 41:4, 958-980. https://doi:10.1080/01402382.2017.1404813

Kriesi, Hanspeter (2018): The Implications of the Euro Crisis for Democracy. Journal of European Public Policy 25 (1), 59-82. https://doi:10.1080/13501763.2017.1310277

Lodge, Martin/Wegrich, Kai (2012): Introduction: Executive Politics in Times of Crisis. In: Lodge, Martin and Wegrich, Kai (eds.) The Executive at Work during Times of Crisis. Basingstoke: Palgrave Macmillan, 1-18.

Milner, Helen V. (1997): Interests, Institutions and Information: Domestic Politics in International Relations. Princeton: Princeton University Press.

Moravcsik, Andrew (1993): Preferences and Power in the European Community: A Liberal Intergovernmentalist Approach. Journal of Common Market Studies 31:4, 473-524. https://doi:10.1111/j.1468-5965.1993.tb00477.x

Moravcsik, Andrew (1997): Taking Preferences Seriously: A Liberal Theory of International Politics. International Organization 51:4, 513-553. https://doi:10.1162/002081897550447

Sanders, David/Toka, Gabor (2013): Is Anyone Listening? Mass and Elite Opinion cueing in the EU. Electoral Studies 32: 13-25. https://doi:10.1016/j.electstud.2012.10.001

Schirm, Stefan A. (2011): Varieties of Strategies: Societal Influences on British and German Responses to the Global Economic Crisis. Journal of Contemporary European Studies 19:1, 47-62. https://doi:10.1080/14782804.2010.535716

Schirm, Stefan A. (2013): Global Politics are Domestic Politics: A Societal Approach to Divergence in the G20. Review of International Studies 39:3, 685-706. https://doi:10.1017/S0260210512000216

Schirm, Stefan A. (2018): Societal Foundations of Governmental Preference Formation in the Eurozone Crisis. European Politics and Society 19:1, 63-78. https://doi:10.1080/23745118.2017.1340397

Schirm, Stefan A. (2020): Refining Domestic Politics Theories of IPE: A Societal Approach to Governmental Preferences. Politics (first published 23 January), 1-17. https://doi:10.1177/0263395719896980

Schmidt, Vivien A. (2015): The Eurozone's Crisis of Democratic Legitimacy. Can the EU Rebuild Public Trust and Support for European Economic Integration? European Economy Discussions Paper No. 15 (European Commission). https://ec.europa.eu/info/sites/info/files/dp015_en.pdf

Schoeller, Magnus G. (2018): The Rise and Fall of Merkozy: Franco-German Bilateralism as a Negotiation Strategy in Eurozone Crisis Management. Journal of Common Market Studies 56:5 1019-1035. https://doi:10.1111/jcms.12704

Smeets, Sandrino/Beach, Derek (2019): Political and Instrumental Leadership in Major EU Reforms. The Role and Influence of the EU Institutions in Setting-up the Fiscal Compact. Journal of European Public Policy. https://doi:10.1080/13501763.2019.1572211

Tagesschau (2013): Streit um Finanzmarktsteuer: Zocker sollen die Zeche zahlen. https://www.tagesschau.de/wirtschaft/finanztransaktionssteuer118.html

The Guardian (2011): German Finance Minister Says too Many Gastarbeiter were Allowed in. https://www.theguardian.com/world/2011/mar/18/german-finance-minister-guest-workers-row

Valelly, Richard M. (2011): Democratic Citizenship. In: Political Science, Oxford Bibliographies. https://doi:10.1093/OBO/9780199756223-0013

Van Loon, Aukje (2018): Domestic Politics and National Differences in Restructuring EU Financial Supervision. European Politics and Society 19:3, 247-263. https://doi:10.1080/23745118.2017.1419598

Van Loon, Aukje (2020): Societal Dynamics in European Economic Governance: A Comparative Analysis of Variation in British and German Governmental Stances. In: Rewizorski, Marek/Jędrzejowska, Karina/Wróbel, Anna (eds.) The Future of Global Economic Governance: Challenges and Prospects in the Age of Uncertainty. Cham: Springer, 119-139.

Van Loon, Aukje (forthcoming): ›Robin Who?‹ Zwischen kollektiven Ideen und materiellen Interessen: die europäische Finanztransaktionssteuer in Deutschland und Großbritannien. Sonderheft NGOs im Prozess demokratischer Politikgestaltung: Strategien und Handlungslogiken zwischen Konflikt und Kooperation. Zeitschrift für Politikwissenschaft.

Wahl, Peter (2014): The European Civil Society Campaign on the Financial Transaction Tax. Global Labour University Working Papers No. 20. www.global-labour-university.org/fileadmin/GLU_Working_Papers/GLU_WP_No.20.pdf

Weiler, Joseph H. H. (2012): In the Face of Crisis: Input Legitimacy, Output Legitimacy and the Political Messianism of European Integration. West European Politics 34:7, 825-841. https://doi:10.1080/07036337.2012.726017

Winnet, Robert, Ward, Victoria and Alleyne, Richard (2011): Archbishop of Canterbury Rowan Williams calls for new tax on bankers. https://www.telegraph.co.uk/news/religion/8863794/Archbishop-of-Canterbury-Rowan-Williams-calls-for-new-tax-on-bankers.html

World Values Survey (2013): Online Analysis. Wave 2010-2014. www.worldvaluessurvey.org/WVSOnline.jsp

Formal citizenship in European constitutions

Kathrin Behrens

1. Introduction

»Citizenship of the Union is hereby established. Every person holding the nationality of a Member State shall be a citizen of the Union« (European Union
1992: 15, art. 8 [1]). With this paragraph, the European Union expresses in the
1992 Maastricht Treaty[1] (European Union 1992) »EU's experiment with a form
of supranational citizenship« (Shaw 2019: 2). In the 1997 Amsterdam Treaty,
however, this experiment was toned down by adding that »Citizenship of the
Union shall complement and not replace national citizenship« (European Union 1997: 27, art. 2 [9])[2]. The European Union's attempt to contest and hence
to restructure the traditional concept of national citizenship is one of many
examples of *citizenship in flux*. Nevertheless, even today European citizenship
is still complementary to national citizenship and not a substitute on a supranational level. More clearly: the opportunities and benefits offered by an
EU-citizenship (for instance freedom of movement, settlement and employment) inevitably depend on the membership to a European member state (for
example Shaw 2019: 1).

The membership to a nation-state as a political community refers to
citizenship as status, one of the two traditional lines of theories on citizenship.
This contrasts with the second classical approach, which broadly refers
to citizenship as activity (for instance Isin 2009. While the first narrative
precisely defines the belonging to a political community, the second focuses
on the function of political and social participation in that specific political

---

1   Origins can already be found in the first treaties of the European Economic Community
of 1957, but not as explicit regulation of European citizenship. Further information can
be found, for instance, in Jacobs (2007).
2   There has been no change in the concept of European citizenship as complementary
to the national citizenship in the Lisbon Treaty of 2009.

community (Kymlicka and Norman 1994: 353-54). Belonging to a nation-state is established by formal membership, represented by legally determined formal citizenship. Consequently, formal citizenship as a legal status includes people to a political community on a formal level, which is necessary in order to have at least the chance of political and social participation in the society of a nation[3]. Both, citizenship as activity and citizenship as status were challenged in the last decades, for instance in discourses on migration(see for instance Bauböck 2019) and globalization (exemplary Staeheli 1999). ?. Yet despite these modern attempts to define and secure citizenship on a global (here: European) level, citizenship on the national level still seems to be indispensable.

This sociological contribution examines the concept of *formal citizenship as status* in its legal dimension through an analysis of European member states' constitutions. On the national level, constitutions are the most basic legal document, and hence they have the potential to legally define the conditions for formal membership, realized as citizenship regulations (Blaustein 1994: 3). Constitutionally regulated formal membership is tied to the privilege of certain (constitutionally secured) rights. These rights, for example in the form of the right to vote or the right to be elected into certain state institutions, contribute significantly to the *formal inclusion*[4] in the community – or the *exclusion* in case of its denial. In this sense and a sociological perspective, *constitutions are highly important legal institutions revealing mechanisms of formal inclusion or exclusion by setting the conditions for formal membership due to citizenship regulations.* In other words, the legal system (potentially) addresses people as citizens and thus formally includes them into a specific social and political community (Luhmann 1995).

---

3   As Schinkel (2010), for example, rightly observes, nation-state and society are not necessarily the same thing. The same applies to their memberships. Whenever formal membership is mentioned in this article, it is always a question of legal belonging to a nation-state qua formal status as a citizen. The possibility of political and social participation and the associated societal belonging results (among other things) from the legally defined rights and duties that go hand in hand with this status. For reasons of space, no further attention can be paid to these consequences in detail.

4   Since this contribution is devoted exclusively to the legal and thus formal construct of citizenship, inclusion/exclusion can only be considered on the formal level. Formal inclusion is achieved through formal membership but does not allow any statements about actual social integration.

Due to the increasing tendency of nation-states to standardize constitutions in terms of content and form (cf. Blaustein 1994), the question arises as to whether formal citizenship and thus legally defined formal inclusion/exclusion follows standardized paths or country-specific patterns – especially in the case of the European Union, in which the need for national regulations is articulated on a supranational level. To sociologically address the topic of *citizenship in flux*[5], the main argument of this paper is as follows: if the formal dimension of citizenship is legally secured on a national level, it could be regulated in national constitutions. Since constitutions are comparatively stable constructs (cf. Elkins, Ginsburg and Melton 2009), the concept of formal citizenship is limited in its dynamic if it is regulated in these documents. Constitutions could thus be interpreted as the ›corset‹ for formal citizenship. Consequently, it can be assumed that formal inclusion/exclusion has a low potential for change. So, the main questions are: is formal citizenship regulated in European constitutions? If so, which dimensions are part of the constitutional regulations? By answering these questions, it can be analyzed if formal citizenship in particular has the potential to flux dynamically.

To outline the legal foundation of formal citizenship, this contribution gives insights into citizenship regulations in constitutional documents on a descriptive level, structured as follows: Firstly, it illustrates a sociological perspective on system-theoretical inclusion/exclusion (Luhmann 1995) to underline its relevance for social order. Secondly, it translates these ideas into the analytical dimensions of formal citizenship in constitutions. Furthermore, the dimensions of formal membership are reconstructed by primary data of a quantitative content analysis of constitutional documents. Thus, this contribution offers an innovative and distinct sociological perspective that provides an understanding of the multidimensional and -faceted concept of citizenship in its explicitly formal expression.

---

5   To answer the question of how constitutionally anchored citizenship regulations have changed over time, an intra-national comparison of various constitutional versions would be required. The current research design of this study does not accommodate the vast complexity needed to internationally compare intra-national constitutional change over time. Instead, the focus is on the international (here European) comparison of formalized citizenship regulations, which is an important aspect for further discussions in the volume.

2. Inclusion and exclusion by formal citizenship

Generally speaking, we can describe inclusion as the multidimensional involvement of people in a community, while exclusion means the opposite; hence,
they are complementary concepts. Inclusion into a social and political community in a *formal dimension* is guaranteed by the legally granted status as citizen. Fahrmeier (2007) describes the *formal dimension of citizenship* as »the legal
definition of a close relationship between individuals and one state, usually
documented in passports or other citizenship certificates. Formal citizenship
[is] [...] a way of defining groups entitled to particular rights [...]« (Fahrmeir
2007: 2). Thus, constitutionally regulated citizenship legally determines formal inclusion that represents the translation of formal citizenship into (the
possibility of) active participation in the social and political arena, which is
crucial for the social and political integration of individuals into society.

One *sociological perspective* on inclusion is given by Systems Theory, the
best-known representatives of which are Parsons (1964) and Luhmann (1995).
While Parsons uses the term *integration* to describe the relationship between
the units of a societal subsystem that ensure its stability and prevent its disintegration (Parsons 1964), Luhmann focuses on the differentiation of *inclusion*
and *exclusion* (Luhmann 1995). He dissociates himself from the concept of integration as he generally assumes that, on the one hand, the *full* integration
of individuals into the functionally differentiated societies in modernity is
impossible. On the other hand, he explains that *multiple inclusions into one or
more subsystems* is possible; which means a simultaneous exclusion from other
subsystems due to the impossibility of full societal inclusion. In this sense,
inclusion refers to the inner side of the system, while exclusion consequently
refers to the outer side (Luhmann 1995: 241). Luhmann does not understand
inclusion as the entire ›incorporation‹ of individual actors[6] into the societal
system, but rather as »the way [...] in which, in the context of communication[7], people are *described*, and thus regarded as relevant,« that is, »the way in
which they are treated as ›persons‹« [translated by author; emphasis in ori-
ginal] (Luhmann 1995: 241). This idea is analogous to Fahrmeier's expression

6   Luhmann (1995) does not actually refer to ›individuals‹ or ›individual actors‹ in the ter-
minology of his systems theory. He rather uses concepts such as ›psychic systems‹ to
address what, in other theories, are the units on the individual level of society.
7   In this context, communication means the final element or specific operation of a societal system (Baraldi, Corsi and Esposito 1997:89).

of »defining groups« (Fahrmeir 2007: 2) that are entitled to a set of rights associated with the status as citizen.

Consequently, with Luhmann's perspective, *exclusion* from a societal subsystem means that the actor is *not a relevant person* for the subsystem. In modern, functionally differentiated societies, exclusion from one subsystem often results in the exclusion from multiple subsystems: losing one's job can result in losing one's flat, which can endanger one's connection to other social institutions (Baraldi, Corsi and Esposito 1997: 81). As Luhmann himself exemplifies, the lack of an identity card is cause to be excluded from social benefits, such as voting and legal marriage (Luhmann 1995: 259-260). The depth of the implications of exclusion can lead to individuals being regarded less and less as persons and as possible communication partners, but only as bodies for which different social conditions apply (Luhmann 1995: 262).

Although this article is explicitly not a system-theoretical examination of citizenship in constitutions, this theoretical excursus serves to clarify the sociological constraints of this article. The question remains, how formal inclusion/exclusion is legally organized. It seems obvious that the rights and duties regarding active participation are crucial for social and political inclusion, and, furthermore, the refusal of such rights leads to exclusion from subsystems such as the economic, judicial or educational systems (and vice versa). Referring again to Luhmann, citizenship (codified by the identity card) is one key mechanism for the claim on social benefits, the right to vote, to be eligible for political office and so on (Luhmann 1995: 259-60), making it plausible to examine citizenship regulations to answer the questions on formal inclusion. Rather than focusing on the political realization of rights indicative of social and political inclusion, this paper seeks to analyze the legal and thus formal dimension of citizenship and hence formal inclusion/exclusion. *Since the formally defined citizenship regulations are the legal translation of formal inclusion, the most important determinant seems to be the granting or denial of citizen status in constitutional documents.*

Following these ideas, the importance of the relationship between the legal definition of formal citizenship in national constitutions and formal inclusion can be summarized as follows: According to Luhmann's ideas, *the legal subsystem addresses the relevant persons by constitutional regulation, especially by formal citizenship as dimension of formal membership. Therefore, constitutional documents can be interpreted as genuine sociological material: they establish social order by mechanisms of inclusion/exclusion and stabilize it over time.* As a result, the constitutional documents seem to be a meaningful empirical basis for the examination of citizenship, since they represent the basis of any legal organization of nation-states. Thus, national constitutions provide an insight into the legal manifestation of how modern nation-states regulate the inclusion of people as legal persons.

3.   Constitutional regulation of formal citizenship

Constitutions as formalized certificates are »the final triumph […] as a solemn result of democratic constitutionalism« [translation by author] (Loewenstein 1969: 137), resulting from the American and French Revolutions. They are the most fundamental written document, legally organizing the social arenas of societies (Grey 1984; Loewenstein 1969; Tschentscher 2011): by regulating the governmental arrangements and thereby setting the frame for political processes, constitutions are highly influential instruments of modern nation-states. Even if there are supranational institutions, for instance the European Union, which provide (at least partially) legally binding laws and treaties, constitutions on the national level still seem to be highly relevant institutions for modern nation-states. This is exemplarily indicated by the fact that the vast majority of countries has a constitution, despite the lack of obligation to have one (Go 2003: 71). Compared to administrative law, they have a special character. Go (2003) for instance states: »Not only are they all packed in a single document, they all specify in one way or another the organisation of political power, the division of governmental labour, the major principles and goals of governance« (2003: 72). Additionally, they are »meant to express an arrangement vastly more complex than those underlying most legal documents: the web of society's basic institutions and ideals« (Grey 1984: 16). In other words, constitutions represent common beliefs and recognized behaviors of a specific community (Loewenstein 1969: 127) as a »system of fundamental norms« [translated by author] (Loewenstein 1969: 129).

Additionally, as constitutions are »not an *ex nihilo* creation« [emphasis in original] (Grey 1984: 16), they can be interpreted as the result of societal negotiation processes as well as the catalyst for future social endeavors, making them *both a result of and a condition for social change*. Here it becomes clear once again why constitutions are relevant empirical data when it comes to *formal citizenship*: On the one hand, the regulations of formal citizenship contained therein are the result of certain social negotiation processes. Thus, the specific regulations of citizenship are the formalized outcome of social and political discourses about membership. On the other hand, they influence, limit and enable social change by legally setting rules and frames for governmental arrangements and thereby determine the social order of society. They set the legal basis for the (passive) status as citizen, which is connected to certain rights and duties for individuals. These in turn form the foundation for the active habitus of citizens. By that, constitutions contribute to the formal inclusion of the members of a specific social and political community and simultaneously foster the social exclusion of foreigners. These mechanisms of formal inclusion and exclusion through the constitutional provision of formal membership are subject to constant negotiation processes. Therefore, the concept of *formal citizenship* itself is result of societal change and at the same time one of its determinants.

Focusing again on the question of *citizenship in flux*, some expectations[8] regarding the forthcoming presentation and discussion of results can be expressed: The ability of constitutions to establish social orders and to stabilize them for a comparatively long period of time determines the *potential for flux in the concept of formal citizenship*. Thus, if these documents contain very specific regulations on formal membership, a tight legal corset and thus a low potential for change can be assumed. If, though, formal citizenship is not regulated on the constitutional level, a capacity for dynamic change can be assumed, without, indeed, being able to say more precisely at this point whether and to what extent this takes place or has taken place.

4.   The data on constitutional citizenship regulation

The following analysis focuses on primary data resulting from a sub-project of the ›OnBound-Project‹ (#316798296 in the DFG database), which aims at an international comparison of religious and national identities. The subproject deals with the significance of religious and national identities in constitutions around the world and was guided by similar approaches that examined different constitutional contents (for instance Fox 2011; Heintz and Schnabel 2006; Schnabel, Behrens and Grötsch 2017). The current study uses the most recent

---

8   These expectations should not be interpreted as research hypotheses that would have to be tested within a statistical analysis.

constitutions available in English language[9], which allows the international comparison of constitutions. However, using translated documents has the disadvantage of potential language distortion: certain formulations, words or semantic details that could be of great interest for the textual analysis of country-specific documents may get lost during the translation process. Due to the aforementioned assumptions, the analysis includes 27 countries that were members of the European Union in September 2017[10]. Four different coders examined the corresponding constitutional documents under the guidance of a codebook developed for this purpose. This codebook mainly contains variables on religion and national identity in constitutional documents, as well as variables on macro information (such as the year of constitutional enactment).

The variables on formal citizenship stem from the block on national identity. According to the basic principles of citizenship (for instance Isin 2009; Shachar 2012), the analysis includes variables on citizenship by birth, by ancestry and by naturalization. These aspects aim at the *acquisition of citizenship*. In addition, the regulation of dual citizenship, the revoking of citizenship and the possibility of extradition operationalize the *stability of citizenship*. Thus, the concept of constitutionally regulated, formal citizenship consists of regulations on acquisition and stability of citizenship. All variables are nominally scaled with the values (0) ›no regulation/no reference‹, (1) ›reference to regulations external law‹, (2) ›not possible‹ and (3) ›possible/possible under certain conditions‹.

Before focusing on the results, it should be explicitly emphasized that the generation and analysis of the constitutional data is a strictly text-based so-

---

9   The online platform of the Comparative Constitute Project (Elkins, Melton and Ginsburg 2010) is the resource for all constitutional documents in English translation. The data were extracted from the constitutions from September 2017 onwards. All constitutional documents were downloaded as pdf files at one point in time, so the document version provided by the Comparative Constitute Project at that time is the respective working version for the analysis. In some cases, there may have been constitutional amendments that were not yet processed by the Comparative Constitute Project at the time of document collection and thus were not yet included in the version used.

10   Austria, Belgium, Bulgaria, Croatia, Cyprus, Czech Republic, Denmark, Estonia, Finland, France, Germany, Greece, Hungary, Ireland, Italy, Latvia, Lithuania, Luxembourg, Malta, Netherlands, Poland, Portugal, Romania, Slovakia, Slovenia, Spain and Sweden. Great Britain is not included, as it does not have a codified constitution.

ciological perspective[11] on constitutional regulations as social phenomenon (Cotterrell 1998). *It is therefore explicitly not a matter of a jurisprudential understanding and interpretation of the constitutional contents.* A jurisprudential interpretation of the constitutions with respect to their regulations of formal citizenship may lead to different results due to different approaches, different perspectives and different focuses. The aim is a *sociological examination* of constitutions as empirical data under the essential assumption that the constitutional content and nature of the formulations provide information about the normative framework of societies and their resulting social order – in this case about the mechanisms of formal inclusion and exclusion. Moreover, the analysis of the formal dimension of constitutional content *does not allow conclusions to be drawn about its ontological qualities* (Loewenstein 1969:154). The aspects of formal citizenship presented here therefore do not provide any information about the implementation in ›reality‹ by the political processes, focusing instead on its formal dimension to describe if and how the legal systems address people as citizens.

5.   Results

The variables relating to formal citizenship are distributed very differently in the examined constitutions, as shown by the number of constitutions that contain the different dimensions of constitutional citizenship regulations (see Table 1). The table shows the counting of the different forms of constitutional regulations (no regulations/external law/not possible/possible) across the different dimensions of citizenship (by birth/by ancestors/by naturalization/dual/revoking/extradition).

---

11   Although a multidimensional analytical approach such as that developed and applied by Witte/Bucholc (2017) is highly plausible and the combination of a legal and cultural-sociological approach can, for instance, provide insights into the relationship between constitutional content and constitutional reality, such an approach would go beyond the scope of this work if all EU member states were to be compared.

Table 1: Number of European constitutions regulating the different dimensions of formal citizenship (N=27).

		n			
		no regulations	external law	not possible	possi-ble
Citizenship	by birth	16	5	1	5
	by ancestors	20	0	0	7
	by naturali-zation	22	4	0	1
	dual	20	4	1	2
	revoking	9	8	1	9
	extradition	7	6	1	13

Source: Own compilation.

One obvious result seems to be that – on the one hand – European consti-tutions do not provide citizenship regulations self-evidently: many constitu-tions (up to 22 for »citizenship by naturalization«) contain no reference to the relevant citizenship dimension. In addition, a considerable proportion (up to 8 for the dimension of »revoking citizenship«) of constitutions refers to regu-lations in external law. Since the present study cannot consider the content and details how external law organizes citizenship in these cases, this does not mean, of course, that those countries do not regulate formal membership at all. It only shows that the different forms of citizenship regulations are not constitutionally regulated by default.

The second fundamental finding is that, on the other hand, European con-stitutions address all the dimension mentioned before at least partially. The strongest contrast can be observed in the explicit constitutional regulation of citizenship by naturalization and the (im)possible extradition from state ter-ritory: while the former is regulated in only one of the constitutions examined here, the regulation of extradition is explicitly formulated in 14 constitutions (impossible and possible).

The country-specific proportions of the constitutional forms of citi-zenship arrangements (»no arrangement«, »external law«, »not possible«, »possible«) differ to such an extent that it is hardly possible to systematically describe meaningful groups of countries with regard to the constitutional arrangement of citizenship[12]. Nevertheless, a rough descriptive classification helps to depict the countries studied, supported by examples of wording from the constitutions.

The large number of constitutions without any references to the various citizenship regulations culminates in those cases which do not have any constitutional reference to citizenship at all. For the European context, it concerns Denmark, France and Luxembourg.

Austria, Belgium, Germany, Greece and the Netherlands contain either no regulation for some of the discussed citizenship dimensions or refer to regulations in external law. For instance, the Dutch Constitution expresses that »Dutch nationality«, the »admission and expulsion of aliens« and »extradition« are regulated »by Act of Parliament« (Netherland's Constitution, 1815 [rev. 2008], art. 2). Here, one can exemplarily see the reference to some citizenship regulations, but without being able to evaluate the content since it is laid down in separate laws.

Estonia, Finland, Malta, Portugal, Romania and Spain have some additional constitutional formulations which allow certain citizenship regulations, partly under certain conditions. The Finnish Constitution is an illustrative example of generally allowing citizenship by birth and prohibiting the release of Finnish citizenship, while simultaneously referring to external law providing details and conditions: »A child acquires Finnish citizenship at birth and through the citizenship of its parents, as provided in more detail by an Act. Citizenship may also be granted upon notification or application, subject to the criteria determined by an Act. No one can be divested of or released from his or her Finnish citizenship except on grounds determined by an Act and only if he or she is in possession of or will be granted the citizenship of another State« (Finland's Constitution, 1999 [rev. 2011], art. 5).

Croatia, Cyprus, Czech Republic, Hungary, Italy, Latvia, Poland, Slovakia and Slovenia do regulate some of the relevant dimensions of citizenship, but without referring to details in external law.

Ireland and Lithuania are the only countries in Europe offering all forms of citizenship regulations: they do not regulate all dimensions of citizenship examined in this study, but do have references to external law, enabling some citizenship regulations and additionally have provisions for impossibilities.

---

12   Table 2 8 in the Appendix gives an overview about the country specific distribution of the different forms of citizenship regulations in European constitutions.

For instance, the Irish Constitution generally provides regulations for citizenship by birth, but also contains formulations restricting this dimension: »Notwithstanding any other provision of this Constitution, a person born in the island of Ireland, which includes its islands and seas, who does not have, at the time of the birth of that person, at least one parent who is an Irish citizen or entitled to be an Irish citizen is not entitled to Irish citizenship or nationality, unless provided for by law« (Ireland's Constitution, 1937 [rev. 2015], art. 9.2).

The Bulgarian and the Swedish cases are exceptional within the scope of this investigation: Bulgaria as it refers to every analyzed dimension of citizenship in its constitution – either by relating to external law or by immediately regulating it. On the other hand, the Swedish Constitution only contains negative regulations concerning the deprivation of citizenship and the extradition of citizens: »No Swedish citizen may be deported from or refused entry into the Realm. No Swedish citizen who is domiciled in the Realm or who has previously been domiciled in the Realm may be deprived of his or her citizenship. (...)« (Sweden's Constitution, 1974 [rev. 2012], ch.2, part2, art. 7).

Discussing the results and considering Luhmann's ideas on the concept of inclusion again, it can be stated that on the national level, only few cases across Europe constitutionally address people as citizens by and for the legal system. In cases where either no reference at all is made on citizenship regulations or only reference is just to regulations or regulatory details in external law, nothing can be said about the country-specific concept of formal inclusion of persons as citizens. Those countries which constitutionally address people as citizens in and by their legal systems, do have a comparatively stable concept of formal inclusion since constitutions are stabilized and stabilizing institutions on the national level. Nevertheless, if one recalls the overall impression of the ›regulatory intensity‹ of the analyzed dimensions of citizenship, the impression remains that formal inclusion by the constitutional addressing of people as citizens is not self-evident for European countries. Constitutionally guaranteed formal inclusion as citizen is the exception, not the rule. This has far-reaching consequences for the individual actor: speaking with Luhmann (1995), the very cautiously formalized inclusion into the legal system on the national level indicates that inclusion into other dependent subsystems of society is only (conditionally) guaranteed in very few cases. Hence, on individual level, social and political participation is not automatically determined by the constitutional regulation of formal membership. One reason for these findings might be that constitutions are more stable concepts than other acts and laws of subordinate character. Considering that *citizenship is in flux* in content and over time, constitutions might not be the best instituti-on to capture the necessary dynamics of this concept. Therefore, it is ques-tionable how secure the concept of citizenship is on the constitutional level. Nevertheless, the formal dimension of citizenship is still one important di-mension of many, and constitutions are highly relevant legal institutions that are comparable in the international context. Thus, the formal dimension of citizenship illustrated by this contribution could serve as a starting point for further perspectives on the concept of citizenship, its critique and analysis.

6. Conclusion

Citizenship in flux – this idea affects many different dimensions of a highly complex concept. One dimension is the possible shift from a national to an international or transnational citizenship, considering for instance the aspi-rations towards European citizenship. However, even this format refers to the nation-state, as can be seen from the formulation in the Amsterdam Treaty (see introduction). Affecting the formal level of citizenship, the focus on the nation-state remains indispensable. Thus, this article deals with the question of the constitutional regulation of formal citizenship on the national level.

Luhmann's systems-theoretical perspective on inclusion/exclusion serves as a theoretical introduction. For the conceptualization of formal citizenship, the legal system constitutionally addresses persons as relevant. By an explo-rative, quantitative content analysis of constitutional documents across the European member states, the formal dimensions of citizenship are illustra-ted. However, the constitutional analysis reconstructing formal citizenship presents *one of several fundamental pillars* of the multidimensional concept of citizenship. Of course, the focus on *formal citizenship* goes hand in hand with the limitation of the perspective on the legal status as a citizen and ignores other dimensions for analytical purposes, such as acts and habitus of citizens (Isin 2009). It is also strictly limited to the abstract level of constitutional law and cannot take into account the constitutional reality: whether the consti-tutionally formulated inclusion by granting formal citizenship status leads to the enabling of the associated rights (and duties) in political realities remains outside the scope of this analysis. At the same time, the study of formal citi-zenship status on the constitutional level contributes to setting the framework for differentiating between different ideal-types[13] of democratic citizen(ship) on the individual level. Consequently, they are highly relevant social institutions for the analysis of the foundation for social and political fragmentation.

Overall, the results can be summarized as follows: First, based on the constitutional data, it can be shown that formalized membership via constitutionally organized citizenship to a state does not follow uniform trends in all its facets. Second, formal inclusion and exclusion are – also on constitutional level – two dimensions that go hand in hand. Third, citizenship seems to be a fluid, dynamic political construction that is only rarely finalized in constitutions. The impression suggests itself that citizenship is a very dynamic mechanism of inclusion and exclusion, which is why constitutions serve as too stable constructs to capture this important aspect of modern societies in its formal-legal dimension. Nevertheless, constitutions are important empirical data when it comes on the regulations of formal membership on the national level: they show that the legal (here: constitutional) regulation of citizenship seems to be a highly complex process, even for modern societies.

The results of this contribution can be followed up by various discussions. First of all, the question arises almost automatically as to the possible implications for political and social science research on democracy and globalization. What does it mean for the democratic process of modern societies if citizenship on the nation-state level is a dynamic construct? Is citizenship still a promising factor for the future in times of globalizing societies? Is an international concept of citizenship suitable for intrastate political processes? The question of the rights and duties associated with constitutionally regulated citizenship is also relevant regarding the perspective of constructing societies. Last but not least, the formal and thus legal dimension of citizenship can be complemented, challenged and criticized by other highly relevant dimensions, as for instance the acts and habitus of citizenship (Isin 2009). This volume provides answers to some of the questions finally raised here. In addition, however, it becomes apparent that citizenship as a political and social concept is not only a historical variable but continues to be not uniformly organized in international comparison, which means that questions of the domestic and international organization of formal membership will continue to arise in the future.

---

13   The assumed ideal-types of democratic citizen(ship) are to be found in the introduction of this volume.

Appendix

Table 2: Country-specific distribution of different forms of citizenship regulations in European constitutions.

country	no regula-tions/no reference	reference to regulations in external law	not possible	possible/under certain conditions
Austria	5	1	0	0
Belgium	5	1	0	0
Bulgaria	0	1	0	5
Croatia	4	0	0	2
Cyprus	4	0	0	2
Czech Republic	5	0	0	1
Denmark	6	0	0	0
Estonia	1	3	0	2
Finland	1	2	0	3
France	6	0	0	0
Germany	2	4	0	0
Greece	2	4	0	0
Hungary	2	0	0	4
Ireland	2	2	1	1
Italy	4	0	0	2
Latvia	4	0	0	2
Lithuania	2	2	1	1
Luxembourg	6	0	0	0
Malta	1	2	0	3
Netherlands	5	1	0	0
Poland	3	0	0	3
Portugal	4	1	0	1
Romania	3	2	0	1
Slovakia	5	0	0	1

Slovenia	5	0	0	1
Spain	3	1	0	2
Sweden	4	0	2	0

Source: Own compilation.

References

Baraldi, Claudio/Giancarlo, Corsi/Esposito, Elena (1997): GLU: Glossar zu Niklas Luhmanns Theorie sozialer Systeme, Frankfurt a.m.: Suhrkamp.

Bauböck, Rainer (2019): Debating European Citizenship. Cham: Springer International Publishing.

Blaustein, Albert P. (1994): Framing the Modern Constitution: A Check-list, FB Rothman.

Cotterrell, Roger (1998): Why Must Legal Ideas Be Interpreted Sociologically? Journal of Law and Society 25: 171-192. https://doi:10.1111/1467-6478.00086

Elkins, Zachary/Ginsburg, Tom/Melton, James (2009): The Endurance of National Constitutions, New York: Cambridge University Press.

Elkins, Zachary/Melton, James/Ginsburg, Tom (2010): The Comparative Constitutions Project (CCP), https://comparativeconstitutionsproject.org

Fahrmeir, Andreas (2007): Citizenship: The Rise and Fall of a Modern Concept, New Haven/London: Yale University Press.

Fox, Jonathan (2011): Religion and State Constitutions Dataset. www.religionandstate.org/

Go, Julian (2003): A Globalizing Constitutionalism? Views from the Postcolony, 1945-2000. International Sociology 18: 71-95. https://doi:10.1177/02685809 03018001005

Grey, Thomas C. (1984): Constitutions as Scripture. Stanford Law Review 37: 1-25.

Heintz, Bettina/Schnabel, Annette (2006): Verfassungen als Spiegel globaler Normen? KZfSS Kölner Zeitschrift für Soziologie und Sozialpsychologie 58: 685-716. https://doi:10.1007/s11577-006-0262-5

Isin, Engin F. (2009): Citizenship in Flux: The Figure of the Activist Citizen. Subjectivity 29: 367-388. https://doi:10.1057/sub.2009.25

Jacobs, Francis G. (2007): Citizenship of the European Union – A Legal Analysis. European Law Journal 13: 591-610.

Kymlicka, Will/Norman, Wayne (1994): Return of the Citizen: A Survey of Recent Work on Citizenship Theory. Ethics 104: 352-381.

Loewenstein, Karl (1969): Verfassungslehre. Tübingen: Mohr (Siebeck).

Luhmann, Niklas (1995): Soziologische Aufklärung 6. Die Soziologie und der Mensch. Opladen: Westdeutscher Verlag GmbH.

Parsons, Talcott (1964): Beiträge zur soziologischen Theorie, Neuwied am Rhein: Luchterhand.

Schinkel, Willem (2010): The Virtualization of Citizenship. Critical Sociology 36: 265-283. https://doi:10.1177/0896920509357506

Schnabel, Annette/Behrens, Kathrin/Grötsch, Florian (2017): Religion in European constitutions – Cases of Different Secularities. European Societies 19: 551-579. https://doi:10.1080/14616696.2017.1334946

Shachar, Ayelet (2012): 48: Citizenship. 1002-1019, In: The Oxford Handbook of Comparative Constitutional Law, Oxford: Oxford University Press.

Shaw, Jo (2019): EU Citizenship: Still a Fundamental Status? 1-17, In: Debating European Citizenship, edited by R. Bauböck, Cham: Springer International Publishing.

Staeheli, Lynn A. (1999): Globalization and the Scales of Citizenship. Geography Research Forum 19: 60-77.

Tschentscher, Axel (2011): Comparing Constitutions and International Constitutional Law: A Primer. University of Chicago Public Law & Legal Theory Working Paper No. 331. https://doi:10.2139/ssrn.1502125

Witte, Daniel/Bucholc, Marta (2017): Verfassungssoziologie als Rechtskulturvergleich: Zur Theorie und Empirie der Analyse von Verfassungskulturen am Beispiel der USA und Polens. Zeitschrift für Rechtssoziologie 37: 266-312. https://doi:10.1515/zfrs-2017-0016

Citizenship regimes and diaspora politics: The case of politically involved Turkish migrants in Germany

Feyza Yildirim-Sungur and Oliver Schwarz

1. Introduction

It has been almost 60 years since workers from Turkey first moved to Germany as part of the labour recruitment agreement between both states. What was planned as a temporary stay of guest workers developed into a permanent settlement of foreigners and changed the country entirely. Whereas the economic integration of Turkish guest workers was successfully realised in a short space of time, their exclusion from political processes has raised questions about membership in political communities of democratic countries (Blatter 2009). Furthermore, the topic of citizenship, especially the expansion of political participation in host country processes, has caused new topics for investigation (Bauböck 2007).

More recently, in 2017, the attendance of Turkish migrants in the Turkish constitutional referendum has led to a considerable discussion about their loyalty to the free democratic basic order of Germany. On the other hand, the call of the Turkish President Recep Tayyip Erdoğan on Turks in Germany to not vote for »Turkey's enemies« in the German federal elections 2017 have caused a heated discussion about the political preferences of Turkish migrants and was perceived as an intervention in Germany's internal affairs. The right to vote depends directly on having the citizenship of the related country. However, as in the case of Turkish migrants residing in Germany, the concept of citizenship (and dual citizenship) has undergone a transformation. This evolution includes both opportunities and challenges (Schmid 2019: 1). In the case of Turkish migrants in Germany, their transnational linkages are perceived as a hindrance for their integration process in Germany. Although some studies show that transmigrants who are more involved in cross-border activities are more likely to participate in the host countries' societal processes (Glick-Schiller 2003; Guarnizo/Portes/Haller 2003; Waldinger 2008), the homeland-related ties of Turkish citizens – especially political ones – are perceived negatively in the German discourse (Faist 1994).

Against this background, our chapter explores the notion of dual citizenship in the context of political participation in more than one country. To accomplish this goal, we follow a qualitative research design based on a single-case study. By analysing the case of Turkish migrants living in Germany, we find that transnational political engagement of migrants is influenced both by the citizenship regime of the receiving country and the diaspora policy of the sending country. With the aim to illustrate the factors influencing the transnational political actions of Turkish diaspora members, a special emphasis is given will be given to institutional and legal regulations of home and host countries. Our main conclusion is that peoples' ties to their home country and interest in what is happening in their country of origin should not be dismissed as a refusal to integrate or as a sign of a lack of loyalty to their county of residence, but should be recognised as a genuine transnational orientation expressed by dual citizenship. The chapter is organised as follows: After a concise literature review in the next section, in section 3 we describe the citizenship regime and integration policy in Germany, before we turn to Turkey's policy towards its citizens abroad in section 4.

2.   Dual citizenship and political participation: A short literature review

Citizenship used to be a unitary concept. Still in the nineteenth century, the idea that a person could be a citizen of two or more states was seen as »an offense to nature, an abomination on the order of bigamy« (Spiro 2016: 3). However, in the twentieth and twenty-first centuries, the view of citizenship as an expression of loyalty, identity, and territorial authority underwent a substantial change. This was especially the case on the European continent. Territorially, the peace treaties that brought the World Wars I and II to an end changed the borders of many countries. With the collapse of the Soviet Union and the disintegration of Yugoslavia, the European landscape changed again. New states emerged and others disappeared. Millions of people were forced to emigrate and/or found themselves as minorities in the territories of newly formed states. In many states, naturalisation was introduced for residents who were not born in the country and an increasing number of migrants could obtain dual citizenship. Others, however, were denied citizenship in their new countries of residence. These developments have promoted a remodelling of the classical concept of unitary citizenship, originated from the sovereign nation state with a well-mappable territory drawn by precisely defined borders (as outlined by Bayer/Schwarz/Stark 2020 in the introduction of this volume).

Legally, the European Convention on Nationality, adopted in 1997, was a major breakthrough for the acceptance of dual citizenship in the international community. The convention explicitly allows for dual or multiple nationality and leaves it to each individual state to grant such a status via national law (Pilgram 2011: 7). Given the importance of nationality as an anchor point for citizenship, this represents an important change in the view of dual citizenship: from strong rejection, via being conceived as an oddity, to general acceptance and even active legal encouragement of the status today (Midtbøen 2019: 296). According to Triadafilopoulos (2007: 35), the principal norm driving the convention is inclusion: »Whereas immigration drove the development of exclusionary citizenship laws at the turn of the twentieth century, it is helping drive the formation of more expansive membership regimes today.« Indeed, in several cases, the convention had a direct effect on the reform of domestic citizenship law. The 2001 Swedish Citizenship Act can be seen as an explicit response to the changing view on multiple nationalities in international law (Howard 2009: 74). Many other European countries also reformed and liberalised their citizenship laws in the late 1990s and early 2000s (de Hart/van Oers 2006: 336-340). According to Sejersen (2008: 553), 61 % of the countries in Europe tolerated dual citizenship in 2005. Since then, the numbers have increased further (Spiro 2016). By 2018, 75 % of all states in the world accept dual citizenship (Vink et al. 2019: 362-363). At the same time, the establishment of EU citizenship has fundamentally changed and contested the classical notion of citizenship (for a further exploration of the concept of EU citizenship, see Schwarz 2020 in this volume).

As often the case in social science, the findings in respect to the impact of dual citizenship on political participation are not clear-cut. Following Verba and Nie (1972), political participation covers four modes, namely voting, campaigning, community-related activities and individual contacts to a public official to achieve a personal goal. Yet, as introduced by Barnes and Kaase (1979), political participation also includes unconventional forms, namely participating in demonstrations, public sit-ins or discussions and the signing of petitions (Stark 2019). In his study on democratic participation among first- and second-generation immigrants in the United States, Ramakrishnan (2005: 6) shows that »immigrants from countries that allow for dual citizenship actually have a higher level of participation than do immigrants from other countries.« However, according to an analysis by Cain and Doherty (2006), U.S. citizens with dual nationality are significantly less likely to register and to vote in comparison to their unitary citizenship counterparts. In accordance to this, the research by Staton, Jackson and Canache (2007a) suggests that dual nationality likely disconnects immigrants from the American political system. However, as the authors reveal in another study, this effect seems to be largely restricted to the first generation of immigrants (Staton/Jackson/Canache 2007b).

Literature on Canadian citizenship has come to different results. For example, Wong (2008) analysed civic participation of transnationals (most of whom are immigrants) and their civic participation in societal organisations. He sees no relationship between transnationalism and active citizenship and further suggests »that far from hindering adaptation to American society, dual citizenship may actually facilitate the cultural and political incorporation of new immigrants who would otherwise fail to naturalise and would remain politically and culturally isolated« (Wong 2008: 95). Mügge (2012) argues in the same way in her study on migrant groups in the Netherlands. She concludes that those migrants with dual nationality are more likely to participate in their host country's political life than those who only have Dutch nationality. An interesting insight is her conclusion that transnational political orientations are often responses to exclusionary citizenship regimes in sending countries – an aspect that has not gained considerable research. In this respect, Østergaard-Nielsen (2003a: 6) has already argued for a »reconsideration of the role of sending countries in international migration that includes but does not overestimate their role in creating transnational economic, social, and political spaces and in turning emigrants and diasporas into a part of national development and democratisation.« Her edited volume offers a comparative study of the policies of sending countries (and homelands) towards their nationals abroad and provides a pioneering study of Turkey's policy towards Turkish citizens abroad (Østergaard-Nielsen 2003b). By using the Turkish and Kurdish communities in Germany as a case study, the author concludes: »Turkey wants its citizens abroad not to assimilate into their receiving countries, but to settle as *Turks*« (Østergaard-Nielsen 2003b: 77). Among the reasons for this is that a settled community of »Euro-Turks«

constitutes an important economic and political resource for the Turkish state. In her case study, Østergaard-Nielsen elaborates a range of measures which are employed to strengthen the economic, political and cultural ties between Turkey and its citizens abroad.

Since then, the focus on diaspora policy has been significantly advanced (Cohen 2008). However, it is difficult to determine the real impact of these policies on the immigrants' political participation in their countries of settlement. In this respect, Østergaard-Nielsen (2016) notes in a more recent publication that diasporas may not automatically respond to the sending countries' outreach. According to her, immigrants are very much aware of the motives and credibility of these efforts and the extent to which they are sensitive to their specific needs. Moreover, she observes, their response depends on the extent to which the political actors of their residence countries »are moving away from the zero-sum debate and the securitization optic on migrant transnationality« (Østergaard-Nielsen 2016: 162).

Drawing on this concise literature review, we now turn to the case of politically involved Turkish migrants in Germany. Generally, case studies provide us with a deep understanding about specific instances (Mabry 2008: 216). Recalling that a single case study is analogue to a single experiment, a single case can be used to confirm, challenge, or extend the theory (Yin 2008: 40). In the following section, we exemplify the German-Turkish case as a critical case. According to Patton (2008: 236), critical cases are cases »that can make a point quite dramatically or are, for some reason, particularly important in the scheme of things«. In other words: »If it happens there, it will happen anywhere,« or, vice, versa, »if it doesn't happen there, it won't happen anywhere« (Patton 2008: 236). It is also important to note that our study only covers one particular form of political participation, namely the participation in elections.

3.   The German-Turkish case: From guest workers to transnational diaspora members

Germany signed its first labour recruitment agreement with Italy in 1955. Later on, the German state authorities set up labour recruitment agreements with Greece (1960), Spain (1961) and Turkey (1961). Similar agreements would then be made with Morocco (1963), Portugal (1964), Tunisia (1965) and Yugoslavia (1968). Only 10 years after the agreement with Turkey, the number of

Turkish workers in Germany was already well over half a million and excee-
ded the one million mark in 1974 (see Figure 1). Because of the law on the
recruitment ban passed in 1973, which was intended to prevent the influx of
further immigrants, many Turkish migrants brought their families to Germany. They feared that this would not be possible later on. This changed the
social structure of the immigrants, which until then had been an almost pure working population. The Turkish resident population rose to just over two
million in 1995. In 2000, 28.2 percent of all foreigners living in Germany were
Turkish citizens. The proportion of Turks has since fallen by more than half,
while the proportion of foreigners from Eastern Europe and the Arab world
has risen. By the end of 2019, 13.1 percent (around 1.5 million) of all foreigners
are Turkish citizens.

Figure 1: Number of foreigners in Germany

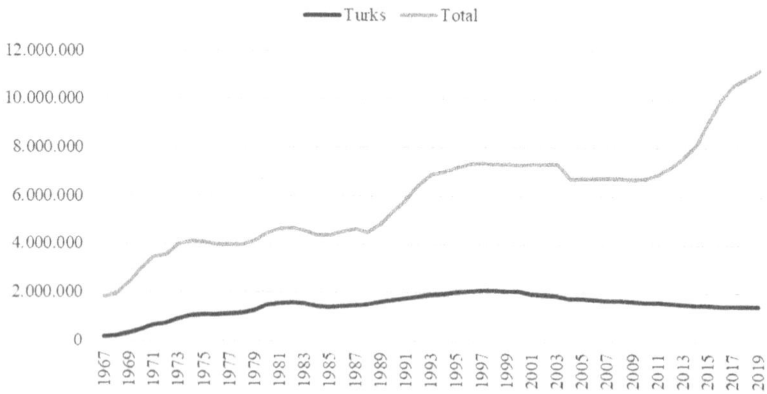

Source: Own compilation based on data from Statistical Office (Destatis 2020a).

However, a decreasing number of statistically recorded Turks is no pro-
of of the decrease in the number of people of Turkish origin in Germany. It
is therefore helpful to differentiate between people with and without a migration background. In general, the definition of migration background includes all immigrant foreigners, naturalised persons, (late) resettlers and the
descendants of these groups born as Germans (Will 2019: 547). Since 2005,
the German Microcensus also distinguishes between the population with and
without a migrant background and currently defines this term as follows: »A
person has a migrant background if he or she or at least one parent does not

possess German citizenship by birth« (Destatis 2019a: 4). According to this definition, 13.3 percent of all people with a migration background living in Germany belong to the Turkish community (see figure 2). Although the proportion of Turks among all migrants living in Germany has slightly fallen in the last few years, Turkish migrants are still representing the second largest group of people in Germany, after the ethnic Germans. Just over half of these people (1.5 million) were born in Germany. Today, the fourth generation of Turkish migrants is growing up in Germany. Despite this, »the integration of Turkish migrants« is still shaping the political discourse in Germany (Berlinghoff 2018).

Figure 2: Number of people with migration background in Germany

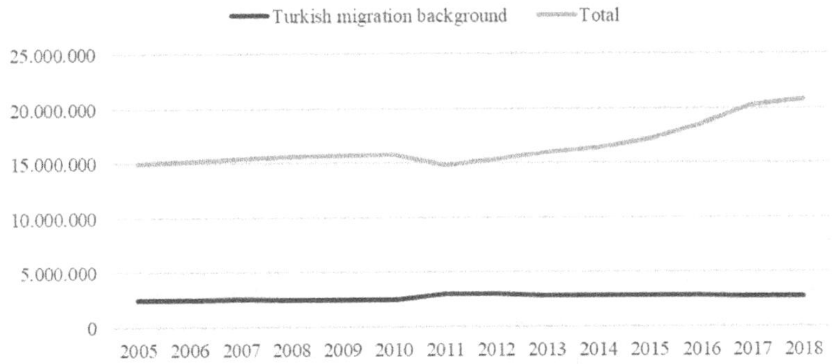

Source: Own compilation based on data from Statistical Office (Destatis 2020b).

From a scientific point of view, the transnational migration paradigm has challenged the concepts of immigration and assimilation (Glick-Schiller 2012: 32). Central to this development was the simple observation that more people are migrating from more places to more destinations. However, migrants do not automatically become »uprooted« from those they »left behind« (Toyota/Yeoh/Nguyen 2007). Transnationalism identifies a multiplicity of migrant networks and communities that transcend received national boundaries (Kivisto 2003). In this respect, the term »diaspora« is central to the study of transnationalism (Tölölyan 1991: 1). In articulating transnational diaspora members, it is no longer assumed that emigrants sever their ties with their countries of origin. Instead, they keep and reconstitute those ties, creating a political dynamic in which both the countries of origin and the countries of residence are becoming mutually influential (Escobar 2004: 66). It is here where dual citizenship relates to the political participation of transnational diaspora members in both political communities, which sheds light not only on multiple memberships but also on multiple loyalties: to the country of residence, the homeland and the transnational community itself. As a consequence, and in the words of Kastoryano (2005: 694), »dual citizenship becomes the institutional expression of and the basis for transnationalism.«

Therefore, it is not surprising, that the issue of dual citizenship plays a major role in the discourse about the integration regime in Germany (Worbs 2008: 24). However, there are no reliable data on how many people in total hold two or more passports. The 2011 Census shows the number of persons with dual citizenship in Germany at 4.26 million (Destatis 2019b). In contrast, the 2018 Microcensus lists 1.87 million persons only. In a breakdown of persons with a migrant background by country of origin, Turkish citizens take the second place with 240.000 behind Poland with 244.000 (Destatis 2019a: 165-168).

Based on the theoretical literature, we expect an increasing political participation of Turkish migrants with dual citizenship both in their country of residence and in their country of origin. However, as our literature review has also revealed, transnational political participation of Turkish migrants seems to be influenced by the citizenship regime of the receiving country and the diaspora policy of the sending country. We therefore start our analysis by describing the citizenship regime and integration policy in Germany, before we turn to Turkey's policy towards its citizens abroad.

4.   Citizenship regime and integration policy in Germany

From 1913 until January 2000, Germany attributed formal citizenship to the principle of *ius sanguinis*. This means German citizenship can be held through blood descent only (Klopp 2002: 41). Attributing citizenship holding to birth by descent illustrates the opposite of *ius soli*, which contains having the citizenship through birth in the country. Due to migration, the need for a legal reorientation of the German citizenship regime was evident for decades, but the political arena was full of divergent opinions concerning how this reformulation should be realised (Brubaker 1992). In 1998, the formation of the German citizenship law gained support by the new red-green government coalition, but main parts of the Christian Democratic Union (CDU) wanted to prevent a reform for reasons of basic reservations. A heated debate was sparked by the intent of the red-green-coalition to introduce dual citizenship. The first draft of the reform of the German citizenship law envisaged the introduction of a dual citizenship, but this attempt failed due to the instrumentalisation of the citizenship issue and the use of this tactic for party-political success.

A prominent reason for this was the success of the signature campaign against the double citizenship of Roland Koch, the CDU's candidate for Minister President in Hessen (Schäfer 1999). At the end, a different version of the dual citizenship emerged, namely the so-called option model (*Optionsmodell*). The option-model allowed children born of foreign parents to hold dual citizenship until adulthood. However, before they reached the age of 23, they have to choose the one or the other citizenship (Ennigkeit 2008: 94-95). Ever since its introduction, the option-model has been a point of discussion, dividing the conservative CDU and the Social Democratic Party (SPD). Therefore, when both parties came together in a grand coalition in the run-up of the parliamentary elections in 2013, the option model was largely abandoned. The result was a new law in 2014 which accepts dual citizenship only for those children, who either have lived in Germany for at least eight years prior the age of 21 and who have attended school in the country for six years or have a German school graduation or completed a vocational training in the country (Worbs 2014: 326-327).

Nevertheless, the year 2000 can be referred to as a fundamental turning point for the integration regime in Germany. This can be seen in the realignment of integration politics; for instance, the initiation of the German Islam Conference in 2006, the National Integration Summit 2007, or the National Integration Plan 2007. However, these positive developments experienced a setback when Thilo Sarrazin, a former SPD-politician, published the book »Germany Abolishes Itself« (*Deutschland schafft sich ab*). The book deals with the alleged negative effects on Germany which, according to Sarrazin, will result from the combination of declining birth rates, a growing underclass and immigration from predominantly Muslim countries. The book topped the German bestseller list for 21 weeks in 2010 and 2011. With his book, Sarazzin stimulated a huge political debate in Germany, targeting foreigners and Muslims (Kelek 2011). In the end, however, the integration of Turks and Muslims was on the public agenda again.

4.1.   The Turkish diaspora in Germany: Politically excluded migrants?

As the foreign population with the highest proportion in Germany, the Turkish guest workers were the main group to be affected by the integration policies and the reformation of the German citizenship law. According to the Federal Statistical Office (Destatis 2020: 170-171), since the introduction of the new citizenship law in 2000, more than 2.2 million people have been naturalised in Germany as of the end of 2018. The most common country of origin for naturalisation is Turkey. Between 2000 and 2018, more than 388.000 Turks got the German citizenship, accounting for more than 17 percent of all naturalisations during that period. However, the number in this group has been falling sharply since 2000. Whereas the number of naturalisations was over 80.000 in the year 2000, it dropped to only 7.000 in 2018. In addition to this, current numbers show that 97.8 percent of Turkish citizens in Germany meet the requirement of becoming a German citizen (i.e. living in Germany for at least 10 years), but they do not apply for naturalisation (Deutsche Welle 2019).

These figures raise the question regarding the identification of the Turkish diaspora in Germany. There are some studies which show that the majority of people with a Turkish migration background feel attached to both their country of residence and origin. Based on structured interviews with 1,065 Turkish migrants in Germany, Kaya and Kentel (2005: 42) show that the so-called »Euro-Turks« see various advantages and disadvantages both in their country of origin and in their country of residence. When asked to which country they feel more affiliated, approximatively 49 % affiliate more with Turkey, 22 % with Germany and 27 % with both countries. In the authors' interpretation, the last number indicates that »Turks no longer essentialise their homeland and they actually challenge the *gurbetçi* discourse common among the Turks in Turkey. They are no longer *gurbetçi*; they have already become active social agents in their new countries. They have actually accommodated themselves in the transnational space bridging the two countries, homeland and hostland« (Kaya/Kertel 2005: 42). A more recent study by the Centre for Studies on Turkey and Integration Research (ZfTI) based on computer assisted telephone interviewing (CATI) comes to similar results. The representative data show that more than 35 % of the Turkish migrants in North-Rhine Westphalia (NRW), where nearly 500.000 people with Turkish citizenship live, find the German and Turkish way of life easy to reconcile (Sauer 2018: 38). However, an earlier study by Özcan (2004), building on data from the German Socio-Economic Panel (GSOEP) and the Microcensus for NRW, has revealed that a majority of both the first and second generation of Turks orient themselves towards permanent residence in Germany. These results have been confirmed by the representative survey »Selected Migrant Groups in Germany 2015« (RAM) of the Federal Office for Migration and Refugees (BAMF). The attachment of Turkish migrants to Germany was higher than the attachment to Turkey in all groups of the survey (Schührer 2018: 6).

However, while the empirical knowledge on the political attachment of the Turkish diaspora in Germany is relatively well-developed, its political participation remains largely under-explored (Schönwälder 2009: 832). One of the first studies that deals with this issue comes from Wüst (2004). For his analysis of the 2002 parliamentary elections in Germany, he took advantage of the monthly Politbarometer surveys. The study shows a slightly lower electoral participation of naturalised Turks (78 %) in comparison to their German-born counterparts (87 %). Formerly Turkish citizens also prefer the SPD more frequently than any other naturalised citizen's group (Wüst 2004: 348-351). A comprehensive study on migrants' political participation has been published by Müssig and Worbs (2012) on behalf of the BAMF. The study's data on the 2002 and 2005 parliamentary elections stem from the European Social Survey (ESS). In addition, the authors use data from the German Longitudinal Election Study (GLES) for the 2009 parliamentary elections. Müssig and Worbs (2012) reveal only minor differences in electoral form of participation between persons without and with a migration background of the first generation. However, these differences could no longer be observed for the second generation born in Germany if they were migrants with German citizenship. The extent of their participation in political life in Germany is comparable to that of persons without a migration background (Müssig/Worbs 2012: 41). Other survey projects allow at least an analysis of partial aspects of migrants' political participation (Wüst/Faas 2018: 10). However, due to the small number of cases, these studies could hardly make reliable statements about the voting behaviour of Turkish migrants in Germany.

Thankfully, this situation has changed with the Immigrant German Election Study (IMGES). For the study, nearly 500 Germans of Turkish origin were randomly selected and interviewed to explain immigrant voter turnout in the 2017 German parliamentary elections. The study shows the voter turnout among Turkish migrants (61 %) was lower than among Germans without a migrant background (76.2 %). 35 % of the Turkish migrants voted for the SPD. Interestingly, in the first generation of Turkish migrants there is a significant correlation between their length of stay in Germany (in years) and their participation in elections: For every ten years of stay, the probability of voting increases by about 10 percentage points. In addition, the study reveals that the voter turnout is almost four percentage points higher for persons with dual citizenship (Goerres/Spies/Mayer 2018: 5). In other words, dual citizenship seems to be beneficial for the increase of the political participation of people with a Turkish migration background in Germany, but how about the political participation of the Turkish diaspora in Turkish elections? Before we turn to this question, we will have a look at the bilateral relations of the home and the host country of Turkish migrants.

4.2.   German-Turkish relations

Since the year 2016, several developments generated political and diplomatic tensions between Germany and Turkey (Eppel 2017). One can say that the first incident was in March 2016, when the German NDR television aired a video with heavy criticism of the Turkish President Erdoğan. As a direct consequence, Ankara summoned the German Ambassador in Turkey, Martin Erdmann, to the Ministry of Foreign Affairs. Shortly afterwards, a second crisis came up because Martin Erdmann attended the first hearing of Cumhuriyet Newspaper's Editor-in-Chief Can Dündar at the Istanbul courthouse, from where he shared posts with the accused on social media. Dündar was arrested on charges of espionage and was found guilty of publishing state secrets. However, Dündar lodged an appeal and the judgement was not final. When the exit ban against Dündar was lifted, he left Turkey for Germany in July 2016, where he has lived and worked in exile ever since. Another major breaking point occurred when the German Bundestag passed a resolution in June 2016, recognizing the Armenian genocide. Shortly afterwards, Turkey denied a German delegation access to the airbase İncirlik, where German troops were stationed as a contribution to the fight against ISIS. The tensions between Ankara and Berlin were taken to a new stage in the run-up to the Turkish constitutional referendum in April 2017. Initially, some campaign rallies by Turkish officials in Germany were allowed. However, German authorities banned Erdoğan from addressing a rally in Cologne via video call with reference to health and safety concerns. The meeting was organized with the aim to protest the coup attempt in July 15.

While the German government initially condemned the coup attempt and expressed its support for democracy in Turkey, these declarations were quickly overlaid by articulated concern and criticism due to the Turkish government's post-coup crackdown. In this context, Ankara criticized Germany for granting asylum to two high-ranking Turkish generals who were wanted by Turkey for their alleged involvement in the coup attempt. In the aftermath of the coup attempt, the Turkish government declared a state of emergency and jailed, dismissed and/or suspended thousands of soldiers, public officials, police officers, teachers, judges and prosecutors. However, the crackdown was also extended to the pro-Kurdish opposition Peoples' Democratic Party's (HDP) and critical media and journalists (HRW 2017: 600). When Ayşenur Bahçekapılı, the AK Party deputy and Parliament Speaker, went to Germany for a visit in December 2016 and was detained at Cologne Airport because she had lost her passport and could only submit a temporary one, further tension came up. This was followed by another crisis. This time, in February 2017, imams of the Turkish-Islamic Union for Religious Affairs (DITIB) in Germany were in the focus of the tension. German authorities claimed that Turkish imams spied on opponents of Turkish President Erdoğan in Germany. This caused a stir about the influence of Ankara on Germany's internal affairs (Maritato 2018: 10). Finally, the crisis reached its peak when German authorities banned the election campaigns of Turkish politicians on German territory during the Turkish constitutional referendum in 2017 and presidential or general elections in 2018. Although a normalisation process started in 2019, the past three years in the German-Turkish relations can be referred to as a period marked by several crises which, in the end, had a pronounced impact on the situation of Turkish migrants in Germany (Baser/Ozturk 2019).

5.   Turkey's policy towards citizens abroad

According to the Presidency for Turks Abroad and Related Communities (YTB 2018), the number of the Turkish diaspora currently exceeds 6.5 million people worldwide. In the first 20 years of the migration of guest workers, most of the activities which were realised through the Turkish state were about consulting activities. Here, social attaches in the Turkish consulates gave advice for guest workers, especially focusing on issues like social rights. At that time, the economic perspective and its advantages for the state were in the foreground of attention. Moreover, this was also the time when Turkish politicians realised that these guest workers would stay abroad since most of them got their families through the family unification process. Additionally, politicians also realised that through the transfer of foreign currency into the Turkish economy, these guest workers would contribute to the Turkish prosperity. Their stay abroad was more beneficial for Turkey than their return (Aydin 2014: 8). As a consequence of the mentioned perception of Turkish politicians, one of the most important steps to influence the Turks living abroad was taken in 1982. In the new constitution of 1982, the nationality legislation was amended and dual citizenship was facilitated for Turkish citizens. Furthermore, the 1982 constitution emphasized the duties of the Turkish state to guarantee that Turkish migrants foster stronger ties to their homeland (Ünver 2013: 184).

The next major development within the policies towards citizens abroad was the establishment of the Turkish-Islamic Union of the Religious Affairs (DITIB) in Germany in 1985. DITIB was under the auspices of the Presidency of Religious Affairs (Ünver 2013: 185). The establishment of a religious organisation was an important step to show that the presence of its citizens abroad was appreciated by the Turkish authorities in the long run. One other significant step was taken at the end of the 1990s. In 1998, two institutions engaging in the topic of Turks abroad, namely the Advisory Committee for Turkish Citizens Living Abroad and the High Committee for Turkish Citizens Living Abroad were founded by the Prime Ministry (Aksel 2013).

5.1. The new diaspora policy under the AKP era

With the takeover of the conservative Justice and Development Party (AKP) in 2002, Turkey's outreach to its citizens abroad was further intensified. Moreover, the political language towards its citizens changed from *gurbetçi/yurtdışı işçi* (guest worker/worker abroad) to *yurtdışı vatandaşlar* (citizens living abroad) and finally to »Turkish diaspora«. According to Ünver, until the AKP period, Turkish migrants living outside Turkey had never been referred to as diaspora (Ünver 2013: 185). The major policy transformation implemented by the AKP government and targeting the Turkish diaspora can be dissected under two different categories. Firstly, the institutional setting, consisting of new state-led coordination mechanisms for its diaspora and, secondly, the electoral setting, like external voting rights. Aydin underlines that three developments are showing this »new« diaspora policy of Turkey. These are: (1) the explicit designation of people abroad who originated from Turkey as a diaspora; (2) that a policy relating to them is embedded in a strategy of public diplomacy being a core element of the present proactive foreign policy; and (3) the connection of this policy with a new view of the nation, compatible with multiple Muslim identities (Aydin 2014: 13).

Although some state-led initiatives and coordination mechanisms dealing with the issues of the Turkish diaspora had been founded in the past, they reached a peak with the creation of the Presidency for Turks Abroad and Related Communities in 2010 (Öktem 2014: 6). After its establishment, Turkey's relations with its citizens living in different parts of the world were firmly based on a more institutional foundation. YTB's responsibilities include defining strategies to meet the needs of the Turkish diaspora and implementing steps in accordance with the planned strategies (Yurtnaç 2012: 4-5). At its foundation, YTB was affiliated to the Turkish Prime Minister. Since Turkey's controversial transition into a presidential government system, the institution is located under the Ministry of Culture and Tourism. Since 2010 it has initiated various activities, mostly with the aim to improve political consciousness, which in turn will enhance political participation, simultaneously contributing to the political, cultural, economic and social life. Finally, the initiatives' goal was to foster closer relations between the diaspora and Turkey on the one hand and between Turkey and the host countries on the other (Ünver 2013: 186).

Another institutional innovation followed with the foundation of the Yunus Emre Institute for Turkish Cultural Diplomacy. The institute is a public institution founded by law in 2007. Its goal is to preserve the Turkish cultural heritage, to promote cultural exchange, to provide educational services on Turkish language and culture and on the country's arts (Aydin 2014: 16). The Yunus Emre Institute can be regarded as an equivalent to the German Goethe Institute or the British Council. Whereas teaching Turkish to the coming generations of Turkish diaspora members seems to be one of the most important priorities, it also aims to build bridges to the Turkish diasporic formations in the receiving countries (Ünver 2013: 187). Whereas the institutional regulations lead to a structural renewal, the AKP has also used several strategies for supporting and strengthening Turkish civil society organisations in Europe and especially in Germany, for example, like the Union of European Turkish Democrats UETD (new name: UID). The reason for these activities is the formation of a pro-government lobby in EU member-states in general and in Germany in particular (Østergaard-Nielsen 2003b: 91). Indeed, mobilizing Turkish migrants through civil society organisations turns out to be successful. UID was one of the main actors in organizing and managing the electoral campaigns abroad (Kuru 2019: 194).

5.2. External voting rights for the Turkish diaspora

One, if not the most decisive, innovation, which was initiated by the AKP government, was the voting right for non-resident Turkish citizens. Turkish nationals living abroad gained the right to vote for the first time in 1987 through amendments to the law on elections and voter registers (Resmî Gazete 1979). However, according to these amendments, citizens were only allowed to cast their votes at border gates and therefore had to enter Turkish territory in order to vote. Thus, it cannot be referred to as an external voting right. In 2008, the election and registration act was once again amended and finally allowed Turkish citizens living abroad the access to voting rights in the country's general elections, presidential elections and referendums (Resmî Gazete 2008). Within this scope, four different options were granted to external voters. These were: (1) by post, (2) border gates, (3) embassies/consulates, and (4) electronically. However, due to the fact that the method of voting by post was perceived as a threat to election security, the Turkish Constitutional Court annulled it. Following this development, the electoral board adopted a resolution in 2011, stating that because of the lack of sufficient infrastructure for voting abroad, non-residents were excluded from the elections in Turkey. Finally, in May 2012, the election law was amended again. This amendment paved the way for the political participation of diaspora members in those countries which are their place of residence (Abadan-Unat et al. 2014).

Turkish diaspora members practiced the out-of-the-country voting for the first time in 2014 during the presidential elections (Köşer-Akçapınar/Bayraktar-Aksel 2017: 148). A look at the numbers and voting preferences of Turkish diaspora members shows a continuous increase of electoral participation since that point of time. Furthermore, their votes were cast mainly in favour of the governing AKP (see Table 1). While it was initially mandatory to arrange an appointment with a consulate or embassy in the country of residence to vote, such appointments were no longer necessary in the 2015 parliamentary elections. However, Turkish citizens abroad still had to travel to a consulate or an embassy closest to their registered international address in order to vote. By 2017, registered expatriates could vote at any embassy or consulate as well as at border polling stations (Sevi et al. 2020: 2). Accordingly, more than 660,000 expatriate voters took part in the referendum, a participation that was achieved again in the 2018 elections.

Table 1: Turkish election results in Germany

Date	Type	Voters	Turnout in %	Winner in %
24.06.2018	Parliamentary	659.132	45,7	55,7 (AKP)
24.06.2018	Presidential	660.341	45,7	64,8 (Erdoğan)
16.04.2017	Referendum	660.666	46,2	63,1 (YES)
01.11.2015	Parliamentary	575.564	40,8	59,7 (AKP)
07.06.2015	Parliamentary	482.753	34,4	53,7 (AKP)
10.08.2014	Presidential	112.705	8,2	68,6 (Erdoğan)

Source: Own compilation based on data from HaberTurk (2014) and Yeni Şafak (2018).

To sum it up, initiating external voting rights to a huge number of non-resident citizens appears to be a success story for the AKP. However, it should not be overlooked that voting patterns in Germany remain diverse (Adar 2019: 19). The numbers of the Turkish authorities do not differ between Turks with single and dual citizenship, or Alevis and Kurds. In the IMGES, for example, less than 42 % of the interviewees with dual citizenship said they had voted. Of these, 78 % percent said they had voted against the constitutional reform. Among those who only had the German citizenship, the overall proportion was just 16 percent in favour of the constitutional reform. The lowest approval was 3 % among the group of Alevis, while still 12 % of the Kurds were in favour of the reform (Goerres/Spies/Mayer 2018: 8).

6. Conclusion

This chapter used the case of Turkish migrants in Germany to illustrate that transnational political engagement of migrants is influenced both by the citizenship regime of the receiving country and the diaspora policy of the sending country. Although the migration process of Turks cannot only be reduced to sending guest workers to foreign countries, the labour migration beginning with the 1960s can be designated as the main factor influencing the creation of the Turkish diaspora today. With more than 6 million diaspora members abroad, the Turkish state began to actively mobilise these people, especially since 2002 with the coming into power of the AKP government. The most decisive change in Turkey's outreach to its diaspora was the granting of voting rights to non-resident citizens. Whereas Germany's opportunity structures for political participation had been closed for Turkish migrants for a long time, the introduction of the option-model represented a fundamental turning point. However, the discussion about dual citizenship and transnational participation still continues today. Moreover, since 2016, there have been several bilateral crises between Germany and Turkey which obviously gave the Turkish diaspora policy an additional impetus. Our study has contributed to the discussion of dual citizenship and the political participation of Turkish migrants by demonstrating that persons who have strong ties to their homeland do not necessarily have to be perceived as having lower ties to their country of residence. It should be highlighted that members of the Turkish diaspora can also have dual loyalties feeding each other. In contrast to the often-negative connotations that go along with a homeland-orientated diaspora, this paints a far more positive picture of the future political involvement of Turkish migrants in Germany. Moreover, the case of Turkish migrants in Germany also suggests that rather than debating the »trouble« of transnational bonds, creating and adjusting the opportunity structures of migrant-receiving societies seems to be a more plausible strategy.

References

Abadan-Unat, Nermin et al. (2014): The Voting Behaviour of Euro-Turks and Turkey's Presidential Elections of 2014, Ankara/Istanbul: Friedrich-Ebert-Stiftung.

Adar, Sinem (2019): Rethinking Political Attitudes of Migrants from Turkey and Their Germany-Born Children. Beyond Loyalty and Democratic Culture, Berlin: Stiftung Wissenschaft und Politik.

Aksel, Damla (2013): Kins, Distant Workers, Diasporas: Constructing Turkey's National Members Abroad. Turkish Studies 15: 195-219. https://doi:10.1080/14683849.2014.926233

Aydın, Yaşar (2014): The New Turkish Diaspora Policy. Its Aims, Their Limits and the Challenges for Associations of People of Turkish Origin and Decision-makers in Germany, Berlin: Stiftung Wissenschaft und Politik.

Barnes, Samuel H./Kaase, Max (1979): Political Action: Mass Participation in Five Western Democracies, Beverly Hills: SAGE Publications.

Baser, Bahar/Öztürk, Ahmet Erdi (2019): Turkey's Diaspora Governance Policies and Diasporas from Turkey in Germany: A Critical Reading of the Changing Dynamics. In: Mete Hatay/Zenonas Tziarra (eds.): Kinship and

Diasporasin Turkish Foreign Policy. Examples from Europe, the Middle East and Eastern Mediterranean, Oslo: Peace Research Institute Oslo, 29-45.

Bauböck, Rainer (2007): Stakeholder Citizenship and Transnational Political Participation: a Normative Evaluation of External Voting. Fordham Law Review Fordham Law Review 75: 2393-2447.

Bayer, Markus/Schwarz, Oliver/Stark, Toralf (2020): Democratic Citizenship in Flux. Introduction and a Conceptual Approach. In: Markus Bayer/Oliver Schwarz/Toralf Stark (eds.): Democratic Citizenship in Flux. Conceptions of Citizenship in the Light of Political and Social Fragmentation, Bielefeld: transcript, 7-22.

Berlinghoff, Marcel (2018): Geschichte der Migration in Deutschland. h ttps://www.bpb.de/gesellschaft/migration/dossier-migration/252241/deu tsche-migrationsgeschichte

Blatter, Joachim (2009): Dual Citizenship and Theories of Democracy. Citizenship Studies 15: 6-7. 769-798. https://doi:10.1080/13621025.2011.600090

Brubaker, Rogers (1992): Citizenship and Nationhood in France and Germany, Harvard University Press.

Cain, Bruce/Doherty, Brendan (2006). The Impact of Dual Nationality on Political participation. In: Taeku Lee/S. Karthick Ramakrishnan/Ricardo Ramírez (eds.): Transforming Politics, Transforming America. The Political and Civic Incorporation of Immigrants in the United States, Charlottesville/London: University of Virginia Press, 89-105.

Cohen, Robin (2008): Global Diasporas. An Introduction, London/New York: Routledge.

De Hart, Betty/van Oers, Ricky (2006): European trends in nationality law. In: Rainer Bauböck et al. (eds.): Acquisition and Loss of Nationality. Policies and Trends in 15 European States (Volume 1: Comparative Cases), Amsterdam: Amsterdam University Press, 317-357.

Deutsche Welle (2019): Alman vatandaşlığına geçişte Türkler ilk sırada. https://p.dw.com/p/3JTeh

Deutsche Welle (2011): Bir kitap yazdı, gündem değişti. https://p.dw.com/p/12JHf

Ennigkeit, Stefan (2008): Gelungene Integration? Zuwanderung und Integrationspolitik in Deutschland und den Niederlanden, Freiburg: Arnold Bergstraesser Institut.

Eppel, Adrian (2017): Making Sense of Rising German-Turkish Tensions. Rome: Istituto Affari Internazionali.

Escobar, Cristina (2004): Dual Citizenship and Political Participation: Migrants in the Interplay of United States and Colombian Politics. Latino Studies 2: 45-69. https://doi:10.1057/palgrave.lst.8600060

Faist, Thomas (1994): How to Define a Foreigner? The Symbolic Politics of Immigration in German Partisan Discourse, 1978-1993. Western European Politics 17: 50-71. https://doi:10.1080/01402389408425014

Glick-Schiller, Nina (2012): The Transnational Migration Paradigm. Global Perspectives on Migration Research. In: Dirk Halm/Zeynep Sezgin (eds.): Migration and Organized Civil Society. Rethinking National Policy, London/New York: Routledge, 25-43.

Glick-Schiller, Nina (2003): The Centrality of Ethnography in the Study of Transnational Migration: Seeing the Wetland instead of the Swamp. In: Nancy Foner (ed.): American Arrivals. Anthropology Engages the New Immigration, Santa Fe: School of American Research Press, 99-128.

Goerres, Achim/Spies, Dennis C./Mayer, Sabrina J. (2018): Deutsche mit Migrationshintergrund bei der Bundestagswahl 2017: Erste Auswertungen der Immigrant German Election Study zu Deutschtürken und Russlanddeutschen, Duisburg: University of Duisburg-Essen.

Guarnizo, Luis Eduardo/Portes, Alejandro/Haller, William (2003): Assimilation and Transnationalism: Determinants of Transnational Political Action among Contemporary Migrants. American Journal of Sociology 108: 1211-1248. https://doi:10.1086/375195

HaberTurk (2014): Cumhurbaşkanlığı Seçimi 2014. https://www.haberturk.com/secim/secim2014/cumhurbaskanligi-secimi/ilce/yurtdisi-almanya-1124

Howard, Marc Morjé (2009): The Politics of Citizenship in Europe, New York: Cambridge University Press.

Human Rights Watch, HRW (2017): World Report 2017. Events in 2016, New York: Seven Stories Press.

Kastoryano, Riva (2005): Citizenship, Nationhood, and Non-Territoriality: Transnational Participation in Europe. PS: Political Science and Politics 38: 693-696. https://doi:10.1017/S1049096505050365

Kaya, Ayhan/Kentel, Ferhat (2005): Euro-Turks: A Bridge or a Breach between Turkey and the European Union? Brussels: Centre for European Policy Studies.

Kelek, Necla (2011): Die postidentischen Deutschen. Frankfurter Allgemeine Zeitung, 31.08.2011, 29.

Kivisto, Peter (2003): Social Spaces, Transnational Immigrant Communities, and the Politics of Incorporation. Ethnicities 3: 5-28. https://doi:10.1177/1468796803003001786

Klopp, Brett (2002): German Multiculturalism. Immigrant Integration and the Transformation of Citizenship, Westport: Praeger.

Köşer-Akçapınar, Şebnem/Bayraktar-Aksel, Damla (2017): Public Diplomacy through Diaspora: The Case of Turkey. Perceptions 22: 135-160.

Kuru, Deniz (2019): Turkish Electoral Campaigns in Germany and the Wider Western Europe as Transnational Practices. In: Ebru Turhan (ed.): German-Turkish Relations Revisited, Baden-Baden: Nomos, 185-206.

Mabry, Linda (2008): In: Pertti Alasuutari/Leonard Bickman/Julia Brannen (eds.): The SAGE Handbook of Social Research Methods, London et al.: SAGE Publications, 214-227.

Maritato, Chiara (2018): Addressing the Blurred Edges of Turkey's Diaspora and Religious Policy: Diyanet Women Preachers Sent to Europe. European Journal of Turkish Studies 27. https://doi:10.4000/ejts.6020

Midtbøen, Arnfinn H. (2019): Dual Citizenship in an Era of Securisation. The Case of Denmark. Nordic Journal of Migration Research 9: 293-309. https://doi:10.2478/njmr-2019-0014

Mügge, Liza (2012): Dual Nationality and Transnational Politics. Journal of Ethnic and Migration Studies 38: 1-19. https://doi:10.1080/1369183X.2012.640003

Müssig, Stephanie/Worbs, Susanne (2012): Politische Einstellungen und politische Partizipation von Migranten in Deutschland, Nürnberg: Bundesamt für Migration und Flüchtlinge.

Østergaard-Nielsen, Eva (2016): Sending Country Policies. In: Blanca Garcés-Mascareñas/Rinus Penninx (eds.): Integration Processes and Policies in Europe. Contexts, Levels and Actors, Heidelberg et al.: Springer VS, 147-165.

Öktem, Kerem (2014): Turkey's New Diaspora Policy: The Challenge of Inclusivity, Outreach and Capacity. Istanbul: Istanbul Policy Center.

Østergaard-Nielsen, Eva (2003a): International Migration and Sending Countries: Key Issues and Themes. In: Eva Østergaard-Nielsen (ed.): International Migration and Sending Countries. Perceptions, Policies, and Transnational Relations, Basingstoke/Hampshire: Palgrave Macmillan, 3-30.

Østergaard-Nielsen, Eva (2003b): Turkey and the ›Euro Turks‹: Overseas Nationals as an Ambiguous Asset. In: Eva Østergaard-Nielsen (ed.): International Migration and Sending Countries. Perceptions, Policies, and Transnational Relations, Basingstoke/Hampshire: Palgrave Macmillan, 77-98.

Özcan, Veysel (2004): Turks in Germany: Aspects of their socio-economic integration. Paper prepared for the conference »Integration of Immigrants from Turkey in Austria, Germany and Holland« Bogazici University Istanbul, 27-28.

Patton, Michael Quinn (2008): Qualitative Research & Evaluation Methods, Thousand Oaks/London/New Delhi: SAGE.

Pilgram, Lisa (2011): International Law and European Nationality Laws, Badia Fiesolana: European University Institute.

Presidency for Turks Abroad and Related Communities, YTB (2018): Genel Bilgi. https://www.ytb.gov.tr/yurtdisi-vatandaslar/genel-bilgi

Ramakrishnan, S. Karthick (2005): Democracy in Immigrant America. Changing Demographics and Political Participation, Stanford, CA: Stanford University Press.

Resmî Gazete (2008): Seçimlerin Temel Hükümleri ve Seçmen Kütükleri Hakkında Kanunun Bazı Maddelerinin Değiştirilmesi. www.resmigazet e.gov.tr/eskiler/2008/03/20080322M1-3.htm

Resmî Gazete (1979): Seçimlerin Temel Hükümleri ve Seçmen Kütükleri Hakkında Kanunun Bazı Maddelerinin Değiştirilmesi. https://www. tbmm.gov.tr/tutanaklar/KANUNLAR_KARARLAR/kanuntbmmc062/kan untbmmc062/kanuntbmmc06202234.pdf

Sauer, Martina (2018): Identifikation und politische Partizipation türkeistämmiger Zugewanderter in Nordrhein-Westfalen und in Deutschland, Essen: Stiftung Zentrum für Türkeistudien und Integrationsforschung.

Schäfer, Albert (1999): Mit Unterschriften gegen die doppelte Staatsbürgerschaft. Frankfurter Allgemeine Zeitung, 04.01.1999, 1.

Schmid, Carol L. (2019): Transnationalism and the Politics of Sending States. The Cases of Italy, Mexico, Turkey, and Ecuador, Lanham et al.: Lexington Books.

Schönwälder, Karen (2009): Einwanderer als Wähler, Gewählte und transnationale Akteure. Politische Vierteljahresschrift 50: 832-849. https://doi:s11 615-009-0158-x

Schührer, Susanne (2018): Türkeistämmige Personen in Deutschland. Erkenntnisse aus der Repräsentativuntersuchung »Ausgewählte Migrantengruppen in Deutschland 2015« (RAM), Nürnberg: Bundesamt für Migration und Flüchtlinge.

Schwarz, Oliver (2020): Public Perception of European Union Citizenship at the Local Level. In: Markus Bayer/Oliver Schwarz/Toralf Stark (eds.): Democratic Citizenship in Flux. Conceptions of Citizenship in the Light of Political and Social Fragmentation, Bielefeld: transcript, 43-62.

Sejersen, Tanja Brøndsted (2008): »I Vow to Thee My Countries« – The Expansion of Dual Citizenship in the 21st century. International Migration Review 42:523-549. https://doi:10.1111/j.1747-7379.2008.00136.x

Sevi, Semra et al. (2020): How do Turks Abroad Vote? Turkish Studies 21: 208-230. https://doi:10.1080/14683849.2019.1607311

Spiro, Peter J. (2016): At Home in Two Countries. The Past and Future of Dual Citizenship, New York: New York University Press.

Stark, Toralf (2019): Demokratische Bürgerbeteiligung außerhalb des Wahllokals. Umbrüche in der politischen Partizipation seit den 1970er-Jahren, Wiesbaden: Springer VS.

Statistisches Bundesamt, Destatis (2020a): Bevölkerung (Zensus), Deutschland, Stichtag, Nationalität, Geschlecht. https://www-genesis.destatis.de/genesis/online?operation=result&code=12111-0001

Statistisches Bundesamt, Destatis (2020b): Migration und Integration. Bevölkerung mit Migrationshintergrund. https://www.destatis.de/DE/Themen/Gesellschaft-Umwelt/Bevoelkerung/Migration-Integration/Publikationen/_publikationen-innen-migrationshintergrund.html

Statistisches Bundesamt, Destatis (2019a): Bevölkerung und Erwerbstätigkeit. Bevölkerung mit Migrationshintergrund – Ergebnisse des Mikrozensus 2018, Wiesbaden.

Statistisches Bundesamt, Destatis (2019b): Migration und Integration. Bevölkerung in Privathaushalten nach Migrationshintergrund und doppelter Staatsangehörigkeit. https://www.destatis.de/DE/Themen/Gesellschaft-Umwelt/Bevoelkerung/Migration-Integration/Tabellen/migrationshintergrund-doppelte-staatsangehoerigkeit.html

Staton, Jeffrey K./Jackson, Robert A./Canache, Damarys (2007a): Dual Nationality Among Latinos: What Are the Implications for Political Connectedness? The Journal of Politics 69: 470-482. https://doi:10.1111/j.1468-2508.2007.00544.x

Staton, Jeffrey K./Jackson, Robert, A./Canache, Damarys (2007b): Costly Citizenship? Dual nationality, Institutions, Naturalization, and Political Connectedness. http://ssrn.com/abstract=995569.

Tölölyan, Khachig (1991): In This Issue. Diaspora 1: 1-2. https://doi:10.1353/dsp.1991.0005

Toyota, Mika/Yeoh, Brenda S. A./Nguyen, Liem (2007): Editorial Introduction: Bringing the ›Left Behind‹ Back into View in Asia: A Framework for Understanding the ›Migration-Left Behind Nexus‹. Population, Space and Place 13: 157-16. https://doi:10.1002/psp.433

Triadafilopoulos, Triadafilos (2007): Dual Citizenship and Security Norms in Historical Perspective. In: Thomas Faist/Peter Kivisto (eds.): Dual Citizenship in Global Perspective. From Unitary to Multiple Citizenship, Houndmills: Palgrave Macmillan, 27-41.

Ünver, Can (2013): Changing Diaspora Politics of Turkey and Public Diplomacy. Turkish Policy Quarterly 12: 181-189.

Verba, Sidney/Nie, Norman H. (1972): Participation in America: Political Democracy and Social Equality, New York: University of Chicago Press.

Vink, Marteen et al. (2019): The International Diffusion of Expatriate Dual Citizenship. Migration Studies 7: 362-383. https://doi:10.1093/migration/mnz011

Waldinger, Roger (2008): Between »Here« and »There«: Immigrant Cross-Border Activities and Loyalties. International Migration Review 42: 3-29. https://doi:10.1111/j.1747-7379.2007.00112.x

Will, Anne-Kathrin (2019): The German Statistical Category »Migration Background«: Historical Roots, Revisions and Shortcomings. Ethnicities 19: 535-557. https://doi:10.1177/1468796819833437

Wong, Loyd L. (2008): Transnationalism, Active Citizenship, and Belonging in Canada. Canadian International Journal 63: 79-99. https://doi:10.1177/00207020080630106

Worbs, Susanne (2014): Bürger auf Zeit. Die Wahl der Staatsangehörigkeit im Kontext der deutschen Optionsregelung, Nürnberg: Bundesamt für Migration und Flüchtlinge.

Worbs, Susanne (2008): Die Einbürgerung von Ausländern in Deutschland, Nürnberg: Bundesamt für Migration und Flüchtlinge.

Wüst, Andreas M. (2004): Naturalised Citizens as Voters: Behaviour and Impact. German Politics 13: 341-359. https://doi:10.1080/0964400042000229972

Wüst, Andreas M./Faas, Thorsten (2018): Politische Einstellungen von Menschen mit Migrationshintergrund, Berlin: Friedrich-Ebert-Stiftung.

Yeni Şafak (2018): Seçim. https://www.yenisafak.com/secim-cumhurbaskanligi-2018/secim-sonuclari

Yin, Robert K. (2008): Case Study Research. Design and Methods, Thousand Oaks/London/New Dehli: SAGE Publications.

Yurtnaç, Kemal (2012): Turkey's New Horizon: Turks Abroad and Related Communities, Ankara: Center for Strategic Research.

Borders of Citizenship? Biopolitics and differential inclusion in local fields of labor and asylum

Thorsten Schlee

1. Introduction

In 2018, 22.3 million third-country nationals resided within the European Union and 17.6 million persons lived in one of the EU member states on 1 January 2018 with the citizenship of another EU Member State (Eurostat 2019). At the same time, 10.9 million foreigners (third-country nationals and Union citizens) were staying in the Federal Republic of Germany (FRG) (Statistisches Bundesamt 2019: 19). Contrary to natural born citizens, migrants can have a variety of legal statuses depending on how they are classified by immigration law. This classification constitutes a system of civic stratification (Morris 2010) that determines the access to social benefits and social services, such as education and qualification measures and health care, and regulates foreigner's legal access to labor markets. Social policy research brought this system in contact with different welfare state regimes and showed a growing differentiation in immigrants' social rights based on entry categories (Sainsburry 2012). Thereby, limited access to social benefits and services are considered to be a nation state's internal instrument of migration control (Bommes/Thränhardt 2010; Atac/Rosenberg 2019). Regardless of the welfare type, nowadays a growing pluralization and differentiation of legal status positioning can be observed in different European Union Member States. This concerns EU citizens' cross-border social rights, the social rights of third country nationals coming to Europe for professional or educational reasons as well as refugees.

Increasing border crossing mobility raises questions of inclusion and exclusion of non-citizens into the social systems, such as the legal system, the political, economic or educational system. Still, it is mainly the national state moderating the access to labor market and social services.

How can we depict the various forms of differential inclusion (Mezza-dra/Neilson 2013) in social and legal systems within the FRG? How can we grasp the simultaneousness of restrictive border practices and the selective liberalization of immigration law and the coincident growing embracement of the migrant population throughout integration policies? Classical concepts of citizenship refer to the state, on a national or nowadays on a European le-vel. While they overestimate the political capacity to integrate society; at the same time they underestimate the power of political rationalities shaping the current migration and membership policies.

In contrast, this contribution argues that recent developments in immi-gration policies and immigration law can and should not be approached from the point of view of state institutions such as citizenship. It outlines the ex-tensive proliferation of status differentiation of migrants into the social sys-tems as an outcome of biopolitical rationality. Moreover we can observe an emerging system of differential inclusion consisting out of overlapping lines of inclusion and exclusion and memberships in flux beyond the institution of citizenship.

(Section 2) Therefore, we first have to consider the »nation form« and the complex interplay of democracy, nationality and welfare state. Citizenship as well as non-citizenship thereby have to be shown as political categories which are producing the problematization of immigration in world society.

(Section 3) Labor market access for asylum seekers and granted refugees is a paradigmatic field to depict the inconsistent and heteronomous outco-me of biopolitical selectivity. Biopolitics can be observed within the European agendas as controlling migration (3.1) as well as, in recent legislation for asyl-um seekers, regulating their access to labor and labor-related social services (3.2). At the same time, this rationality produces conflicting legal spheres and institutions in multi-scaled policy areas.

(Section 4) Based on local case studies, the contribution gives an insight into the contradictious effects of immigration policies on the local level.

2.   The national social state

Talking about the borders of citizenship implies to talk about migration and the concept of the nation state. This starting point follows a trend in migration research that Nieswand calls the decentralization of migration. That means not only to deal scientifically with the challenges of migration and ›integration‹ of migrants into a new society, but also with the structural and world social dynamics which produce the specific forms of problematization and handling immigration (Nieswand 2016: 285).[1]

The international political system is segmented in nation states. The concept of a nation state is the historical-political form of organizing society. Like every form of unity, the nation is an imagined unity that needs to be materialized. It materializes in symbols as well as in technical artefacts. In the course of the 18th century and mainly the 19th century, nations began writing and producing its histories and curating their specific heritage. Emblematically, the United States' history – it's unity and difference – is set in scene in the National Mall in Washington D.C (Manow 2018). Thereby the nation can constitute its unity in different ways. In the German case, the nation established itself as a mainly ethnically defined union against particular political entities. In the French case, the nation did not answer to particularism but to the misuse of power, which was not exercised by the people, but by some privileged (Bommes 1999: 109-115). The national history of statehood makes it always possible to emphasize the somehow politically or culturally unified people. The end of the cold war also revitalized the accentuation of nationalist patterns of identifying and unifying. In a liberal sense, former member states of the Warsaw Pact abolished communist dictatorship but developed more and more an intensive and externally-endangered and ethnically-defined unity. Both pathways, the liberal democratic and the ethnical, are possible patterns to fill the empty signifier nation, so that, for example the 1989 German national-liberal slogan »We are the people« (»Wir sind das Volk«) soon turned out to be a xenophobic phrase (Glück 2018).

As Earth is almost completely covered by territorially defined nation states, the individual states as well as an international state system successfully monopolize the legitimate means of movement. Therefore, the state assigns his citizens with documents: »the notion of national communities must be codified in documents rather than merely imagined« (Torpey 2010: 6) and it interpellates (Althusser 2016: 85) citizens as voters, pupils, taxpayers or soldiers.

---

1   Problematization is a Foucauldian term (Foucault 1996: 78; Foucault 2004b: 114f) that describes an angle, which is less interested in the problem definitions based on existing institutions and more focused on the observation of forms of knowledge and practices producing the problems of migration.

Democracy describes power relations. The concept of a nation describes a form of unity in the context of other unities. Both evolve in parallel to the welfare state. The construct of a welfare state is the active agent, trying to implement the modern promises of permanent economic growth, consumption and wealth. A national social state (Balibar 2010: 25) represents the two sides of state activity: the welfare state regulating social conflicts and reproducing the relations and means of production and the nation form (Balibar 2011), which is the symbolic form of a both sacrificed and secularized unity.

This welfare state is far from being an universalistic form. Moreover, its concrete spatial and historical shape depends on the societies' mode of production (e.g. fordistic and post-fordistic), the political system, the nation's political parties and, last but not least, the economic growth (for an overview: Myles and Quadagno 2002).The post-war Keynesian welfare state emerged as an answer to the rise of socialist movements among industrial workers and in the cold war against the socialist block. For some time in the post-war period, it seemed to be the political solution for societal contradiction by successfully regulating the conflict between labour and capital. At the same time, it guaranteed the stability of a nation and linked social and political rights within the institution of citizenship, thereby producing insiders and outsiders. Rights, equality and social protection on the one hand and the expectation of loyalty and obligation on the other hand mutually tie together state and citizens (Bommes 1999: 125).

The welfare state's objective is less the legal term of the people than the sociological and empirical term of the population (Foucault 2004b: 114). The invention of the population is based on forms of statistical knowledge, producing this empirical artefact in visualized numbers, curves and statistics. Differently to the people or the nation, the governed population is subject to multiple divisions, based on nationality, on gender, on age, or class composition as well as on different territorial developments in segregated spaces (Jessop 2016: 35). The statistical observation of the population enables to handle and govern objectives like birth rates, family structures, migration, education, vocational training and so on. By governing the population, the welfare state moderates chances of inclusion into and exclusion from the social systems and legitimates itself with the objective to guarantee public wealth and social equality between state citizens. While the welfare state legitimates itself with the promise of growing wealth and equality, it is less interested in inequality between the states. Moreover, the relative equality within the state makes the inequality between the states invisible (Stichweh 1998: 51), as elected politicians are primary obliged to the well-being of their voters and not to the well-being of the rest of the world. Enduring cross-border migration contradicts the assignment of people to territorial states. Enduring cross-border mobility brings the tension between insiders and outsiders into the nation state's territory and points at the central tension between particularistic-social rights, which are exclusively bounded by national membership, and the drivers producing enduring cross-border mobility, such as post-colonial conflicts and international system of labour division.

The question of inclusion and exclusion in legal, political and social rights is politically contested and historically alterable. Referring to the form of democracy, it arises questions of voting, representation and political inclusion (Bausch 2015). Referring to the nation, it evokes questions of loyalty and unity. Referring to the welfare state which governs the statistically produced population based on economic knowledge (Foucault 2004a: 164-165), it induces a debate about costs and benefits of migration, about push and pull factors and about inequality between state citizens, immigrants and their descendants. With this shortly outlined co-evolution of the nation form in mind, the welfare state and the self-description as democracy, the following section depicts an evolving system of differential inclusion not only between citizens and non-citizens, but also between different groups of migrants within the state. Thereby it focuses on legislation concerning refugees' labor market access and argues that welfare state refugee policies are following biopolitical calculations. It also shows the outcome of these policies on a local level.

The research was conducted in three selected German municipalities which differ in their organizational framework to govern labor markets and in their size. Finally, they are located in three different federated states (*Bundesländer*), with differing legal responsibilities, policy objectives for refugee integration and, last but not least, with varying resources of public services. The eight expert interviews in each municipality (n=24) aim to grasp the partly contradictory organizational rationalities and reactions on forced migration. The research focusses on methods of coordinating federal actors, like the local employment agency or the regional department of the Federal Bureau of Migration and Refugees, with municipalities administration, such as the municipal immigration office (*Kommunale Ausländerbehörde*) or integration offices, and with the welfare market actors implementing the integration courses or measures of activation. The selected data for this contribution highlight questions of identifying and the contradictions and interplay between the local labor administration and the municipal immigration offices.

3.   Border extensions: the case of labor market access of refugees in Germany

The paradoxical nation form produces the problematization of immigration that the national social state tries to solve and control at the same time. The term »differential inclusion« describes the increase of »differentiation and selectivity of human mobility« (Könönen 2018: 55; see also Morris 2010: 9-12). This tendency can be observed in the evolution and growing complexity of immigration law. Immigration law assigns legal status, identities and motives of mobility based on the differentiation of citizens and aliens, and is thereby the productive instrument to »categorize and individualize« (Balibar 2009) non-citizens. At the same time, it extends external state borders into the inner side of the nation state or the respective political union. This suffix is necessary because the nation state´s migration policy – and by this, the immigration law itself – became more and more part of inter-state formations reacting to the mobility of world's societies. In the German case, immigration law does not consist in a single code, but in a complex intersection of legal spheres, mainly the Residence Act (AufenhthG), the Asylum Law (AsylG), the Second, the Third or the Eight Book of the Social Code (SGB II, III and VIII) and the Asylum Seekers Benefit Act (AsylbLG). Figure 1 shows the differentiation of legal residence status for foreigners, based on the attribution of motives to enter the country.

3.1.   From deterrence to managing migration

In this context, asylum is one attributed reason to achieve a residence permit. Nowadays relevance of refugee law as a form of protection only makes sense with the development of border and passports controls, visas restrictions and an uprising technical infrastructure directed to control the population's movements (Behrman 2018; Behrman 2019: 284).

In the post-war era, asylum was based on the Art. 16, para. 2 cl 2 of the German Constitution (*Grundgesetz* – GG), which provided protection against political persecution, as well as on the Geneva Convention, which grants protection to people who have a »well-founded fear of being persecuted for rea-

Figure 1: Attribution of motives to stay

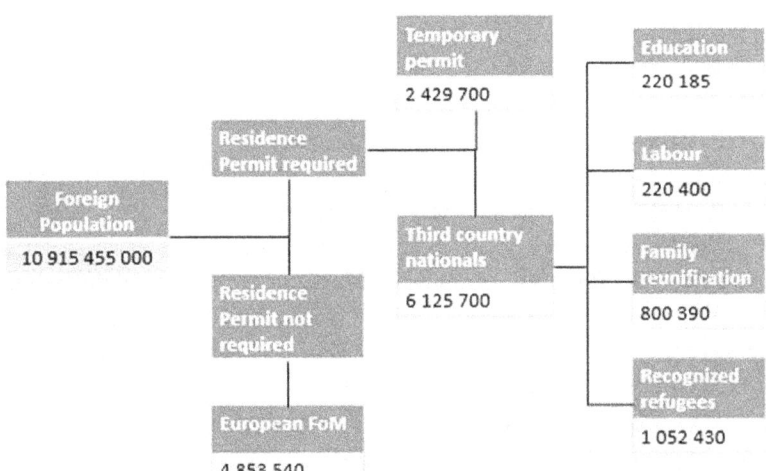

Source: Author's compilation based on Statistisches Bundesamt 2019 and BT-Drs
19/8258

sons of race, religion, nationality, membership of a particular social group or
political opinion.« National as well as international law needs to be implemented. The set of laws, regulations, institutions and procedures that implement
asylum law in the Federal Republic of Germany can be called a system of asylum enforcement. Under the circumstances of the old Art. 16 of the German
Constitution, the asylum enforcement system was the nation state's singular
and probably failed instrument to control asylum migration. It relied on deterrence throughout mobility restrictions, work ban and a differentiation of
access into the social security systems. These restrictive instruments should
avoid giving incentives to ›abuse‹ asylum. These policies led to the paradox
situation that »the country with the world's most liberal asylum law was also
the one with most illiberal asylum practice« (Joppke 1997: 294).

The growing numbers of asylum seekers in the course of the armed conflicts in former Yugoslavia led not only to new debates about asylum, but also
to pogrom-like violent crimes and the so-called asylum compromise. With
the new version of Art. 16a of the GG, asylum grant no longer depends on the
flight motive, but on the escape route. Art. 16a (2) of the GG cannot be invo-
ked by those who enter federal territory of a Member State of the EC (EU) or

another third country in which the application of the Geneva Convention and the European Convention on Human Rights is ensured. This new regulation is already applied in the context of the developing European migration policies (Münch 2013: 76).

Within an emerging European migration law, the Maastricht Treaty did not only transform former foreigners into union citizens with legal rights, a certain degree of political rights and quite limited social rights; it also declared asylum and migration policies to a matter of common interest. Within the Amsterdam treaty, the member states committed themselves to develop a Common European Asylum System. What we can observe evolving on a European level since then, is an institutional architecture of making border, which at the same time follows a certain rationality described as migration management. This semantics indicates a significant shift in migration policies, which from now on follows the two-folded aims to simultaneously combat illegal migration and foster the wanted forms of migration (Buckel 2012: 90). The managerial semantics promises leadership, rationality, control, effectiveness and the problem-solving capacity. This new frame is due to the realization that migration ›flows‹ cannot be prevented by single nation states; moreover, the mobility of world societies cannot and shall not be prevented at all. The semantics of ›flows‹ and ›waves‹ and other frequently water-related metaphors show a rationality which is geared towards the naturalized population (Meyer/Purtschert 2017: 156).

The opposite of controlled and managed migration is uncontrolled migration. Uncontrolled migration is illegal migration, from people trying to reach Europe in order to seek asylum or achieve another residence permit. The European Visa policies, which have been designed with the Schengen Agreement, are producing the ›flows‹ of illegalized migration and made it impossible to reach Europe via legal pathways. Uncontrolled migration is linked to security issues (»heightened terrorist activities«; European Commission 2018: 6), to a lack of integration into the society (the problem of unity) and to the ›humanitarian efforts‹ to protect migrants from smugglers and other forms of exploitation on their route.

The Migration Management rationality is astonishingly clear. Foucault calls this kind of rationality and technique *biopolitical*. Biopolitics target on the enhancement of the natural processes of the population. The natural processes of the population are determined by the reality of human beings who act economically and who are coordinated by market mechanisms and exchange. For the modern era, the market is the true reality of society (Vogl 2002: 371) and also the biopolitical knowledge is based economically. According to this reality, biopolitical rationalities take care of every individual being (Foucault 1981) and thereby raise the productivity and strength of the body politics within a hostile global environment. Biopolitics includes investment in the human capital of societies. As education, activation labor market measures or preventive health promotion, immigration policies are a sort of investment in societies' collective human capital. Bröckling (2017: 333) recently quoted, if life was subordinated to economic calculations, and became a function of investment, disinvestment would be death. On the other hand, body politic is permanently endangered by people who lack the capacity to integrate, who cannot adapt to the shared life styles and mainly who are not expected to meet the requirements of the market. This attribution intersects with racial differentiations. They can be observed on a global scale but also within the European Union, where harsh divisions between wanted and unwanted (so called poverty-driven) migration are constructed (Ulbricht 2017: 271). As outcomes of colonial history, economic rationality and racist attributions are mutually linked. In the case of Germany as in other western European countries (Lafleur 2018), European freedom of movement is more and more problematized as uncontrolled migration. This problematization leads to a legislation limiting the access to social service in order to control movements with social legislation and with restrictive local organizational practices (Riedner 2017: 101).

The technical and institutional outcome of this biopolitical rationality is a multi-scaled apparatus dealing with immigration issues. In a functional way, this apparatus is scientifically described as a multi-level governance system ?; in a more distanced sense it is grasped as a heteronomous migration regime (Pott/Rasch/Wolf 2018). The theoretical framework of Governmentality Studies degrades the state and also the evolving European state apparatus to a set of technical instruments based on a political rationality. In consequence, it is not »the old nation state« which tries to control the processes of bordering, but an institutional ensemble of a supranational migration apparatus consisting of diverse European authorities and jurisdictions, including not only the European Union institutions or the administrations of the member states, but also private actors (like formal or informal transport companies and enterprises) and humanitarian agencies (de Genova 2017: 17). Most researchers stress the nation state's loss of capacity to control migration within this architecture, while it is rarely pointed out that this is more a transformation of exercising power than an attempt to abolish the claim to sovereign control. On the contrary, an »orderly management of migration flows« has to be ensured. Sovereign control in this context means the attempt to extend the governance of human mobility by the capability to institute, personalize and interpellates human beings, and that depends on calculations concerning the expectable exploitability of human capital.

The narrative of asylum misuse led to a set of administrative measures that, still today, will not give disincentives for asylum migration (SVR 2019a: 71). Taking in account not only asylum and residence law, but also the different fields of social (mainly the books of the social code) and employment regulation (BeschV), the processes of bordering do not only concern the nation state's or nowadays Europe's external border, but also different administrations and levels within the nation states. The following section shows the intrastate attempts to govern and to exploit human mobility and analyzes the relevant legislative changes for asylum seekers concerning the labor-related issues.

3.2. Incentives and compulsions

Labor market access for refugees in Germany is caught between migration policies and an activating labor market policy. Migration policies intend to govern migration based on a push-pull model. In contrast to this, activation policies rely on investment in human capital with the intention to produce a self-responsible workforce that is not dependent on social benefits and try to increase the labor market supply side.

Access to labor-related social services and to the labor market depends on different factors. The first of them is the outcome of the asylum procedure. It is the Federal Office for Migration and Refugees (BAMF) that decides in its regional branches on the legal status of third country nationals in the FRG. It is affiliated with the Ministry of the Interior and also organizes and implements the federal language courses, so-called integration courses.[2] The Janus-faced Migration and Refugee Office plays roles as gate keeper and as main actor to provide the first step to an ideally modelled integration process (OECD 2017: 24).

---

2   This course is directed to all foreigners living in Germany. It includes language learning (normally 600h, or 900h or 400h) and an orientation part, which aims to provide daily life skills and knowledge about the legal system (100h) (cf. Integration Course Regulation – *Integrationskursverordnung*). The access is restricted to refugees with officially recognized status as refugees or refuges who are expected to be recognized (§ 44 AufenthG).

There are mainly five possible outcomes of the asylum procedure: being recognized as entitled to protection under

1. the Geneva Convention (§ 3 AsylG),
2. the asylum article (§16a GG) or
3. the subsidiary protection regime (§ 4 AsylG),
4. In addition, rejected asylum seekers can fall within the national ban on deportation, or
5. their asylum application can be rejected and they are subject to deportation (see figure 3).

Most refugees are recognized under the Geneva Convention. The old Art. 16 of the German Basic Law quantitatively no longer plays a role. Recognized asylum seekers have full access to the labor market and to labor market measures. The distinction between different types of protection has only indirect consequences, for example, being recognized under subsidiary protection hinders family reunification (§ 140 (3) AufenthG) and the duration of the recognition is first limited for one year.

The second crucial factor for the labor market access for refugees is the duration of the stay. In this context, the European Reception Directive is the most extensive European intervention into the national social state. Member states obligate themselves to grant access to medical care and a human standard of living. Labor market access must be granted not later than nine months after the time of the application (Art. 15 Abs. 1, European Reception Directive). German legislation even reduced this time to three months (§ 61 Abs. 2 AsylG), but not without making exceptions. § 61 Abs. 1 AsylG bans people living in an initial reception center as well as people from secure states of origin from access to labor. People who are not officially tolerated and who shall be deported (60 000 persons) (SVR 2019b) are also under work ban. These prohibitions can contradict the Art. 15 of the Reception Directive.

The legislation responding to the forced migration in the years 2014 to 2016 tried to facilitate and accelerate labor market access for refugees. The legal packages passed in 2015 and the following years are not easily to be categorized as either being dominantly liberal or restrictive. Moreover, they include restrictive measures for some refugees and liberal measures for others. They

- extended the list of secure states of origin (§ 61 (1) AsylG), from which refugees have no chances to be granted asylum in Germany,
- opened legal pathways for people from Serbia, Montenegro, Albania, Bosnian and Herzegovina to migrate with an existing contract for labor purposes to Germany (26 Abs. 2 BeschV),
- invented the notion of the »good perspective to stay« that enables people to participate at the integration course during the ongoing asylum procedure and to accelerate processes of language learning and, thereby, of labor market integration.

The law liberalizes access to social services for asylum seekers who are expected to stay and who will be recognized as refugees; it is restrictive for asylum seekers from countries with a recognition rate of less than 50 %.

The Integration Law of 2016, which is also a legal package concerning the Second and the Third Book of the Social Code and the Residence Act as well as the Asylum seekers benefit Act (AsylblG), is once more a combination of pressure and incentive to act economically. It introduced

- an obligation to remain at the assigned place of residence for three years (§ 12a AufenthG) and makes at the same time an exception for people who work, study or start a vocational training. The residence obligation is introduced because of spatial differentiation in Germany and the misgiving that due to local housing markets, spatial segregation would be intensified (Bt-Drs. 18/8829, p: 3), although the positive effects of mobility restrictions are scientifically doubted (IAB 2019).
- possibilities to reduce social benefits for asylum seekers and tolerated persons if they do not cooperate (§ 1 (4 and 5) AslyblG).
- measures of activating labor market policies for rejected refugees.
- a permission to stay for the duration of an apprenticeship of three years and for two more years of work.

The law of 2016 was revised in 2019. It extends the possibilities to acquire a permanent residence permit in Germany through work. It points at the increasing quantity of people who got their application for asylum rejected but still stayed in Germany for different reasons (IAB 2019). This affects both refugees who start a vocational training and tolerated refugees who are in employment relationships and provide their own livelihood. This legislation opens new pathways to acquire a permanent residence in Germany.

The rejected asylum seekers, who are subject to deportation and who nonetheless permanently live in Germany, are the most troublesome group of third country nationals.

Figure 2: No residence permit

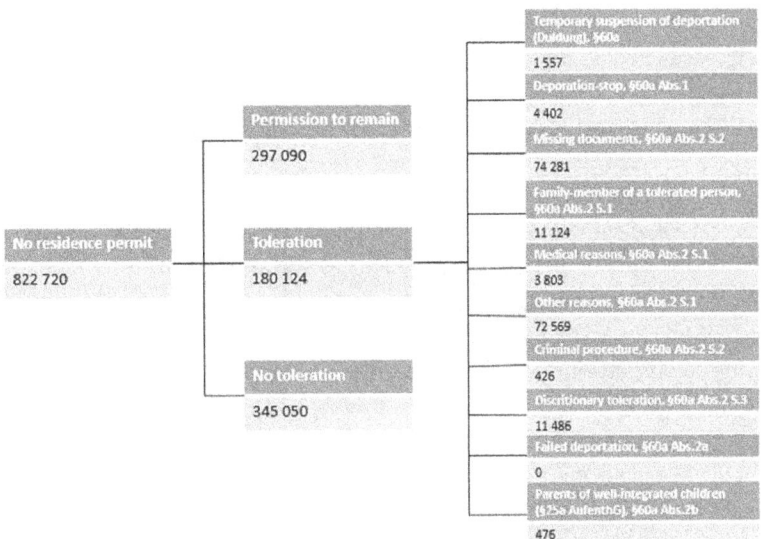

Source: Author's compilation based on Statistisches Bundesamt 2019 and BT-Drs 19/8258.

There are about 180 000 asylum seekers who are rejected and have a temporary permission to stay. In addition to the 300 000 people who have an authorization to stay in the country for the duration of the asylum procedure, there are also 345 000 third-country nationals who have no permission to stay (see Figure 3). These people have no access to the integration courses. They remain within the asylum seekers benefit act and have no access to the activating labor market measures of the local job centers.

The renewed law is dedicated to people who are well-integrated. In this context, integration mainly stands for individual success in education and work (Schammann 2017b: 751). While residence laws until now attributed the motives to stay in Germany, it now establishes a new selectivity within these causes. This selectivity is based on educational and economic capacity. Hannes

Schamman (2017b) called this a meritocratic turnaround, now also present in asylum policies.

The always two-sided legislation does not miss to implement repressive measures at the same time. Currently, a new legal package is negotiated which aims to facilitate and accelerate deportations, e.g. in cases of substance misuse or other crimes. The law mainly affects people who do not cooperate with the administration in identifying them: »German authorities need to know who resides in *our* [emphasis added] country. The obligation to present a travel document has to be enforced, especially for tolerated refugees« (BMI 2019: 2).

The managing migration agenda interrelated with the discourses of demographic change and the interest to increase the supply of workforce to the labor market now also affect the residence law for asylum seekers. The multiplication of entitlements to stay in Germany can be seen as borders within the nation state, increasing the selectivity of asylum-related human mobility. Recent legislation packages open the access to social services and labor for people who have been assessed as worth investing in. In contrast to the growing complexity of the different immigration-related legal spheres, the core of this legislation is not very sophisticated at all. It follows a classical model of conditioning, i.e. it promises incentives to act in an expected manner on the one hand and works with threats, compulsion and deportation on the other hand. The Janus-faced migration apparatus fosters education and training and enables people to live their lives in peace, democracy and wealth. At the same time this apparatus works at the borders of legality, always trying to expand these borders in order to push back illegal and useless lives. The following section outlines the contradictions of these policies in focusing on the legislation and on central local actors implementing this legislation for people whose asylum application has been rejected.

4. Questions of identifying: Tolerated refugees between the rationalities

After being recognized as a refugee, the asylum seekers fall under the jurisdiction/legislation of the Second Book of Social Code, mostly until they find work. There have been 990 000 people in February 2019, from whom 598 000 are capable to work (BA 2019: 14). All activating labor market measures are now opened to them. It is important to recognize that tolerated refugees do not fall under the legislation of the Second Book of the Social Code (SGB II), which provides basic income and tries to enable people to find work by individual training. In contrast, tolerated refugees receive their basic income from the municipalities and do not leave the jurisdiction of the Asylum Seekers Benefits Act, so municipalities continue to be financially responsible for this category of refugees. Thus, municipalities have to deal with the consequences of restrictive national politics and implement integration policies besides the policies of nation states (Scholten 2019).The following section shows how local institutions deal with these persons.

The focus on local fields of labor and asylum (Etzold 2017) follows a growing interest in local varieties (Schammann 2017a) in order to grasp the complex interplay of actors from different policy fields in multi-scaled arrangements. In a functional sense, research stresses the local capacities to solve problems; in a more political sense, researchers emphasize the local autonomy in shaping integration policies. »Solidarity Cities« give room to new political ideas apart from nation states violence (Neumann 2019).

The following section depicts the core of control that is the power to decide on and interpellate one's identity. The chapter focuses on the labor-related role of the municipal immigration offices[3] and thereby shows the tension between migration policies and activating social policies.

Whilst the Federal Office for Migration and Refugees (BAMF) decides on the legal status of asylum seekers and organizes the integration courses as well as other language learning measures, it is subject to the 16 federal states (Länder) to implement the residence law. They supervise the municipal immigration offices and determine the responsibilities to implement the federal law. The federal state of Bavaria, for example, organizes deportations and is responsible for all rejected asylum seekers. In contrast, in the state of North Rhine-Westphalia the municipal immigration offices deal with these issues (for example ZustVAuslR-BY; Zust AVO NRW).

There are more than 500 municipal immigration offices within the FRG, which have, corresponding to the inhabitants and the local immigration situation, quite different personnel resources (Bogumil/Hafner/Kastilian 2017: 29). These organizations suffer from a structural personnel shortage. That is due to the growing immigration-related tasks and the depicted differentiation of motives to remain in Germany. As one local expert illustrates, it is hard

---

3   The municipal immigration office (Kommunale Ausländerbehörde) is quoted as MIO.

to attract staff to implement the residence law, which is for many administrators less attractive than working in an integration'-related field (Frankfurter Rundschau 2019). At the same time, the residence law intersecting with labor law is a complex and very unstable legal sphere. The legislative furor in the field produces legal uncertainty. An expert quotes:

> »A colleague compiled a list of all legislative changes within the last five years. You have to say: that is unbelievable. At the beginning, one tried to facilitate deportation; afterwards one tried to facilitate the possibilities to stay. The Articles 25a and b were added to approve integration efforts. Well, that is also some years ago now. That is all not stable over time. You cannot say that the government tried to complicate the lives of foreigners. That would not be true, moreover sometimes in this direction sometimes in another direction. Overall: I cannot identify a direction within this legislation« (MIO, June 2018).

Political legal activism, under pressure to prove the political ability to act, at the same time produces uncertainty in law implementation. In this sense, Eule (2017: 177) quotes that the municipal immigration offices are not only a crucial actor in the field but also – due to legislative uncertainty and their decision-making scope – an unpredictable player.

Until 2005, it was only the labor administration who examined if there were preferential applicants for a job vacancy which was to be filled by a foreigner. This examination privileged nationals and European citizens and aimed to prevent the labor market from wage reductions caused by immigration. Since the 2005 immigration law, the municipal immigration offices have to permit work for foreigners. That is a shift in responsibilities from welfare state actors to migration control actors (Goebel 2019: 109). Municipal immigration offices only consult the labor administration in select cases to verify the labor market situation, but it is the immigration office which grants the permit to work.

In the case of rejected refugees who are tolerated (§ 60 para. 2 AufenthG), the employment legislation quotes that these persons *can* receive a work permit after three months of residence within the FRG (§32BeschV). Mostly local authorities grant this permit, because it reduces the costs for social benefits that municipalities need to cover. On the other hand, by allowing rejected refugees to work in Germany it becomes increasingly difficult to deport them. Deportation is the core of the BAMF decision. The longer people live and work in Germany, the harder it is to deport them. People acquire social rights, they get children who are in school, they marry nationals or other foreigners with possibly differing legal status. In short: they integrate themselves into society. In legal terms, this is taken into account as individual efforts to integrate in society (§ 25a and § 25b AufenthG) and influences the decision to deport rejected refugees or to extend their toleration:

> »Sure, if someone has been working in Germany for some seven or eight years, it will be hard to deport this person. Normally we think, we can deport for two, maximum three years; if we don`t succeed within three years, it will be hard to deport (MIO, June 2018)«

Identification is the crucial issue in this context and current legislation mainly addresses this question. Within the 180 000 people who are tolerated, there are about 74 000 people who have no identity papers and 72 000 people who are tolerated out of unspecific »other reasons« (Bt-Drs. 19/8258: 38). Looking at the 2018 refugee migration to Germany, we can observe that out of the 83 000 people who applied for asylum for the first time, there were 48 000 (or 54 %) without identity papers, coming e.g. from Nigeria, Iran or Afghanistan (Bt-Drs. 19/8701). More than 90 % of refugees from these states of origin arrive in Germany without identity papers. This is due to different reasons, for example, the lack of registration and passport systems, the loss of their papers en route to Europe – and it could also be a strategy to stay in Germany, as the systems gives incentives to cover the identity:

> »Well, that's like it is: If people do not relinquish their identities, we cannot deport but afterward these people will also not acquire a permanent permission to stay. These people remain tolerated. When we find out who they are, we`ll deport them, yes, I would say it is like this. Sure, this is contradictory. It means in effect they can receive a permission to stay, when we know who they are. But the problem is: if we know who they are, we will deport them« (MIO, January 2018).

The legal consequences are harsh. People are under employment ban, if the reasons that prevent from deportation can be accounted to them (§ 60a para. 6 cl. 1 Nr. 2). In addition, these people have the obligation to stay at their attributed places. They have no chances to receive the mentioned toleration for causes of vocational training or employment (see above). Until today, in some cases the vocational training gave reason to receive a toleration status. The new legislation waives this opportunity (SVR 2019b) and quotes that, after finishing the vocational training, these people will still be obliged to clear their identities. The newest legislation emphasizes that it is not worth disguising identities and therefore gives incentives not to lie and implements restrictive measures based on a suspicion. This kind of messages sent in form of deterrence did not prevent people to seek asylum in Germany until today. In contrast: it institutionalizes exclusion and generates precarious immigrants.

However, the new legislation tries to specify what »collaboration« to clear one's identity means. It is a difficult issue because people who fled from their country of origin normally cannot easily return and even the contact with an embassy is not always reasonable. With this in mind, the scope of the decision of the municipal immigration office shifts to the question whether a person without identity papers fulfills the obligations of cooperation to clear the identity. The local varieties of implementing these questions lead to further efforts in some federal states to centralize migration policies (Niedersachsen 2019).

Other local players also observe this scope of decision. The local branch of the Federal Employment Agency (BA) is the local labor office. It is responsible for the labor market integration of tolerated people as well as for people who are expecting their asylum decision. The respective Third Book of the Social Code defines its purposes as »the promotion of employment that should counteract the emergence of unemployment, shorten the duration of unemployment and support the balance of supply and demand in the education and labor market« (§ 1 SGB III). Tolerated people need a permission to work from the foreigners' office:

> »Sure, for tolerated refugees and these, who are still in the asylum procedure, they have this clause in their papers, saying that the local immigration office needs to give permission to start working. Everybody is uncertain in this issue. The applicants, the entrepreneurs, the voluntary-helpers, and also, we are unsure. We never can precisely predict, if the immigration office will give the permission. [...] They began to rely on these identity questions and they began to stress, that they do not open a perspective to stay, for people they do not know who they are. There were some refugees, they started their training yet and then, suddenly, the permission was not extended any longer. Also, the work-permission: there were some people who have been working for a year and then their permission to stay was not prolonged. That

means we have people receiving social benefits and they want to work. I really do not understand it« (Public Employment Service, January 2018).

The velocity of legal chances in this field does not only produce an opacity of decisions and actions and a certain degree of contingency in these decisions, but also leads to structural mutual misunderstandings.

5. Conclusion

Differential inclusion is a concept to empirically grasp the proliferation of legal status beside the normality of citizenship. This is necessary because the various forms of inclusion and exclusion are becoming normality beside full citizenship rights. Differential inclusion is not a new phenomenon, concerning the continuity of differing legal positions within a nation state as well as the non-formal mechanisms of exclusion like ethnicity and gender. What is new is the pluralization of legal status positioning caused by a growing selectivity of human mobility. Economic calculations are the center part of these biopolitical calculations. The local labor administration and the municipal immigration office are only two stakeholders with differing legal bases and organizational rationalities shaping the local fields of asylum and labor. They coproduce social policies (Bakoben et al. 2019) together with the local branches of the Federal Migration and Refugee Office, with social worker, volunteers, teachers, security agencies, lawyers, economic actors who are very interested in the labor force of refugees (especially the Chamber of Crafts). The local fields of labor and asylum are highly fragmented between differing rationalities and interests. The depicted rationality of identifying in order to control migration and the activation paradigm is accompanied by the municipalities' interest in integrating refugees to avoid social spending. It remains a scientific task to empirically outline these overlapping and partly conflicting interests and rationalities within the local fields of labor and asylum.

The blindfold of these institutions – that means in this case the legal and organization-centered concept of differential inclusions – is obvious. It emphasizes the productivity of immigration law but covers the multiple subject positions and thereby the »subjective viewpoints of border crossing and struggles« (Mezzadra/Neilson 2013: 166) completing the institutional side of differential inclusion. Beside the historical dimension of the struggle for rights (see Tischmeyer in this volume) and the state's formal citizenship legislation (see Behrens in this volume) as well as the legislation beyond citizenship which is shown in this contribution, it is the »enactments of citizenship« and the political actions that appropriate legal and institutional frameworks for one's own purposes (see Rzadtki in this volume), completing a political understanding of citizenship.

However, the depicted biopolitical rationality and selectivity is far from being an ›immigrant issue‹ only. The borders of citizenship and the legal pathways in society are, in a figurative sense, the venue where the notion of belonging is negotiated and where we can observe the human selectivity of societies based on powerful self-descriptions of societies in economic terms. Biopolitics affect democratic institutions and thereby the institution of citizenship in their core. Economic and biopolitical calculations do not answer Kelsens (1963: 49) question »who actually belongs to the people« – which is an eternal question of democracy – in legal terms. They rely on unlimited commodification and assess humans based on accounted exploitability. The consequences of this contemporary transition from legally-oriented to economy-based rationalities is hardly predictable, but like every hegemonic project it is contested.

References

Althusser, Louis (2016): Ideologie und ideologische Staatsapparate. Teil 1, Hamburg: VSA-Verl.

Ataç, Ilker/Rosenberger, Sieglinde (2019): Social Policies as a Tool of Migration Control, In: Journal of Immigrant and Refugee Studies (17), 1-10.

Bakoben, Sandrine/Rumpel, Andrea/Schlee, Thorsten (2019): Koproduktion lokaler Sozialpolitik für und durch Geflüchtete. Wege in die sozialen Dienste. Duisburg (IAQ-Report, 2019-08).

Balibar, Étienne (2009): Europe as Borderland. Environment and Planning D: Society and Space 27, 190-215. https://doi:10.1068/d13008

Balibar, Étienne (2010): Kommunismus und (Staats-)Bürgerschaft. Überlegungen zur emanzipatorischen Politik. In: Alex Demirovic/Stephan Adolphs/Serhat Karakayali (eds.), Das Staatsverständnis von Nicos Poulantzas: Der Staat als gesellschaftliches Verhältnis, Baden-Baden: Nomos, 19-34.

Balibar, Étienne (2011): The Nation Form: History and Ideology, In: Immanuel M. Wallerstein/Étienne Balibar (eds.), Race, Nation, Class. Ambiguous Identities, London, New York: Verso, 86-106.

Bausch, Christiane (2015): Demokratie, Migration und die Konstruktion des Anderen, In: Renate Martinsen (ed.), Ordnungsbildung und Entgrenzung. Demokratie im Wandel, Wiesbaden: Springer VS, 221-238.

Behrman, Simon (2018): Law and Asylum. Space, Subject, Resistance. Milton: Routledge (Law and Migration).

Behrman, Simon (2019): Refugee Law as a Means of Control. Journal of Refugee Studies 32, 42-62. https://doi:10.1093/jrs/fey016

BMI (2019): Geordnetes Rückkehrgesetz. Draft for a Secount Law to Improve the Obligation to leave the country. Berlin.

Bogumil, Jörg/Hafner, Jonas/Kastilian, Andre (2017): Städte und Gemeinden in der Flüchtlingspolitik. Welche Probleme gibt es und wie kann man sie lösen? Essen: Stiftung Mercator.

Bommes, Michael (1999): Migration und nationaler Wohlfahrtsstaat. Ein differenzierungstheoretischer Entwurf, Opladen: Westdeutscher Verlag.

Bommes, Michael/Thränhardt, Dietrich (2010): Introduction: National Paradigms of Migration Research. In: Michael Bommes/Dietrich Thränhardt (eds.), National Paradigms of Migration Research, Göttingen: V&R Unipress, 9-40.

Bröckling, Ulrich (2017): Gute Hirten führen sanft. Über Menschenregierungskünste, Berlin: Suhrkamp.

Buckel, Sonja (2012): Managing Migration. Eine intersektionale Kapitalismusanalyse am Beispiel der Europäischen Migrationspolitik. Berliner Journal für Soziologie 22, 79-100.

Bundesagentur für Arbeit (BA) (2019): Fluchtmigration, Nürnberg, https://statistik.arbeitsagentur.de/Statistikdaten/Detail/201904/fluchtmigration/fluchtmigration/fluchtmigration-d-0-201904-pdf.pdf

Deutscher Bundestag (2019): Gesetzesentwurf der Bundesregierung. Entwurf eines Zweiten Gesetzes zur besseren Durchsetzung der Ausreisepflicht, Drucksache 19/10047, https://dip21.bundestag.de/dip21/btd/19/100/1910047.pdf

Etzold, Benjamin (2017): Capitalising on Asylum – The Reconfiguration of Refugees to Local Fields of Labour in Germany, In: Refugee Review 3, 82-102.

Eule, Tobias G. (2017): Ausländerbehörden im dynamischen Feld der Migrationssteuerung. In: Christian Lahusen/Stephanie Schneider (eds.), Asyl verwalten. Zur bürokratischen Bearbeitung eines gesellschaftlichen Problems, Bielefeld: transcript, 175-194.

European Commission (2018): Communication from the Commission to the European Parliament, the European Council and the Council: Managing Migration in All its Aspects: Progress Under the European Agenda on Migration, COM (2018) 798 final, Brussels.

Eurostat (2019): Migration and Migration population statistics, https://ec. europa.eu/eurostat/statistics-explained/index.php?title=Migration_and_ migrant_population_statistics

Foucault, Michel (1981): Omnes et singulatim: zu einer Kritik der politischen Vernunft. In: Daniel Defert/Francois Ewald (eds.), Schriften in vier Bänden. Dits et Escrits. Band IV, 165-198. Suhrkamp.

Foucault, Michel (1996): Diskurs und Wahrheit: die Problematisierung der Parrhesia. 6 Vorlesungen gehalten im Herbst 1983 an der Universität Berkeley/Kalifornien, Berlin: Merve.

Foucault, Michel (2004a): Geschichte der Gouvernementalität. I. Sicherheit, Territorium, Bevölkerung, Vorlesung am College de France 1978-1979, Frankfurt a. M.: Suhrkamp.

Foucault, Michel (2004b): Geschichte der Gouvernementalität. II. Die Geburt der Biopolitik, Vorlesung am College de France 1978-1979, Frankfurt a.M.: Suhrkamp.

Frankfurter Rundschau (2019): Frankfurt will mehr Personal für Ausländerbehörde, https://www.fr.de/frankfurt/frankfurt-am-main-ort28687/fran kfurt-personalmangel-auslaenderbehoerde-11559449.html

Genova, Nicolas de (2017): The Borders of »Europe«. Autonomy of Migration, Tactics of Bordering, Durham, London: Duke University Press.

Glück, Hannes (2018): Wir sind das unmögliche Volk! In: Thomas Alkemeyer/Tobias Peter/Ulrich Bröckling (eds.), Jenseits der Person. Zur Subjektivierung von Kollektiven, Bielefeld: transcript Verlag, 95-112.

Goebel, Simon (2019): Push back und pull down. Arbeit als Steuerungsinstrument der Asylpolitik. In: Alexandra David/Michaela Evans/Illeana Hamburg et al. (eds.), Migration und Arbeit. Herausforderungen, Problemlagen und Gestaltungsinstrumente, Opladen/Berlin/Toronto: Barbara Budrich, 105-129.

Hinterberger, Kevin F. (2018): A Multi-Level Governance Approach to Residence Rights of Migrants and Irregular Residence in the EU. European Journal of Migration, 182-204.

Institute for Employment Research (IAB) (2019): Zum Gesetzentwurf der Bundesregierung zur Entfristung des Integrationsgesetzes. Stellungnahme des IAB zur Anhörung im Ausschuss für Inneres und Heimat des Deutschen Bundestags am 3. Juni 2019 (IAB-Stellungnahme, 08/2019), Nürnberg, http://doku.iab.de/stellungnahme/2019/sn0819.pdf.

Jessop, Bob (2016): The state. Past, Present, Future, Cambridge, UK, Malden, MA: Polity Press.

Joppke, Christian (1997): Asylum and State Sovereignty. A Comparison of the United States Germany, and Britain. In: Comparative Political Studies 30, 259-298.

Kelsen, Hans (1963): Vom Wesen und Wert der Demokratie. Neudruck der zweiten, umgearbeiteten Auflage von 1929, Aalen: scientia Verlag.

Könönen, Jukka (2018): Differential Inclusion of Non-Citizens in a Universalistic Welfare State. In: Citizenship Studies 22, 53-69.

Lafleur, Jean-Michel/Mescoli, Elsa (2018): Creating Undocumented EU Migrants through Welfare: A Conceptualization of Undeserving and Precarious Citizenship. In: Sociology 52 (3), 480-496.

Manow, Philip (2018): Die National Mall in Washington D.C. – Einheit und Differenz des demokratischen Souveräns. In: Sebastian Huhnholz/Eva Marlene Hausteiner (eds.), Politische Ikonographie und Differenzrepräsentation, Leviathan Sonderband 34, 182-195.

Mezzadra, Sandro/Neilson, Brett (2013): Border as Method, or, the Multiplication of Labor, Durham: Duke University Press.

Meyer, Katrin/Purtschert, Patricia (2017): Migrationsmanagement und die Sicherheit der Bevölkerung. In: Patricia Purtschert/Katrin Meyer/Yves Winter et al. (eds.), Gouvernementalität und Sicherheit. Zeitdiagnostische Beitrag im Anschluss an Foucault, Bielefeld: transcript, 150-172.

Morris, Lydia (2010): Asylum, Welfare and the Cosmopolitan Ideal. A Sociology of Rights. London: Routledge.

Münch Ursula (2013): Asylpolitik in Deutschland. Akteure, Interessen, Strategien. In: Peter Schimany/Stefan Luft (eds.), 20 Jahre Asylkompromiss: Bilanz und Perspektiven, Bielefeld: transcript, 69-86.

Myles, John/Quadagno, Jill (2002): Political Theories of the Welfare State. In: Social Service Review March 2002, 34-57.

Nieswand, Boris (2016): Die Dezentrierung der Migrationsforschung, In: Kerstin Kazzazi/Angela Treiber/Tim Wätzold (eds.), Migration, Religion, Identität. Aspekte transkultureller Prozesse, Wiesbaden: Springer, 283-297.

Niedersachsen (2019): Kleine Aufgabe zur schriftlichen Beantwortung gemäß § 46 Abs. 1 GO LT mit Antwort der Landesregierung. NL-Drs.184631.

Neumann, Mario (2019): Die Solidarität der Städte. Episode 1: Städte als Orte einer neuen politischen Phantasie, https://www.rosalux.de/publikation/i d/39792/die-solidaritaet-der-staedte/, (12.05.2019)

OECD (2017): Finding their Way. Labour Market Integration of Refugees in Germany, https://www.oecd.org/els/mig/Finding-their-Way-Germany.p df from 03.2017.

Offe, Claus (1984): Contradictions of the Welfare State. Melbourne: Hutchinson.

Pott, Andreas/Rass, Christoph/Wolff, Frank (eds.) (2018): Was ist ein Migrationsregime? Pionierstudien und Referenztheorien, Wiesbaden: Springer VS.

Riedner, Lisa (2017): Aktivierung durch Ausschluss. Sozial- und Migrationspolitische Transformationen unter den Bedingungen der EU Freizügigkeit. In: Movements Journal 3, 90-108.

Sachverständigenrat deutscher Stiftungen für Integration und Migration (SVR) (2019a): Bewegte Zeiten: Rückblick auf die Integrations- und Migrationspolitik der letzten Jahre. Jahresgutachten 2019, Berlin.

Sachverständigenrat deutscher Stiftungen für Integration und Migration SVR (2019b): Stellungnahme zum Entwurf eines Zweiten Gesetzes zur besseren Durchsetzung der Ausreisepflicht (Geordnete-Rückkehr-Gesetz), Berlin.

Sainsbury, Diane (2012): Welfare States and Immigrant Rights: Oxford University Press.

Schammann, Hannes (2017a): Stadt, Land, Flucht. Konzeptionelle Überlegungen zum Vergleich städtischer Flüchtlingspolitik in Deutschland, In: Marlon Barbehön/Sybille Münch (eds.), Variationen des Städtischen – Variationen lokaler Politik. Wiesbaden: Springer VS, 91-117.

Schammann, Hannes (2017b): Eine meritokratische Wende? Arbeit und Leistung als neue Strukturprinzipien der deutschen Flüchtlingspolitik. In: Sozialer Fortschritt 66, 741-757.

Schiller, Maria (2019): The Local Governance of Immigrant Integration in Europe. The State of the Art and a Conceptual Model for Future Research. In: Tiziana Caponio/Peter Scholten/Ricard Zapata-Barrero (eds.): The Routledge Handbook of the Governance of Migration and Diversity in Cities, London, New York: Routledge Taylor & Francis Group (Routledge Handbooks), 204-215.

Scholten,Peter (2019): Two Worlds Apart? Multilevel Governance and the Gap Between National and Local Integration Policies. In: Tiziana Caponio/Peter Scholten/Ricard Zapata-Barrero (eds.): The Routledge Handbook of the Governance of Migration and Diversity in Cities, London, New York: Routledge Taylor & Francis Group (Routledge Handbooks), 157-167.

Statistisches Bundesamt (2019): Ausländische Bevölkerung. Ergebnisse des Ausländerzentralregisters, https://www.destatis.de/DE/Themen/Gesellschaft-Umwelt/Bevoelkerung/Migration-Integration/Publikationen/Downloads-Migration/auslaend-bevoelkerung-2010200187004.pdf?__blob=publicationFile&v=3 from 15.04.2019.

Stichweh, Rudolf (1998): Migration, nationale Wohlfahrtsstaaten und die Entstehung der Weltgesellschaft. In: Michael Bommes/Jost Halfmann (eds.), Migration in nationalen Wohlfahrtsstaaten. Theoretische und vergleichende Untersuchungen, Osnabrück: Univ.-Verl. Rasch.

Tischmeyer, Christian (2020): Exclusive Citizenship as Basis for Chauvinistic Nationalism. A Historical Institutionalist Perspective on the Ruling Rationales of Liberal Regimes, In: Markus Bayer/Oliver Schwarz/Toralf Stark (eds.), Democratic Citizenship in Flux. Conceptions of Citizenship in the Light of Political and Social Fragmentation, Bielefeld: transcript, 15-32.

Torpey, John (2010): The Invention of the Passport. Surveillance, Citizenship and the State, Cambridge: Cambridge University Press.

Ulbricht, Christian (2017): Ein- und Ausgrenzungen von Migranten: zur sozialen Konstruktion (un-)erwünschter Zuwanderung. Kultur und soziale Praxis, Bielefeld: transcript.

Vogl, Joseph (2002): Kalkül und Leidenschaft. Poetik des ökonomischen Menschen, München: Sequenzia Verlag.

Activist citizens beyond dichotomies: Migrant rights activism in Hamburg

Lea Rzadtki

1. Introduction

Border, migration, and asylum policies have, over the last years, continued to tighten dramatically (Ataç et al. 2015: 3; Lister 1997: 44; Nicholls/Uitermark 2017: 2f.; Schwenken/Ruß-Sattar 2014: 15f.). At the same time, refugees and migrants are organizing themselves, protesting, and claiming rights on broader scales (Johnson 2015: 5f.; McGuaran/Hudig 2014: 28; Nyers/Rygiel 2014: 204f.). While citizenship is often merely addressed as a legal status, critical citizenship perspectives underline that citizenship is fundamentally about who can be and who is framed as political (Rygiel et al. 2015: 4). These perspectives propose a decoupling of citizenship from the nation-state which, however, does not mean that they ignore that the nation-state remains the dominant empirical reality shaping citizenship (Brubaker 2015: 7). Instead, they reveal that this link is not natural and can, therefore, be conceptually questioned (Lazar/Nuijten 2013: 3). Critical citizenship approaches often explicitly focus on non-citizens' struggles over citizenship and, thereby, shift attention to transformations and appropriations of this concept.

In this chapter, I follow this direction by taking a closer look at migrant rights groups in Hamburg. My empirical data show that these groups engage in more than just publicly visible protest actions and that they are more heterogeneous than the often-formulated focus on non-citizens suggests.[1] I will conceptually develop these two observations with regards to citizenship: exploring the relation between what is considered political and citizenship, thereby further challenging the public/private dichotomy, and looking at how

---

1   In fact, this is why I refer to migrant rights as the more inclusive term beyond formal categorizations.

groups deal with multiple internal differences, moving beyond the simplifying German/refugee dichotomy. Subsequently, I will also link these observations to existing literature dealing with similar dynamics, namely (Black and post – colonial) feminist perspectives. Such theories have so far not been broadly linked to critical citizenship studies and, even though my contribution can only be a first step, it points out a direction that should be further explored.

2. Critical citizenship studies

Migration currently dominates public and academic debates. Even before recent polarizations, particularly after the long summer of migration 2015, it has often mainly been discussed as a problem that democratic nation-states face (Rother 2016: 3). The focus has often been on how migration could be limited (Earnest 2008; Hammar 1990), or on how (democratic) home and receiving countries could handle its consequences (Benhabib 2004; Schulte 2009). Simultaneously, globalization and migration have been constructing different realities. Hammar introduced the notable concept of the »denizen« showing one of such dilemmas in long-term residents not having basic political rights (1990: 13). Perspectives, such as autonomy of migration, have been central in criticizing such limiting views, based on the currently dominant restrictive border regimes of the global North. Methodological nationalism is one central critique: »As a result of methodological nationalism and the ethnic lens, researchers often approach the terrain of the nation-state as a single homogeneous national culture, while defining a migrant population as a community of culture, interest and identity« (Glick/Schiller 2012: 29). The supposedly inherent linkage of territory, cultural, and political community assumes nation-states to be »bounded, autonomous and decontextualizable units« (Calhoun 1999: 218), thus, leaving it unquestioned as unit of analysis and defining empirical frame (Castles/Davidson 2001: 15; Cohen 1999: 249). This is relevant for the study of citizenship because such lenses take its linkage to the nation-state for granted and conceptualize actors solely through their positioning in this setting. Therefore, Mikuszies et al. summarize the resulting need to develop alternative perspectives raised by critical citizenship studies:

»The consensus of this debate is that a link of citizenship and ethnically-founded nationality, going hand in hand with modern statehood, contributes to migrants being excluded. This results in the need to develop new forms of citizenship to do justice in more inclusive ways to this changed situation« (Mikuszies et al. 2010: 99 [Translated by the author]).

In fact, citizenship research has been engaged in exploring supranational (Beck/Grande 2006; Borja 2000; Kochenov 2012; Shaw 2003), sub-national (Hess/Lebuhn 2014; Kewes 2016; Purcell 2003; Smith/McQuarrie 2012), or multi-layered models of citizenship (Nicholls 2013). Such foci open fruitful debates on more inclusive models of citizenship and are explored in other contributions in this edited volume. However, while these research strands start to decouple citizenship from the nation, they mainly differentiate between different or shift the debate to other policy levels. Critical citizenship studies stand for questioning state-centered perspectives as such (Holston 1999b: 157; Köster-Eiserfunke et al. 2014). They move beyond citizenship as a legal status by shifting the attention to migrants as political agents and, therefore, to their practices of citizenship (Holston 1999a: 1f.; Lazar/Nuijten 2013: 3; Nyers 2015: 34).

As discussed in the introduction to this volume, Engin Isin distinguishes between three forms of citizenship. Citizenship as a *status* refers to formal citizenship and constructs exclusive categories of (non-)citizens (Isin 2008: 17). Citizenship as *habitus* presupposes the legal definition but focuses on traditional political participation. According to Isin, habitus is the long-term making of citizens and, therefore, a passive »[acting] out already written scripts« (2009: 381; 2008: 17). As opposed to this, *acts* of citizenship »create a scene« (Isin 2009: 381). They »[transform] subjects into claimants of rights over a relatively short period of time« (Isin 2008: 17) and »break routines, understandings and practices« (Isin 2009: 379). Through such a conceptualization, formal »non-citizens« can actually enact and transform citizenship because it acknowledges that, just as the nation-state, citizenship is not a neutral concept: »we think it is important to insist that the political and juridical inscriptions of citizenship are the products of social, cultural, political and institutional conflicts and struggles« (Clarke et al. 2014: 104). So while it is, of course, essential that there is research engaging in current regulatory systems, it is as important not to ignore less institutionalized forms and imaginaries of citizenship. Nyers claims that rather than being about »expanding or widening [...] the space of citizenship and belonging [...], [migrant citizenships] indicate that a significant, if uncertain, transformation has already occurred with this basic political category« (2015: 34).

Increasingly, research on migrant rights struggles all over the world captures a political agency and relations mostly ignored by traditional views on citizenship, emphasizing citizenship as an unfinished transformative process (Clarke et al. 2014: 177). Given that this is already a considerable step, I argue that dynamics dealing with differences within these movements have received little attention so far and still lack conceptualization. My aim is to contribute to current critical citizenship debates by starting to link empirical observations of this to insights from (Black and post-colonial) feminist theories. These insights are often not explicitly integrated in current discussions on citizenship because they are not focusing on migration. However, they address similar dynamics of inequalities like the ones migrant rights groups are facing so they can help to advance conceptualizations of citizenship in this context as well.

3. Activism by, with, and for migrants

3.1. Methodology

This chapter is based on my dissertation research for which I follow a constructivist grounded theory methodology (GTM) after Charmaz (2014) and Bryant (2017). Their constructivist approach emphasizes an interpretive philosophical background, understanding data and analysis as socially constructed and context-specific (Hildenbrand 2011: 556). Constructivist GTM is understood as a systematic, abductive, and comparative methodology aimed at building middle-range theory (Bryant 2017: 89ff.; Peters 2014: 6). The abductive logic stands for a constant shifting between data and theory, making the approach neither purely inductive nor deductive (Bryant 2017: 278). Applying this logic to my research, this means that I developed sensitizing concepts based on a preliminary literature review which I used as starting points for generating data. These data were analyzed through different coding techniques which eventually involved their confrontation with existing literature. Constant comparison, therefore, means that data generation and analysis inform each other (Bryant 2017: 200): Data are confronted with other data and with theory, developing the analytical conceptualization. As a consequence, in GTM, the conceptual and the empirical dimension are closely intertwined: »in some sense, the researcher is simultaneously puzzling over empirical materials and theoretical literatures« (Schwartz-Shea/Yanow 2012: 27). In this chapter, I develop two empirical and conceptual aspects from my doctoral research and link them to existing literature.

3.2.   Field and case selection

My research focuses on activist groups engaged for migrant rights in Hamburg, Northern Germany. Hamburg has the second-biggest European port, making it an important center of economic power and historically also one of migration. Despite its partly very rich society, Hamburg has traditionally been a social-democratic city but is also known for its radical left neighborhoods. With its about 1.8 million inhabitants it is a relevant urban metropolis which »spatially concentrates« the resources and relations which movements draw on (Nicholls/Uitermark 2017: 8).

For my research, I regularly accompanied three activist groups (and a few more on an occasional basis) in their meetings and activities for two years (2017-2019). My data consist of field notes from this participant observation and twelve in-depth interviews with activists.[2] Groups and interview partners were selected purposively, based on the sensitizing concepts and my own political involvement. The size of the groups cannot be determined with precision. For regular meetings, there were usually between five and fifteen people. The groups differ in their concrete topical focus and forms of organizing[3] but they all engage for migrant rights, are or aim at being mixed with regards to the legal status of the people involved, and explicitly consider themselves political. The actual composition varies: one group focuses on women; another one is predominantly white German, most groups involve multiple kinds of migrants. Both in regard to the activists involved in the groups and those interviewed, there is a balanced range of legal status, age, race, and gender.[4]

---

2   When referencing my data, the systematization works as follows: »IDI« stands for in-depth interview, followed by the participant (e.g. »IDI_P02«); »PO« means participant observation, followed by group and fieldnote (e.g. »PO_G03_12«).

3   The majority of the groups is self-organized, i.e. they are no legal entity and run through political engagement. One is a registered association including two part-time paid positions.

4   Following Bakewell and Brubaker, I try to move »beyond categories« because often by sorting people by categories, e.g. nationality, they are reduced to only one ascribed identity (Bakewell 2008: 445; Brubaker 2013: 6). According to Holston, indeed, citizenship has been established as one dominant categorization (1999a: 1f.). Here I mostly address people as »activist citizens« or »activists« in order to not reduce them to their legal status. As this chapter is centrally about differences, that does not mean, however, that I ignore the existence or significance of these categories. When using them, I rather try to take a critical view on them.

3.3.   Positionality

Constructivist GTM is very apt for exploratory research of marginalized activism. Ethical reflections about positionality, privilege, and relations between researcher and participants are central to my research. Given the limited extent of this chapter, I leave it at saying that I am trying to conduct
my research as critically self-reflexive as possible. I have gained many insights
from interpretive research, activist scholarship, participatory and ethnogra-
phic approaches, post-colonial and feminist theories but also, and particularly, from conversations and discussions with and within the groups themselves. I am constantly reflecting and negotiating my position in and vis-à-vis
these groups as a white academic holding a German passport and an involved
activist.

4.   Activist citizens re-negotiating citizenship

As previously discussed, critical citizenship studies have led to an increasing
awareness of how important it is to involve the perspectives of those excluded from citizenship. Most conceptual advances have been made by observing
the actual struggles over citizenship in societies, for instance by women and
Black civil rights activists. The latest focus on migrants builds on these conceptual advancements but also brings new perspectives which still need further exploration. In 2007 Lister observed that citizenship debates tend to be
very conceptual, identifying an »empirical void« (2007: 58). I would argue that
empirical engagement with the lived realities and struggles of migrants has
been constantly growing in the recent past. However, migrants are a group
that is often externally and internally excluded from citizenship, raising further challenges, and their political struggle is much more diverse than often
depicted. In the following, I discuss how variety in activities and activists im-
pacts on our conceptual view of citizenship and how such a perspective can
be advanced by involving (post-colonial and Black) feminist theories.

4.1.   Variety in activities: How everyday politics enable citizenship

When observing the activities of the migrant rights groups, it quickly becomes clear that these go beyond classically »political« and partly blur with what
might be referred to as »social« ones. Groups engage in the traditional politi-

cal dimension of the public. »Going outside«, »[making] the situation public, [...] [giving] an awareness about the situation« are central concerns which are classically aimed at through demonstrations, public events, or conferences (IDI_P08, l. 113-131; IDI_P01, l. 474-479). Activists want to »[hold] up a mirror to society« (IDI_P04, l. 596-604), »[transport] things publicly« (IDI_P06, l. 496-508) but also mobilize people (PO_G06_05, l. 25-32). Through these societal goals, activists engage in a reciprocal relationship with the state. They make direct demands to politicians, such as the closure of a certain camp, stopping racist police controls, or obtaining freedom of movement (PO_G01_06, p.76; PO_G01_17, p.99).

Simultaneously, groups and individuals are addressed by the state in multiple ways, making the relationality reciprocal: isolation (IDI_P15, l. 453-462), criminalization (IDI_P03, l. 1244ff.), deportation (IDI_P01, l. 136-139; IDI_P06, l. 745-749), or tightening of migration laws (IDI_P03, l. 901-905; IDI_P04, l. 428-441). Many activists distinguish this confrontational relationship to the state from pure *humanitarian* work of other societal actors, which according to them is unpolitical, uncritical (IDI_P06, l. 136-144; IDI_P08, l. 689-697; PO_G06_01, p.73) and »moves within the limits of the law« (IDI_P03, l. 999-1001). This statement underlines that migrants are often criminalized, pointing out that what is termed *social* or *humanitarian support* adheres to given rules and laws without questioning them. In this sense, some activists make a clear distinction between what is political and what is not.

However, many activists simultaneously distinguish between social and political work within their own group contexts. Social work, then, are activities dealing with individual problems, i.e. support and care practices (IDI_P03, l. 1017-1022; IDI_P08, l. 676-688). The difference some activists make is that their own social practices consciously undermine the current state of things. Many activists clearly articulate that they see the conditions in which migrants have to live as a purposefully imposed isolation by the state (PO_G05_05, p.51). They live in camps from various months to years, which not only impedes them to live a normal life due to lack of privacy and self-determined routines, but also makes it unlikely to properly arrive in Hamburg through working, meeting locals, or learning German. So providing housing, legal support, or language courses to (illegalized) people becomes a direct challenge to the state (IDI_P01, l. 312-316; IDI_P03, 594-598;

IDI_P04, l. 299-302). Most of the urgencies addressed like this are so basic that addressing them becomes political in itself.[5]

Additionally, through spending time together, creating spaces to cook or relax, the migrants' structurally imposed isolation is undermined as well (IDI_P11, l. 313-316; IDI_P14, l. 732-742; IDI_P15, l. 144-158; PO_G01_3, p. 18; PO_G06_04, p. 17; PO_G09_02, l. 42-49). In that sense, giving people without perspective some hope can be political: »It [our activities] cannot change anythings. But ... [...] the people's mood is become good and the people is become [...] hopeful« (IDI_P01, l. 279-284). One activist names these activities »micro politics« (IDI_P14, l. 507). This underlines that the political action in these contexts takes place on an everyday level that might often not be identified as such. The classically vertical relationality of citizenship between the state and the individual appears to be more complex when accepting this.

The empirical reality of a complex mixture of activities shows that it is not enough to focus discussions about citizenship on legal rights claims. This is also reflected in some publications which observe this dimension of everyday politics as resisting or even undermining state (b)orders, defining them as »invisible practices« (Ataç et al. 2015: 7), »imperceptible politics« (Köster-Eiserfunke et al. 2014: 191f.), or »a wider collective practice that is transformative and underpinned by a logic of resistance« (Piacentini 2014: 177). Such observations point out that a broader conceptual link of the political and citizenship is needed.

The employed vocabulary already emphasizes the proximity to feminist struggles and theories of citizenship. Ruth Lister's notion of a feminist perspective on inclusive citizenship is illuminating in this context: »A key tenet of feminist citizenship theory is that understanding lived citizenship involves a challenge to the public-private dichotomy that underpinned the traditional association of citizenship with the public sphere« (2007: 55). She emphasizes that feminist fights cannot take place without the ground-work of everyday politics for satisfying »human needs« and, thereby, »[promoting] autonomy« (Lister 1997: 16). Similarly, Martin et al. call for paying more attention to the »social basis of political action, and to recognize otherwise-overlooked actions that create social change« (2007: 91). Kabeer argues that we should generally take a more multi-dimensional view on rights. Especially concerning

---

5   Nevertheless, it is also important to underline that, especially for people in such conditions, joining a group is not necessarily a political choice but one in search of concrete support (IDI_P07, l. 257-266; IDI_P07, l. 312-317; IDI_P15, l. 209-220).

citizenship debates, rights are often reduced to political and civil ones, as opposed to social, economic, and cultural rights. Kabeer claims: »When they [people] protest, their protests are not confined to one or the other of these spheres, but tend to staddle them both« (2005: 15). These feminist perspectives on citizenship can easily be linked back to observations from my field where one activist describes very vividly:

»We were very political but the people realized that we also need humanitarian support to sustain our fight. And you can see people try to open their doors, you know, [...] because they know that we need at least [a place] to sleep. So [...] in this sense you can say that the humanitarian support motivated our political struggle« (IDI_P08, l. 680-685).

In the case of feminist fights, women were formally included but actually excluded so that we can speak about an *internal* exclusion. This exclusion has been famously revealed by the claim »the personal is political« (Hanisch 2006), which broadens notions of the political: individual problems are structural. When discussing citizenship in the context of migration, in addition to internal, there very obviously is also *external*, exclusion. People are excluded from the categorization citizenship, or even more basically residency, and thereby lack basic rights. The realization that individual problems actually have structural roots and are, thus, public in nature is one that explains the insistence of activists to frame their social support activities as political as well (IDI_P06, l. 483-491; IDI_P11, l. 476-479; IDI_P15, l. 592-602).

This does not mean that the political and citizenship should be conflated. Indeed, Lister argues that citizenship is enacted publicly: »not all politics necessarily counts as citizenship, for the latter, in its political sense, implies active political participation, albeit broadly defined« (1997: 28). However, the acts in less visible settings are still central to conceptions of citizenship as they enable the political fight in the first place and question the status quo. Again, it is Lister who observes that it might be less about the place where somebody is acting and more about what the action is about and which consequences it has (2007: 57). This fits to the notion that groups are doing more and less visible work simultaneously, meaning that for them, even though not the same, a broad understanding of the political cannot be disentangled from citizenship: »It's that the human being is complex ... and composed by all these things. And [Name 76] also said that [...] cooking is politics too. [...] The human being eats ..., it needs friendships, relationships ... and the human being has to realize itself, right? So all of this comes in. All of this makes politics« (IDI_P17_1, l. 879-887 [Translated by the author]).

Migrant rights activists engage in a wide range of activities, moving beyond a dichotomy between public and private, which calls for a broadening of
the understanding of the political and results in being able to consider what
Isin terms *acts of citizenship* as citizenship at all. It should be explored further
how the different dimensions of political action interact and can constitute
citizenship.

4.2.   Intersection of differences: How inequalities shape citizenship

The migrant rights groups I have accompanied are composed of activists with
a variety of legal statuses (IDI_P06, l. 897-911; IDI_P11, l. 309-313; PO_G06_02,
p.15). This is the most visible and often defining of various differences in the
activist groups: It is not merely about distinguishing between Germans and
migrants, as there is a variety of migrants involved. These include so-called
»regular migrants«, refugees formally granted asylum, and several illegalized
groups, to name just a few. This variety in statuses also results in very real
differences between these groups and their access to language classes, job
market, or other kinds of rights (IDI_P01, l. 556-571; IDI_P05, l. 1366-1382).
Supporting this notion, one activist underlines in a meeting: »It's important
that it's the system that is dividing people through different treatments and
statuses« (PO_G02_06, p.68).

Similarly, some German activists are read as migrants, based on their physical appearance, and thereby, experience racism and discrimination as well.
Moving beyond legal status, the activist groups are still highly diverse. Classical systems of oppression, such as race, gender, and class intersect with each
other, and are complemented by further differences in the context of these
activist groups. Next to having different legal statuses, socio-economic, cultural, and political backgrounds, activists also differ in their aims, interests,
and necessities. Some activists point out how women are basically excluded
from activist groups because there is no childcare or due to the choice of
meeting places and times (IDI_P05, l. 818-825; IDI_P07, l. 49-55; PO_G06_02,
p.14). Language also emerges as a challenge because, even when interpretation is organized, people depend on others, can only participate indirectly and
time-lagged (IDI_P06, 1021-1030; IDI_P14, l. 875-885; PO_G02_9, p.109). It oc-
curs that those in need of interpretation are seated in a corner in order not to
disturb the rest of the group, a practice which has been framed as »a symbolic mechanism of exclusion« (PO_G02_9, p.110). Finally, local knowledge and
experience centrally determine how much someone depends on others:

»[U]sually these meetings are pretty much ... ›oh, we have these problems‹. And then [how] can we fix it, and usually [it is] the Kartoffel[6] or the ... [...] so-called supporters, activists, that have their contacts. And it's really important that they do ... but I would like to get to a point where, as [Name 9] said [...], I don't need to ask [Name 7] [...] to write the [finance] application for me« (IDI_P05, l. 867-874).

It is an expressed aim of the groups to work together on equal terms (IDI_P06, l. 897-911; IDI_P08, l. 439-443; IDI_P11, l. 309-313; PO_G06_02, p.15). This is most explicitly voiced concerning the interaction between Germans and refugees but, as the previous examples have shown, it is not limited to it. On the other side, legal status often concurs with many of these differences so inequalities are constantly present in the groups.[7] Actually challenging them is difficult because dependencies constantly reproduce power gaps and hierarchies: »[T]hey [supporters] want to contribute and their contribution in some ways might not be in the interest of the self-organized group, of the refugees group« (IDI_P08, l. 355-369). To be able to challenge such dynamics, intersectional differences have to be recognized: »we are all activists, but at the same time we need to recognize certain things« (IDI_P05, l. 150-159).

My data show that some of these activist groups realize that they are reproducing inequalities, for instance when not organizing interpretation or childcare. Of course, in most cases they cannot undo the inequalities themselves but they can openly engage with the existing power structures and develop strategies of alleviating them. Self-organization of refugees and migrants, sometimes through settings which are exclusive to them, is one step sometimes mentioned as empowering (IDI_P03, l. 317-325; IDI_P05, l. 1360-1366; IDI_P08, l. 90-99; PO_G01_05, p. 49; PO_G02_5, p.51). One group started to experiment with technical devices making interpretation a less excluding process within the group conversation (PO_G01_33, l. 27-50). Another one decided to buy speakers and an amplifier so that they were not dependent anymore on other (German) groups providing them (PO_G02_07, p. 79). However, such reflections are often »swallowed« by the emerging everyday urgencies.

---

6   Potato, used to refer to white Germans.
7   Nevertheless, there are examples to demonstrate that legal status is not the one and only factor: It is often the migrants themselves who provide interpretation, local knowledge has to be acquired by everyone moving to Hamburg, Black people are not necessarily migrants, and a lack of childcare can also exclude German (single) parents.

My empirical observations underline that there is a plurality of differences within activist groups which intersect with each other, resulting in power imbalances and challenges these groups are constantly struggling with. Acknowledging but challenging the differences, one can say, captures the ways these activist groups in Hamburg deal with their positionalities. Some to a higher, some to a lesser extent, they engage in a continuous process of (re-)negotiating possibilities and necessities. Some publications in studies of social movements and critical citizenship raise similar issues. Weldon argues that internal politics are over-representing privileged instead of marginalized groups in many movements (2011: 5). This is particularly central in struggles over citizenship because migrants are externally and internally excluded and work in highly heterogeneous constellations. Glöde and Böhlo acknowledge the difficulty which inequalities pose to joint political action (2015: 79), Fadaee critically reflects the dominance of European activists' priorities (2015: 734). Kewes, Ataç, and Steinhilper emphasize problematic dependencies and patronization (Ataç 2016: 642; Kewes 2016: 264; Steinhilper 2017: 81f.).

Black and post-colonial feminist perspectives offer valuable insights into such complex constellations of intersecting inequalities. The Combahee River collective strongly shows the differences within feminist but also Black struggles by stating that »we have in many ways gone beyond white women's revelations because we are dealing with the implications of race and class as well as sex« and by referring to negative reactions of Black men to Black feminism (Combahee River Collective 1977). Ell Ooks argues similarly, showing that it had first to be pointed out how »racism had shaped and informed feminist theory and practice« (2000: 16). Today, intersectionality is an established concept which captures the interaction of multiple power systems. It also emerged from this increasing awareness for segmented life and movement realities that imposing homogeneity to all people supposedly included in a certain category or movement reproduces privileges and inequalities:

»[T]his interdependency between individual and group rights can often serve to undermine the capacity of subordinated members of subordinated groups to press for their individual rights when to do so appears to divide the collective struggle for recognition or to play into hegemonic discourses which denigrate such groups« (Kabeer 2005: 14).

Ünsal explicitly refers to migrant rights activism when she criticizes that we mostly engage with the supporter/refugee distinction, ignoring intersectional power structures: »We should respect the different realities and recognize the discriminations in the movement« (2015: 15). Indeed, according to

Lister, pretending unity without acknowledging differences »[reinforces] the very exclusion against which these groups are fighting« (1997: 30). Overlooking that the migrant rights struggle is composed by a variety of differently categorized people means marginalizing those suffering from essentializing categories anyhow. These insights from different struggles call for a conceptualization of citizenship not only in its relationality between state and individual (Lister 1997: 3). Kabeer emphasizes a horizontal view of citizenship as follows: »one which stresses that the relationship between citizens is at least as important as the more traditional ›vertical‹ view of citizenship as the relationship between the state and the individual« (2005: 23). What the focus on migrant rights groups adds is that this relationality expands beyond the formal citizen. In all their diversity, the groups try to constructively deal with inequalities and resulting hierarchies. Johnson describes this as mutual recognition and solidarity: »It enables a relationship of mutual support and protection that uses the security of the citizen, but does not reduce or subordinate the power of the migrant« (2015: 16f.). This element of mutual solidarity is also reflected in a field note from a meeting: »Then [Name 9] said [...]: Everybody is giving and supporting with different things so in the end it becomes working together for a common goal« (PO_G06_02, p.12).

In aiming at this, it is central to recognize the intersectionality of different positions. It is not about a dichotomy that should be brought together but about engaging with complex relationalities among individuals that act together. While some positions might be specific to these migrant rights groups, I argue that citizenship studies pay too little attention to groups' internal complexities and the resulting excluding dynamics. Feminist, Black, and post-colonial perspectives have long emphasized the diverse nature of activist struggles and intersectional identities and are, thus, a promising point of reference that should be explored further in the current debates on citizenship.

5. Conclusion

Approaching discussions on citizenship through migrant rights groups clearly has conceptual implications. As I have shown, critical perspectives have long argued for less state-centered models and explicitly criticized the taken-for-granted linkage between political agency and formal citizenship. What I hope to have added through this contribution is, firstly, that looking at the everyday reality of these activist struggles leads to a broader conceptualization of the political which enables us to better capture the range of activities discussed as »acts of citizenship«. The vertical relationality between state and individual becomes more complex from such a perspective. To frame individual support politically means acknowledging personal situations as structural and, thus, questioning current citizenship regimes further. Secondly, these struggles are intersectionally heterogeneous contexts which are shaped by externally impo-sed, essentializing categorizations that are reproduced in internal dynamics of inequalities and exclusion. Exploring the ways through which groups deal with this introduces a horizontal dimension of citizenship. By linking these context-specific insights to existing literature from (Black and post-colonial) feminist perspectives, we can start to intersectionally explore conceptualizati-ons of citizenship beyond dichotomous distinctions of inclusion or exclusion.

Therefore, I argue that it is reasonable to relate such perspectives more systematically to migrant rights activism. Nevertheless, linking this to the li-ved realities of activists is challenging because especially on an individual level they are simultaneously fighting for – if not citizenship, then certainly for-mal rights – and against citizenship in terms of current policies constituting it (Erensu 2016: 665). Therefore, I want to mention that conceptualizing such struggles as citizenship does not help migrant activists: their *real* status does not change. While they are addressed as activist citizens and conceptualized as political actors, their precarious realities remain: people are transferred, deported, discriminated. One could, then, question whether citizenship con-stitutes the right frame of analysis for researching these struggles. However, acknowledging the transformations of citizenship that feminist and Black ac-tivists have already reached, adds an important corrective in that it reinforces the observation that no concept of citizenship is ever fixed or neutral. Every concept evolves over time and builds on others that are equally constructed. So ultimately, I would argue that a conceptualization of these struggles through citizenship, on the one hand, does justice to the truly inspiring agency these people enact and, on the other hand, calls into question a dominant but con-structed paradigm which completely shapes their lives. Stretching the con-cept of citizenship in this way is essential for taking a critical stance on the dominant supposedly neutral views underlying it.

References

Ataç, Ilker (2016): ›Refugee Protest Camp Vienna‹: Making Citizens Through Locations of the Protest Movement. Citizenship Studies, 20(5), 629-646. https://doi:10.1080/13621025.2016.1182676

Ataç, Ilker/Kron, Stefanie/Schilliger, Sarah/Schwiertz, Helge/Stierl, Maurice (2015): Kämpfe der Migration als Un-/Sichtbare Politiken. Movements. Journal Für Kritische Migrations- und Grenzregimeforschung, 1(2), 1-18.

Bakewell, Oliver (2008): Research Beyond the Categories: The Importance of Policy Irrelevant Research into Forced Migration. Journal of Refugee Studies, 21(4), 432-453. https://doi:10.1093/jrs/fen042

Beck, Ulrich/Grande, Edgar (2007). Cosmopolitan Europe. Cambridge: Polity Press.

Benhabib, Seyla (2004). The Rights of Others: Aliens, Residents and Citizens. Cambridge: University Press.

Borja, Jordi (2000): The Citizenship Question and the Challenge of Globalization: The European Context. City, 4(1), 43-52. https://doi:10.1080/713656996

Brubaker, Rogers (2013): Categories of Analysis and Categories of Practice: A Note on the Study of Muslims in European Countries of Immigration. Ethnic and Racial Studies, 36(1), 1-8. https://doi:10.1080/01419870.2012.729674

Brubaker, Rogers (2015): Grounds for Difference. Harvard University Press.

Bryant, Antony (2017): Grounded Theory and Grounded Theorizing: Pragmatism in Research Practice. Oxford University Press.

Calhoun, Craig (1999): Nationalism, Political Community and the Representation of Society: Or, Why Feeling at Home is not a Substitute for Public Space. European Journal of Social Theory, 2(2), 217-231. https://doi:10.1177/13684319900200005

Castles, Stephen/Davidson, Alastair (2001): Citizenship and Migration: Globalization and the Politics of Belonging (3rd Edition). Palgrave.

Charmaz, Kathy (2014): Constructing Grounded Theory 2nd Edition, California: Sage.

Clarke, John/Coll, Kathleen/Dagnino, Evelina/Neveu, Catherine (2014): Disputing Citizenship, Bristol: Policy Press.

Cohen, J. L. (1999). Changing Paradigms of Citizenship and the Exclusiveness of the Demos. International Sociology, 14(3), 245-268.

Combahee River Collective (1977): Combahee River Collective Statement. http s://combaheerivercollective.weebly.com/the-combahee-river-collective-statement.html

Earnest, David (2008): Old Nations, New Voters: Nationalism, Transnationalism, and Democracy in the Era of Global Migration, Albany: State University of New York Press.

Erensu, Asli Ikizoglu (2016): Notes From a Refugee Protest: Ambivalences of Resisting and Desiring Citizenship. Citizenship Studies, 20(5), 664-677. https://doi:10.1080/13621025.2016.1182677

Fadaee, Simin (2015): The Immigrant Rights Struggle, and the Paradoxes of Radical Activism in Europe. Social Movement Studies, 14(6), 733-739. http s://doi:10.1080/14742837.2015.1070336

Glick Schiller, Nina (2012). Transnationality, Migrants and Cities: A Comparative Approach. In: Anna Amelina/Devrimsel D. Nergiz/Thomas Faist/Nina Glick Schiller, Beyond Methodological Nationalism: Research Methodologies for Cross-Border Studies, London: Routledge, 23-40.

Glöde, Harald/Böhlo, Berenice (2015): Der Marsch der protestierenden Flüchtlinge von Würzburg nach Berlin und ihr Protest bis heute. Forschungsjournal Soziale Bewegungen 28(4): 75-86. https://doi:10.1515/fjsb-2015-0410

Hammar, Tomas (1990): Democracy and the Nation State: Aliens, Denizens, and Citizens in a World of International Migration, Avebury: Gower Pub Co.

Hanisch, Carol (2006): The Women's Liberation Movement Classic with a New Explanatory Introduction. www.carolhanisch.org/CHwritings/PIP.html.

Hess, Sabine/Lebuhn, Henrik (2014): Politiken der Bürgerschaft. Zur Forschungsdebatte um Migration, Stadt und Citizenship. Sub\urban. Zeitschrift Für Kritische Stadtforschung 2(3): 11-34. https://doi:10.36900/suburban.v2i3.153

Hildenbrand, Bruno (2011). Mediating Structure and Interaction in Grounded Theory. In: Antony, Bryant/Kathy, Charmaz (eds.), The SAGE Handbook of Grounded Theory, London: Sage. 539-564.

Holston, James (eds.) (1999a): Cities and Citizenship, Durham: Duke University Press.

Holston, James (1999b): Spaces of Insurgent Cities. In: James, Holston (eds.), Cities and Citizenship, Durham: Duke University Press, 155-173.

Isin, Engin F. (2008): Theorizing acts of citizenship. In: Engin F., Isin/Greg M., Nielsen (eds.), Acts of citizenship, London: Palgrave Macmillan, 15-43.

Isin, Engin F. (2009): Citizenship in flux: The figure of the activist citizen. Subjectivity 29(1): 367-388. https://doi:10.1057/sub.2009.25

Johnson, Heather L. (2015): These Fine Lines: Locating Noncitizenship in Political Protest in Europe. Citizenship Studies 19(8): 951-965. https://doi:10.1080/13621025.2015.1110287

Kabeer, Naila (2005): Inclusive Citizenship: Meanings and Expressions, London: Zed Books.

Kewes, Andreas (2016): Urban Citizenship-Oder: Über den Versuch, dem »System« auf Augenhöhe zu begegnen. In: Stefan Rother (ed.), Migration und Demokratie, Wiesbaden: Springer VS, 139-160.

Kochenov, Dimitry (2012): EU Citizenship: From an Incipient Form to an Incipient Substance? The Discovery of the Treaty Text. European Law Review 37(4): 369-396.

Köster-Eiserfunke, Anna/Reichhold, Clemens/Schwiertz, Helge (2014): Citizenship zwischen nationalem Status und aktivistischer Praxis. Eine Einführung. In: Lisa-Marie Heimeshoff/Sabine Hess (eds.), Grenzregime II: Migration- Kontrolle- Wissen: Transnationale Perspektiven, Berlin: Assoziation A., 177-196.

Lazar, Sian/Nuijten, Monique (2013): Citizenship, the Self, and Political Agency. Critique of Anthropology 33(1): 3-7. https://doi:10.1177/0308275X 12466684

Lister, Ruth (1997): Citizenship: Feminist Perspectives, London: Palgrave Macmillan.

Lister, Ruth (2007): Inclusive Citizenship: Realizing the Potential1. Citizenship Studies 11(1): 49-61. https://doi:10.1080/13621020601099856

Martin, Deborah G./Hanson, Susan/Fontaine, Danielle (2007): What Counts as Activism? The Role of Individuals in Creating Change. Women's Studies Quarterly 35(3/4): 78-94.

McGuaran, Katrin/Hudig, Kees (2014): Refugee Protests in Europe: Fighting for the Right to Stay. Statewatch Journal 23(3/4): 28-33.

Mikuszies, Esther/Nowak, Jörg/Ruß, Sabine (2010): Die politische Repräsentation von schwachen Interessen am Beispiel von MigrantInnen. In: Ute Clement (ed.), Public Governance und schwache Interessen, Wiesbaden: VS Verlag für Sozialwissenschaften.

Nicholls, Walter J. (2013): Fragmenting Citizenship: Dynamics of Cooperation and Conflict in France's Immigrant Rights Movement. Ethnic and Racial Studies 36(4): 611-631. https://doi:10.1080/01419870.2011.626055

Nicholls, Walter J./Uitermark, Justus (2017): Cities and Social Movements: Immigrant Rights Activism in the US, France, and the Netherlands, 1970-2015, Oxford: John Wiley & Sons, Ltd.

Nyers, Peter. 2015. »Migrant Citizenships and Autonomous Mobilities.« Migration, Mobility, & Displacement. 1 (1): 23-39. https://doi:10.1 8357/mmd11201513521

Nyers, Peter/Rygiel, Kim (2014): Citizenship, migrantischer Aktivismus und Politiken der Bewegung. In: Lisa-Marie Heimeshoff/Sabine Hess (eds.), Migration – Kontrolle – Wissen: Transnationale Perspektiven, Berlin: Assoziation A., 197-216.

Ooks, Ell (2000): Feminism is for Everybody: Passionate Politics, Boston: South End Press.

Peters, Ina (2014): Too Abstract to Be Feasible? Applying the Grounded Theory Method in Social Movement Research, GIGA – German Institute of Global and Area Studies, 247.

Piacentini, Teresa (2014): Everyday Acts of Resistance. The Precarious Lives of Asylum Seekers in Glasgow. In: Katarzyna Marciniak/Imogen Tyler (eds.), Immigrant Protest: Politics, Aesthetics, and Everyday Dissent, New York: State University of New York Press, 169-187.

Purcell, Mark (2003): Citizenship and the Right to the Global City: Reimagining the Capitalist World Order. International Journal of Urban and Regional Research 27(3): 564-590. https://doi:10.1111/1468-2427.00467

Rother, Stefan (ed.) (2016): Migration und Demokratie, Wiesbaden: Springer VS.

Rygiel, Kim/Ataç, Ilker/Köster-Eiserfunke, Anna/Schwiertz, Helge (2015): Governing through Citizenship and Citizenship from Below. An Interview with Kim Rygiel. Movements Journal Für Kritische Migrations- und Grenzregimeforschung 1(2).

Schulte, Axel (2009): Demokratie und Integration: Zwischen dem Ideal gleicher Freiheit und der Wirklichkeit ungleicher Macht – eine Studie mit Blick auf Norberto Bobbio, Münster: LIT.

Schwartz-Shea, Peregrine/Yanow, Dvora (2012): Interpretive Research Design: Concepts and Processes, London: Routledge.

Schwenken, Helen/Ruß-Sattar, Sabine (eds.) (2014): New Border and Citizenship Politics, London: Palgrave Macmillan.

Shaw, Jo (2003): The Interpretation of European Union Citizenship. The Modern Law Review 61(3): 293-317. https://doi:10.1111/1468-2230.00145

Smith, Michael Peter/McQuarrie, Michael (eds.) (2012): Remaking Urban Citizenship: Organizations, Institutions, and the Right to the City, New Jersey: Transaction Publishers.

Steinhilper, Elias (2017): Politisiert in der Migration, vernetzt in der Stadt. Transnationaler politischer Protest von Geflüchteten in Berlin. Forschungsjournal Soziale Bewegungen 30(3): 76-86.

Ünsal, Nadiye (2015): Challenging ›Refugees‹ and ›Supporters‹. Intersectional Power Structures in the Refugee Movement in Berlin. Movements. Journal für Kritische Migrations- und Grenzregimeforschung 1(2).

Weldon, Laurel S. (2011): When Protest Makes Policy: How Social Movements Represent Disadvantaged Groups, Michigan: University of Michigan Press.

Who belongs to ›the people‹?
The societal boundaries of national and European notions of citizenship

Carsten Wegscheider and Roula Nezi

1. Introduction

The process of European integration increasingly challenges the concept of national citizenship through the development of a supranational citizenship derived from countries' membership in the European Union. While nation states and borders gradually lose their political and societal significance, policies aimed at deepening and promoting further integration give rise to a backlash against the European Union. This backlash evolved around the significance of national and European citizenship and is mainly related to the conditions for belonging to ›the people‹.

Today's concepts of citizenship distinguish between nation and state due to the rise of supranational and multicultural states, where identities are developed alongside citizenship (McCrone/Kiely 2000). While this has not been the case in the past, in contemporary democracies there is a clear distinction between citizenship and nationality. The concept of citizenship denotes a person's legal status and thus regulates the legal criteria and conditions for the acquisition of citizenship. The concept of nationality, on the other hand, refers to a person's identity and thus to the subjective feeling and individual construction of belonging. However, we know little about the extent to which the citizens' (political) identities influence their attitudes towards and perceptions of different notions of citizenship.

Previous research suggests two widespread notions of citizenship among citizens – *ethnic* and *civic* – which are both related to the development of nation states in Europe. The ethnic definition of citizenship considers ancestry as the most important criterion for inclusion, and eventually members of the nation share a common cultural heritage such as religious beliefs (Smith 1991). In contrast, the civic definition entails that citizenship can be acquired through efforts to join the group and adherence to legal norms (Reeskens/Hooghe 2010). For this reason, ethnic notions of citizenship tend to be considered as highly exclusive: if you are not born into it (*the country*), you cannot acquire it (Ignatieff 1994). This dichotomy of ethnic and civic notions of citizenship can be transferred to both the national and the European level. These differences into citizens' perceptions of symbolic boundaries[1] are reflected upon the legal criteria and prerequisites for obtaining citizenship, but also in the societal and individual construction of (political) identities.

In our analysis we argue that citizen attitudes regarding requirements for citizenship depend upon their political identity.

Accordingly, individuals with a strong national identity should support restrictions on the conditions for acquiring citizenship at both the national and the European level. Individuals with strong European identity should support limitations at the European level. On the other hand, we expect that the citizens' sharing cosmopolitan views – people who emphasize equality and oppose the idea of state borders – will reject both national and European restrictions on the conditions for citizenship. To identify the societal boundaries of the different concepts of citizenship in European societies, we analyze the causes of ethnic and civic notions of national and European citizenship among citizens and provide an answer to the following question: *what are the causes of citizens' ethnic and civic notions of national and European citizenship?*

In our analysis we use data from the second pre-release of the European Values Study (EVS) 2017, which covers 20 member states of the European Union[2]. Using Bayesian hierarchical models, we examine the causes of ethnic and civic notions of national and European citizenship. Our empirical results confirm the importance of political identity for the support of restrictions on the conditions for acquiring citizenship. While political identity determines the support or rejection of national and European restrictions on citizenship, social liberal values and anti-immigration attitudes are also very important

---

1   Symbolic boundaries are considered the lines that include and define some people, groups, and things while excluding others (Epstein 1992: 232).

2   Though our initial goal was to include more waves and to extend the time span of our analysis, unfortunately, previous waves do not include the battery of questions about citizens` attitudes towards European citizenship.

factors. Furthermore, the results suggest that both notions of European citizenship are comparatively more inclusive to their national counterparts, although the degree of inclusiveness is ultimately determined by the distinction between the ethnic and civic dichotomy. This chapter is structured as follows: In the next section, we briefly review the literature on different notions and levels of citizenship and formulate our theoretical argument. Subsequently, in the third section, we introduce the data and methods we are using. In the fourth section, we present our empirical results, while we discuss the societal and political implications of our findings in the final section.

2.   Notions of citizenship

According to the basic assumption of political culture research, the stability of a political system rests on the congruence between the political culture and institutionalized structures (Almond/Verba 1963) and is thus largely dependent on the *political support* of its citizens (Easton 1965, 1975). A political system only receives support if it is responsive to the political orientations and attitudes of its citizens (Pickel/Pickel 2006, 2016). Besides their support for *political authorities* and the *political regime*, a certain degree of social cohesion among citizens and their willingness to collectively solve political problems is crucial for the survivability of a political system (Easton 1965, 1975; Norris 1999, 2011). The political system only receives support if the citizens' ideas about the belonging of certain groups to the people coincide with the actual composition of society. Notwithstanding the importance of the concept of *political community* for political culture research, there are different ideas about who constitutes a political community and how it should be defined.

In our analysis we define political community as *a group of people who respect commonly agreed habits of making and implementing political decisions* (Deutsch 1954). This means, in other words, groups of people with a common sense of belonging and obligations (Anderson 1991; Deutsch 1966; Wright 2011). The immediate implication is that a political community and its social cohesion are characterized by a *shared sense of identity, and mutual loyalty among citizens* (Almond et al. 2008; Brubaker 2004). Social cohesion is thus based on a societal agreement on which social groups belong to the political community. However, there are different notions about what kind of boundaries these *imagined communities* (Wright 2011) are based on and which criteria are used to determine the belonging or exclusion of people.

2.1.   The national and European dimension of citizenship

In modern democracies, the symbolic boundaries and criteria by which membership to a political community is regulated are inevitably linked to the concept of citizenship (Simonsen/Bonikowski 2019). In addition to a bundle of legal rights and (political) participation, citizenship regulates the belonging of and the relationship between citizens and the political system (Bellamy, Castiglione and Santoro 2004). Thereby, the »socially constructed sameness« (Kunovich 2009: 576) among the members of a political community can have different origins, forms and rules.

Since the contemporary political world is dominated by nation states, access to state resources is primarily granted through *national citizenship* regulations (Kunovich 2009). According to this traditional understanding, citizenship is tied to a historically grown *national identity* and defined by a common ethnicity, language, history, culture or the use of the same territorial area (Almond et al. 2008). This inclusiveness and exclusiveness of national identity also illustrates the social closure of the concept of national citizenship (Brubaker 1992).

While this may be true, the process of European integration increasingly challenges the concept of national citizenship, with the aim of developing a common European identity and thus a supranational citizenship (Nezi 2010; Nezi 2009; Shore 2004). The European citizenship is linked to the idea of an open and liberal society in which legal rights and political participation are detached from the national identity, and citizenship is regulated by civil and political norms rather than ethno-cultural criteria (Habermas 1992).

The European notion of citizenship meets the demands of cosmopolitanism – a worldview according to which all human beings belong to a single community based on shared morality (Smith 1998). Cosmopolitans, as supporters of the EU are often characterized, support a world without national borders and emphasize the equality of all humans for which rights should not be restricted based on certain individual characteristics (Merkel 2017). In this regard, European citizenship enables the development of dual identities and promotes integration and unity among European societies by breaking down prejudices (Curtis 2014). At the same time, European citizenship only simulates an openness to the world, since the inclusion and exclusion of people is simply raised to the level and borders of the European Union (Kunovich 2009). For this reason, it is questionable whether European citizenship is more inclusive compared to national approaches.

The conflict between national and European notions of citizenship is particularly important in the light of recent political developments, especially due to the backlash generated by the enforcement of European citizenship (Brubaker 2017). This backlash fosters the rise of populist radical right parties, who claim to bring power back to the national sovereign – ›the people‹. Further to the political and societal conflict around the national and European notions of citizenship, an additional conflict developed over the *ethnic and civic conditions* associated with the democratic privilege of citizenship. In particular, liberal and authoritarian nativist ideas of citizenship compete with each other. While political liberalism supports the idea of absorbing elements from other cultural traditions and integrating different ethnic groups, authoritarian nativism defines citizenship primarily through ethnic components and is exclusive towards members of out-groups (Lubbers and Coenders 2017; Mudde 2007; Rydgren 2007).

2.2. The ethnic and civic dichotomy of citizenship

The societal conflict over the requirements for obtaining citizenship is based on two fundamental principles and legal rights for the acquisition of citizenship. The first one is the right of the soil, *jus soli*, according to which citizenship is granted to everyone born in the country, regardless of ethnicity. According to the analysis by Brubaker (1992), France is a classic example of a country following the principle of jus soli. In contrast, Germany is a classic example of a country following the principles of *jus sanguinis* – the law of blood. In this case, citizenship can only be obtained if a person is of national descent.

Previous research on nationalism suggested that citizens' notions of citizenship follow the principles of jus soli and jus sanguinis and can be distinguished between an *ethnic* and a *civic* dimension (Brubaker 1992; Kohn 1944; Kunovich 2009; Reeskens/Hooghe 2010; Shulman 2002; Simonsen/Bonikowski 2019). The ethnic notion of citizenship includes »relatively fixed attributes, such as race, ethnicity, native-born status and national ancestry, as well as deeply socialised cultural traits like religious beliefs« (Simonsen/Bonikowski 2019: 4). The civic notion of citizenship encompasses transformable and assimilating ideas such as respect for national political institutions and laws, adaptation to cultural traditions or learning the national language (Lubbers/Coenders 2017; Simonsen/Bonikowski 2019; Smith 2001). These self-conceptions of collective in-group identity therefore include the symbolic boundaries and criteria for belonging to a nation (Bail 2008). However, these two dimensions of citizenship are not necessarily mutually exclusive, because individuals may hold both notions at the same time (Lubbers/Coenders 2017).

2.3.   Hypotheses: Causes of notions of citizenship

In addition to the question on citizens' perceptions of the requirements for obtaining citizenship, there is also the question on the causes of the competing perceptions of citizenship. Our main argument is that the societal boundaries of notions of citizenship are based on individual political identities. The social identity theory (Tajfel 1982; Tajfel/Turner 1979) predicts that identification with a particular group (in-group) strengthens negative attitudes towards members of what they define as an out-group. In our analysis, we expect different effects of political identities on notions of national and European citizenship:

We distinguish between three territorial levels individuals can identify with; the national, the European and the global level. The national level refers to the country in which a person lives (Lubbers/Coenders 2017; Smith 2007). Individuals strongly identifying with their country are more likely to hold negative attitudes towards people who do not hold the national citizenship. Moreover, strong nationalist attitudes are also associated with the restriction of certain groups on the European level to avoid jeopardizing national and European homogeneity. Therefore, *we expect that citizens strongly identifying with their country will also support limitations on the requirements for acquiring both the national and the European citizenship, albeit with a stronger effect at the national level* (H1a).

Due to the importance of the development of European integration, identification with Europe is our second political level. We expect people who strongly identify with Europe to be more likely to stand up for an open and liberal (national) society compared to nationalists, since the idea of a European identity corresponds more to the desire of a cosmopolitan society. On the other hand, we expect that strong levels of identification with Europe also lead to a desire to restrict the privilege of citizenship towards non-Europeans. For these reasons, *we expect that citizens identifying with Europe are more likely to reject national restrictions on the conditions of acquiring citizenship, but more likely to advocate requirements for obtaining European citizenship* (H1b).

As a third political level, we refer to the identification with a cosmopolitan global citizenship (Merkel 2017; Smith 1998). According to cosmopolitanism, all humans are equal and belong to a single community based on a commonly shared morality. The idea of cosmopolitanism thus rejects (national) borders and the exclusion of people on the basis of individual characteristics. In this case, *we expect that citizens identifying with the world are more likely to reject any limitation of the conditions for acquiring national and European citizenship* (H1c).

Based on a social-psychological perspective, we control for social identities which also distinguish between *us* and the supposed *others*. Drawing on the approach of social capital, social trust in in-groups and out-groups are suitable indicators for the binding and bridging of social capital (Putnam 2001). While strong in-group trust is positively associated with a sense of community within a group, strong out-group trust also strengthens the bridging between social groups with different characteristics. Thus, in-group trust should be associated with negative attitudes towards members of out-groups, while out-group trust should increase tolerance towards out-groups. Accordingly, *we expect that people with high levels of in-group trust are more likely to support restrictions on national and European citizenship, while people with high out-group trust should be more likely to reject restrictions on national and European citizenship* (H2).

Previous research has already shown that nationalism is accompanied by prejudice, xenophobia and racism (Brubaker 1992; Kunovich 2009). However, populist radical right parties often argue that they are the defenders of social liberal values against the treat of immigration. In fact, their authoritarian and nativist ideology also contradicts these values, and these parties often represent illiberal values themselves (Akkerman 2005; Brubaker 2017; Mudde 2007; Rydgren 2007). Accordingly, citizens with positive attitudes towards immigration and supporting social liberal values, such as gender equality and gay rights, should be more likely to be tolerant towards members of out-groups (Heinisch/Wegscheider 2020; Stark et al. 2017). Therefore, *we expect citizens with negative attitudes towards immigration to support restrictions of the conditions for national and European citizenship, while citizens with social liberal values reject these restrictions* (H3).

3.   Research design

In our analysis, we use data from the second pre-release of the fifth wave of the European Values Study (EVS 2019). This data covers 37.277 European citizens from 20 member states of the European Union: Austria, Bulgaria,

Croatia, Czech Republic, Denmark, Estonia, Finland, France, Germany, Hungary, Italy, Lithuania, the Netherlands, Poland, Romania, Slovakia, Slovenia, Spain, Sweden, and Great Britain. This latest version of the EVS offers the opportunity to analyze individual attitudes towards citizenship at the national and the European level.

Our main dependent variables measure the ethnic and civic dimensions of national and European citizenship. Respondents were asked on a four-point-scale to express their own views on how important they consider to be certain characteristics of belonging to their country or to Europe. To analyze the ethnic notion of national citizenship, we use questions measuring the importance of *having been born in the country* and *having country's ancestry*[3]. In addition to the equivalent questions relating to Europe, which are used to construct the ethnic notion of European citizenship, we also included a question on religious identity in our analysis. Existing research has demonstrated the importance of religion and especially of Christianity at the European level for ethnic attributions (Brubaker 2017). The above-mentioned questions measure the importance of *being born in Europe, having European ancestries*, and *being a Christian*[4].

To develop a more comprehensive model, we included two additional dependent variables analyzing the civic dimensions of national and European citizenship. The national dimension of civic citizenship consists of three measures gauging the importance of *respecting the country's political institutions and laws, speaking the national language*, and *sharing the national culture*. The civic dimension of European citizenship is constructed based on a measure asking respondents how important it is in their view to *share the European culture*.

Multidimensional phenomena such as citizenship are often difficult to measure accurately, because they are characterized by a wide range of dimensions. The civic dimension of citizenship, for example, consists of three indicators that are not ranked in any particular order – political institutions and laws, the national language, and the national culture. These three dimensions should be combined into a single indicator that measures individual attitudes towards the national dimension of civic citizenship. In soci-

---

3   The exact wording of the question is the following: Some people say the following things are important for being truly [NATIONALITY]. Others say they are not important. How important do you think each of the following is?

4   People differ in what they think it means to be European. In your view, how important is each of the following to be European?

al sciences, this is typically achieved by index construction. Indices combine indicators representing different dimensions of the same phenomenon. There are two main approaches to index construction; the addition of variables and the reduction of variables (Reckien 2018). In our analysis, we follow the approach of the addition of variables and only consider variables that have been identified as influential in already existing studies (Brubaker 1992; Kunovich 2009; Reeskens/Hooghe 2010; Shulman 2002; Simonsen/Bonikowski 2019). These variables are then summed up and normalized (Reckien 2018).

With response to our research question, we included variables measuring the concepts of *attachment with the country, Europe and the world, social identity, anti-immigration attitudes and social liberal values.* To measure the level of attachment with their country, Europe and the world, we use a series of variables measuring how close respondents feel to their *country, Europe* and *the world*[5]. Furthermore, we add a dichotomous variable indicating whether the respondent has the *nationality of the country or not*[6].

Social identity is operationalized by a battery of questions asking how much people trust the so-called in-groups and out-groups[7]. We measure in-group trust through the respondents' trust in their *family, people in their neighborhood,* and *people they know personally.* In contrast, we measure out-group trust as the respondents' trust in *people they meet for the first time, people of another religion* and *people of another nationality. Anti-immigration attitudes* are measured using a battery of questions asking whether immigrants *take away jobs from nationals, make crime problems worse,* and are a *strain on a country's welfare system*[8]. For

---

5   People have different views about themselves and how they relate to the world. Using this card, would you tell me how close do you feel to…?
6   Do you have [COUNTRY'S] nationality?
7   I would like to ask you how much you trust people from various groups. Could you tell me for each whether you trust people from this group completely, somewhat, not very much or not at all?
8   Please look at the following statements and indicate where you would place your views on this scale?

social liberal values, we use attitudes towards *gender equality*[9] and whether respondents consider *homosexuality, abortion,* and *divorce* as always justifiable[10].

All measures included in the analysis are re-coded so that positive values indicate that the phenomenon under study is present. To provide a detailed example, when we construct an index to measure the level of support for gender equality, positive values indicate that the respondent price gender equality as very important. The same logic holds for the index measuring anti-immigration attitudes; higher values indicate that the individual holds negative attitudes towards immigration.

In addition to the indices described above, we include a series of variables proven to have a strong impact on how citizens define citizenship. Existing studies have stressed the importance of *political ideology* and *education*. As a proxy for *political ideology*, we use the left-right sale[11] and for *education* the highest formally completed level of education[12]. Furthermore, we control for the age, income, and gender of the respondent[13].

In our analysis, we move beyond existing scholarship in comparative politics by employing a Bayesian hierarchical model. Bayesian approaches have several advantages, especially when individual attitudes are nested within countries. This is especially the case when the number of countries included in the analysis is less than 20, as in our analysis (Stegmueller 2013).

To test our hypotheses, we use a linear hierarchical model where individuals are nested within countries. To statistically acknowledge the differences among the included countries, we use a varying intercept model. We use the so-called *non-informative prior* distributions, meaning that our model utilizes the data to inform the model and to estimate each parameter[14]. The mathe-

---

9   For each of the following statements I read out, can you tell me how strongly you agree or disagree with each. Do you strongly agree, agree, disagree, or strongly disagree? A man's job is to earn money; a woman's job is to look after the home and family; On the whole, men make better political leaders than women do; A university education is more important for a boy than for a girl; On the whole, men make better business executives than women do.

10   Please tell me for each of the following whether you think it can always be justified, never be justified, or something in between, using this card.

11   In political matters, people talk of »the left« and »the right«. How would you place your views on this scale, generally speaking?

12   What is the highest educational level that you have attained?

13   This dummy has the value one for a female respondent.

14   Additionally, the regression coefficient β is given a normal prior distribution with a mean value of 0 and a standard deviation of 1.

matical equation y_{ij} $\alpha_j + \beta x_{ij} +$ ₍ᵢ₎ represents the linear model where y is our dependent variable, ‚denotes the constant term of the regression that is varying across countries (j), x represents the respective independent variable measured at the individual level (i), while ε represents the error term.

4. Empirical results

Our results from the Bayesian hierarchical models are visually presented in Figures 1 and 2[15]. Figure 1 presents the determinants of ethnic and civic notions of national citizenship. Based on our literature review, we expected that citizens strongly identifying with their country will also support restrictions on the requirements for acquiring national and European citizenship (H1a). The results suggest that, as expected, national identity, operationalized as the level of attachment to the country, is an important determinant for both the ethnic and civic components of national citizenship. From the three levels of identity considered – national, European and the world – only the variables at the national level are statistically significant for both dimensions of national citizenship. While, contrary to our expectations, European identity shows no significant results (H1b), people who identify with the world are less likely to advocate restrictions on national citizenship based on ethnic characteristics (H1c).

With respect to our hypothesis related to the social identity theory (H2), our results confirm that the level of identification with in-groups and out-groups influences perceptions towards citizenship. Individuals who express higher levels of trust to their in-groups are in favor of restrictions on citizenship. Individuals expressing high levels of trust in out-groups reject these restrictions. From this perspective, citizens who hold a nationalist notion of citizenship strongly identify with their in-groups while showing a high level of detachment from out-groups.

---

15   In the Appendix we included a series of tables reporting the coefficients associated to our models.

16   Notes: Plots show standardized coefficients from Bayesian hierarchical models and 95 % credible intervals. See online appendix for full tables and results (Tables 1 and 2). If the interval crosses the horizontal line drawn at 0 in the horizontal axis, it means that the estimated coefficient is not significant.

17   Notes: Plots show standardized coefficients from Bayesian hierarchical models and 95 % credible intervals. See online appendix for full tables and results (Tables 3

Figure 1: Explaining notions of national citizenship

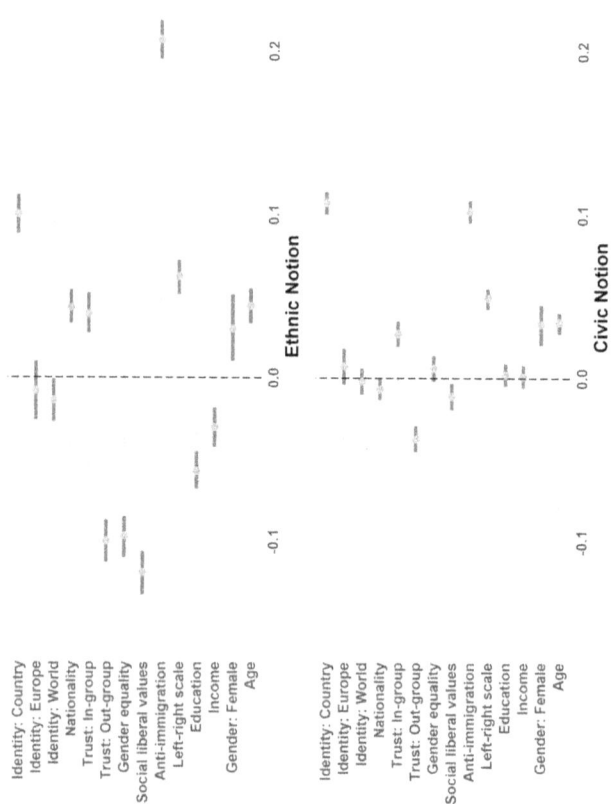

Source: Own compilation[16]. Data: European Values Study (EVS 2019).

Anti-immigration attitudes are considered a very strong component of nationalism with coefficients of 0.2 for the ethnic and 0.1 for the civic dimension of national citizenship. Accordingly, it is important for people who

---

and 4). If the interval crosses the horizontal line drawn at 0 in the horizontal axis, it means that the estimated coefficient is not significant.

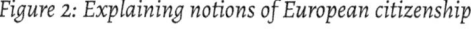

Figure 2: Explaining notions of European citizenship

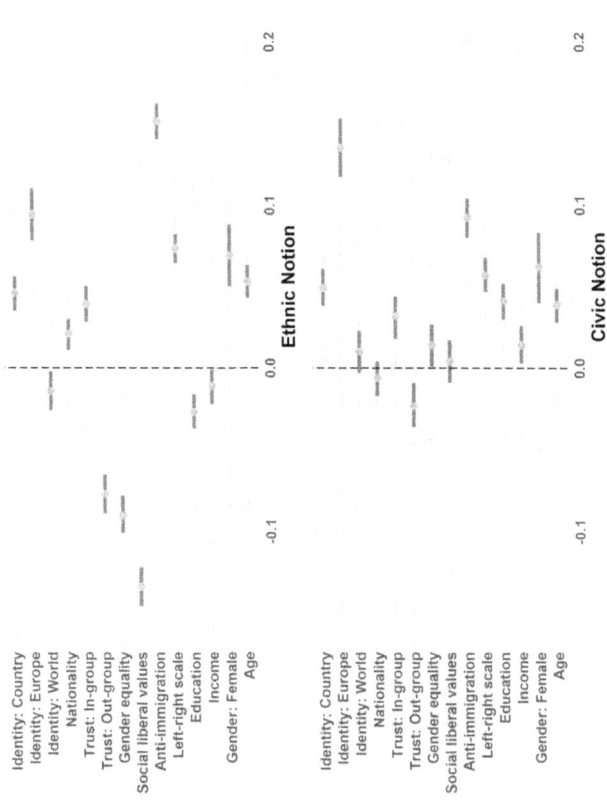

Source: Own compilation[17]. Data: European Values Study (EVS 2019).

hold negative attitudes towards migration that the barriers to acquire national citizenship are very high, regardless of whether the conditions are ethnic or civic. Anti-immigration attitudes are also an important component of
right-wing ideology and nationalism, and this relationship is also reflected
in the strong negative relationship of nationalism with social liberal values
and attitudes towards gender equality. While people with progressive attitu-

des towards social liberal values and gender equality are less likely to support ethnic conditions for acquiring national citizenship, the effects for civic notions are less pronounced for social liberal values and not significant for attitudes towards gender equality (H3). Thus, it can be concluded from this analysis that the civic dimension of national citizenship is more inclusive than ethnic notions, at least in relative terms.

Figure 2 illustrates the results of our models analyzing the ethnic and civic notions of European citizenship. Our analysis suggests that the determinants of citizenship are similar at both levels of analysis – national and European. The most important difference is that individuals expressing a strong European identity tend to be more likely to hold ethnic and civic notions towards European citizenship. This confirms our assumption that the European dimensions of citizenship are similarly exclusive, and that exclusion is transposed on the European level (H1b). As expected, strong levels of identification with citizens' respective country are associated with higher levels of exclusion at the European level (H1a). While the effect of identification with the world is not significant for the civic notion, we see that people who have a global identity are less likely to support ethnic conditions for European citizenship (H1c).

Compared with the results for ethnic and civic notions of national citizenship, we find similar results for the effects of the levels of trust in in-groups and out-groups, anti-immigration attitudes as well as attitudes towards gender equality and social liberal values on the respective European dimension. We constantly observe the same patterns for the European notions of citizenship as for the national ones. Conservative values (H3) and the demarcation against members of out-groups (H2) go hand in hand with the support for people's exclusion due to certain characteristics from acquiring citizenship. However, while our findings confirm that civic beliefs towards citizenship are less exclusive compared to ethnic ones, our results also suggest that European notions of citizenship are more inclusive compared to their national counterparts.

The results displayed in Figures 1 and 2 confirm our first hypothesis (H1) regarding the effect of political identity: People strongly identifying with their country are more likely to support restrictions of the conditions for national and European citizenship, with a stronger effect at the national level (H1a). Furthermore, citizens who identify with Europe are more likely to advocate exclusion at the European level, while we do not find any significant effects at the national level (H1b). In contrast, our findings for the cosmopolitan world view are statistically significant only for the ethnic dimension of national and European citizenship and partly confirm our expectation that people who identify with the world are less likely to support any restrictions on national and European citizenship (H1c).

Our analysis confirms that people with strong levels of trust in in-groups are more likely to support restrictions on national and European citizenship, while people with high trust in out-groups are more likely to reject restrictions on national and European citizenship (H2). Furthermore, anti-immigration attitudes are strongly related to the support of ethnic and civic restrictions of national and European citizenship, in contrast to those expressing liberal ideas (H3).

5.   Conclusion and discussion

The purpose of this study was to examine the causes of ethnic and civic notions of citizenship at two discrete levels of identification – the national and the European. We argued that each notion of citizenship is present at the national and the supranational level and that political identity determines the support or rejection of restrictions on citizenship at the respective level. While the ethnic notion of citizenship includes relatively fixed attributes such as national descent (Simonsen and Bonikowski 2019), civic notions encompass transformable and assimilating ideas of inclusion (Lubbers and Coenders 2017; Simonsen and Bonikowski 2019; Smith 2001).

To test our hypotheses, we used recent data from the European Values Study 2017 (EVS 2019) covering 20 member states of the European Union and employed Bayesian hierarchical models to provide robust results. Our empirical results suggest that political identity matters for supporting restrictions to citizenship. Individuals with a strong national identity support restriction of citizenship at both national and European level, while individuals with a strong European identity support restriction of citizenship at the European level. From this perspective, both levels of citizenship are exclusionary. However, conservative values and anti-immigration attitudes are more important for holding restrictive notions of citizenship. Our findings suggest that European concepts of citizenship are more inclusive than their national counterparts, but that exclusiveness is rather based on the distinction between the ethnic and civic dichotomy.

Our results thus illustrate two important findings: First, restrictions on citizenship, whether at the national or at the European level, are always associated with an exclusionary mindset that contradicts the idea of an open and liberal society. Second, while civic notions are more inclusive than ethnic notions of citizenship, both ideas are exclusive in absolute terms. It is therefore necessary to develop concepts of citizenship that include a liberal and open world view and do not exclude specific groups based on certain characteristics, thereby jeopardizing the social cohesion of a political community, whether organized at the national or supranational level.

Important questions for further research include the analysis of the inclusiveness and exclusiveness of the civic and European dimensions. Another important question relates to the notions of citizenship that people represent with cosmopolitan world views. Furthermore, the question arises whether authoritarian ideas are related to certain notions of citizenship, and whether concepts of citizenship which are also represented by different political parties influence the voting behavior of individuals. Thus, this analysis provides an important approach for future research on the societal and political implications of the concepts of nationalism and citizenship.

References

Akkerman, Tjitske (2005): Anti-immigration Parties and the Defence of Liberal Values: The Exceptional Case of the List Pim Fortuyn. Journal of Political Ideologies 10(3): 337-354. https://doi:10.1080/13569310500244354

Almond, Gabriel A./Powell, G. Bingham Jr./Dalton, Russell J./Strøm, Kaare (2008): Comparative Politics Today: A World View, New York: Pearson.

Almond, Gabriel A./Verba, Sidney. (1963): The Civic Culture: Political Attitudes and Democracy in Five Nations, Princeton: Princeton University Press.

Anderson, Benedict (1991): Imagined Communities. Reflections on the Origin and Spread of Nationalism, London: Verso.

Brubaker, Rogers (1992): Citizenship and Nationhood in France and Germany, Cambridge: Harvard University Press.

Brubaker, Rogers (2004): In the Name of the Nation: Reflections on Nationalism and Patriotism. Citizenship Studies 8(2): 115-127. https://doi:10.1080/1362102042000214705

Brubaker, Rogers (2017): Between Nationalism and Civilizationism: the European Populist Moment in Comparative Perspective. Ethnic and Racial Studies 40(8): 1191-1226. https://doi:10.1080/01419870.2017.1294700

Curtis, K. Amber (2014): Inclusive versus Exclusive: A Cross-National Comparison of the Effects of Subnational, National, and Supranational Identity. European Union Politics 15(4): 521-546. https://doi:10.1177/1465116514528058

Deutsch, Karl Wolfgang (1954): Political Community at the International Level, New York: Doubleday.

Deutsch, Karl Wolfgang (1966): Nationalism and Social Communication: An Inquiry into the Foundations of Nationality, Cambridge: MIT Press.

Easton, David. (1965): A Systems Analysis of Political Life, New York: John Wiley & Sons.

Easton, David (1975): A Re-Assessment of the Concept of Political Support. British Journal of Political Science 5(4): 435-457.

Epstein, Cynthia Fuchs (1992): Tinkerbells and Pinups: The Construction and Reconstruction of Gender Boundaries at Work. In: Michéle Lamont/Marcel Fournier (eds.), Cultivating Differences. Symbolic Boundaries and the Making of Inequality, Chicago: University of Chicago Press, 232-256.

EVS (2019): European Values Study 2017: Integrated Dataset (EVS 2017). GESIS Data Archive, Cologne. ZA7500 Data file Version 2.0.0, https://doi:10.4232/1.13314

Habermas, Jürgen (1992): Citizenship and National Identity: Some Reflections on the Future of Europe. Praxis International 12(1): 1-19.

Heinisch, Reinhard/Wegscheider, Carsten (2020): Disentangling How Populism and Radical Host Ideologies Shape Citizens' Conceptions of Democratic Decision-Making. Politics and Governance 8(3), 32-44. https://doi:10.17645/pag.v8i3.2915

Ignatieff, Michael (1994): Blood and Belonging: Journeys into the new Nationalism, New York: Macmillan.

Kohn, Hans (1944): The Idea of Nationalism: A Study in its Origins and Background, New York: Macmillan.

Kunovich, Robert M. (2009): The Sources and Consequences of National Identification. American Sociological Review 74(4): 573-593. https://doi:10.1177/000312240907400404

Lubbers, Marcel/Coenders, Marcel (2017): Nationalistic Attitudes and Voting for the Radical Right in Europe. European Union Politics 18(1): 98-118. https://doi:10.1177/1465116516678932

McCrone, David/Kiely, Richard (2000): Nationalism and Citizenship. Sociology 34(1): 19-34. https://doi:10.1177/S0038038500000031

Merkel, Wolfgang (2017): Kosmopolitismus versus Kommunitarismus: Ein neuer Konflikt in der Demokratie. In: Phillip Harfst/Ina Kubbe/Thomas Poguntke (eds.), Parties, Governments and Elites, Wiesbaden: VS Verlag, 9-23.

Mudde, Cas (2007): Populist Radical Right Parties in Europe, Cambridge: Cambridge University Press.

Nezi, Roula/Sotiropoulos, Dimitri A./Toka, Panayiota (2010): Attitudes of Greek parliamentarians towards European and national identity, representation, and scope of governance. South European Society and Politics 15(1): 79-96.

Nezi, Roula/Sotiropoulos, Dimitri A./Toka, Panayiota (2009): Explaining the Attitudes of Parliamentarians towards European Integration in Bulgaria, Greece and Serbia: Party Affiliation, 'Left-Right' Self-placement or Country Origin? European-Asia Studies 61(6), 1003-1020.

Norris, Pippa (ed.) (1999): Critical Citizens: Global Support for Democratic government, Oxford: Oxford University Press.

Norris, Pippa (2011): Democratic Deficit: Critical Citizens revisited, Cambridge: Cambridge University Press.

Putnam, Robert D. (2001): Bowling alone: The Collapse and Revival of American Community, New York: Simon & Schuster.

Reckien, Diana (2018): What is in an Index? Construction Method, Data Metric, and weighting scheme determine the Outcome of Composite social vulnerability Indices in New York City. Regional Environmental Change 18(5): 1439-1451.

Reeskens, Tim/Hooghe, Marc (2010): Beyond the Civic-Ethnic Dichotomy: Investigating the Structure of Citizenship Concepts across thirty-three Countries. Nations and Nationalism 16(4): 579-597. https://doi:10.1111/j.1469-8129.2010.00446.x

Rydgren, Jens (2007): The Sociology of the radical Right. Annual Review of Sociology 33(1): 241-262.

Shore, Cris (2004): Whither European Citizenship? European Journal of Social Theory 7(1): 27-44.

Shulman, Stephen (2002). Challenging the Civic/Ethnic and West/East Dichotomies in the Study of Nationalism. Comparative Political Studies 35(5): 554-585. https://doi:10.1177/0010414002035005003

Simonsen, Kristina Bakkær/Bonikowski, Bart (2019): Is Civic Nationalism Necessarily Inclusive? Conceptions of Nationhood and Anti-Muslim Attitudes in Europe. European Journal of Political Research 10(1): 1-23. https://doi:10.1111/1475-6765.12337

Smith, Anthony D. (1998): Nationalism and Modernism, London: Routledge.

Smith, Anthony D. (1991): National Identity, Reno: University of Nevada Press.

Smith, Rogers M. (2001): Citizenship and the Politics of People-Building. Citizenship Studies 5(1): 73-96. https://doi:10.1080/13621020020025204

Smith, Tom W. (2007): Social Identity and Socio-Demographic Structure. International Journal of Public Opinion Research 19(3): 380-390.

Stark,Toralf/Wegscheider, Carsten/Brähler, Elmar/Decker, Oliver (2017): Sind Rechtsextremisten sozial ausgegrenzt? Eine Analyse der sozialen Lage und Einstellungen zum Rechtsextremismus. Papers 2/2017. Berlin: Rosa-Luxenburg-Stiftung.

Stegmueller, Daniel (2013): How Many Countries for Multilevel Modeling? A Comparison of Frequentist and Bayesian Approaches. American Journal of Political Science 57(3): 748-761. https://doi:10.1111/ajps.12001

Tajfel, Henri (1982): Social Psychology of Intergroup Relations. Annual Review of Psychology 33(1):1-39. https://doi:10.1146/annurev.ps.33.020182.000245

Tajfel, Henri/Turner, John (1979): An Integrative Theory of Intergroup Conflict. In: William G. Austin/Stephen Worchel (eds.), the Social Psychology of Intergroup Relations, Monterey: Brooks/Cole, 33-47.

Wright, Matthew (2011): Policy Regimes and Normative Conceptions of Nationalism in Mass Public Opinion. Comparative Political Studies 44(5): 598-624. https://doi:10.1177/0010414010396461

Can nationalists be democratic citizens in the age of global migration? Boundaries of political community and their impact on liberal orientation in EU societies

Merve Schmitz-Vardar

1. Introduction

Migration has a structuring and transforming effect on societies. Structuring in the way that the political collective is formed by a new composition. Transforming, as the demands placed on the political system are more heterogeneous. Especially the (new) composition of the political community on territorially constituted borders can have far-reaching consequences for liberal democracies (Foroutan 2019: 144). Even with a critical perspective, nations are necessary in the contemporary situation because transnational democracy or supranational democracy do not work (Fukuyama 2018). In less critical position, studies show that democracies need national identity to be able to operate (Eger/Valdez 2015; Helbing 2009; Manent 2013). Democracy is based on solidarity in the community and one of the historically dominant sources of group formation work through national identification (Pickel/Pickel 2018). Therefore, every construction of a perceived *in*group is linked to the exclusion of a perceived *out*group (Tajfel/Turner 1979). Exclusive and discriminatory forms of nationalism are not conducive to liberal democracy. Hence, the following question arises: What does the construction of the ingroup mean for democratic values? As the dependent variable, liberal-democratic regime support is at the centre of the analysis.[1]

---

1 Special thanks go to Cemal Öztürk for the permanent constructive discussion, especially in the conceptualisation of the dependent variable.

The normative-theoretical position is that democratic societies function based on mutual recognition of their members as free and equal citizens (Habermas 1998), which includes supposed others such as migrants, homosexuals or women, and offers possibilities to combine political culture research and the theory of social identity. While the former argues that an indicator – identification with the national political community – provides information about the cohesion of a society (Pickel/Pickel 2018), the latter cognitive-psychological approach (Tajfel/Turner 1979) assumes a fundamental distinction between »us« and the supposed »others«. Based on these considerations, the following research question is examined: How do including and excluding ideas of identity, trust, and belonging affect democratic value orientation of EU citizens? EU countries were selected based on the essentially normative principles such as human rights, liberal freedoms, respect for human dignity and the principles of equality and solidarity. These guiding principles serve both as internal self-assurance and as an external maxim for action (Schneider 2015: 313). Varying reactions of (potential) immigrant societies – during the most recent migration movement in 2015 – emerge from different community conceptions which function as identity markers and influence the construction of a perceived in- and outgroup. The main hypothesis assumes that exclusionary ideas of community – regarding identity, trust and belonging – promote the rejection of democratic values and thus endanger the political support for a democracy of the people. Additional independent variables focus on the relationships between resentments towards migrants, homosexuals as well as gender equality and the suspected lower democratic orientation of the people. The analysis is based on the pre-release data of the European Value Study 2017 (EVS) and includes the following 20 member states: Austria, Bulgaria, Croatia, the Czech Republic, Denmark, United Kingdom, Estonia, Finland, France, Germany, Hungary, Italy, Lithuania, Netherlands, Poland, Romania, Slovakia, Slovenia, Spain, and Sweden. The results of descriptive statistics, correlations, and country-spread OLS-regressions are expected to reflect the link between political communities and their importance for liberal-democratic regime support.

2. Understanding democratic citizenship as liberal-democratic regime support and socio-psychological sources

From the perspective of political culture research, I will develop a conceptual approach for the anthology topic of democratic citizenship. First of all, it seems useful to clarify the term »citizenship« and link it to other terms and concepts like denizenship (Hammar 1990; Turner 2016) and democratic value orientation (Welzel/Alvarez 2014).

Citizenship is primarily understood as a mechanism of legal equality in which a state »formally defines its citizenry, publically identifying a set of persons as its members and residually designating all others as noncitizens, or aliens« (Brubaker 1992: 21). With the identification of members and non-members, citizenship is both internally inclusive and externally exclusive. As an institution, it is an instrument of social closure. However, nation-states are not only home to their »own« citizens. Immigrants, regardless of the reasons for migration, are residents as well and become part of the system and political unity, for example by paying taxes. These considerations refer to the territorial closure associated with citizenship (Brubaker 1992: 23, 27). The inclusion of non-members as *denizens* is an essential element of democratic states and for a democratic understanding of citizenship.

> »The concept of denizenship is a serviceable addition to the array of concepts describing the ambiguities of modern social and political membership (...). More precisely, denizens, as migrants, are often more dependent on human rights and not citizenship for protection« (Turner 2016: 687).

The crucial difference between citizens and denizens is the necessity of residence. Denizens are simply described as someone who lives in a certain place and thus presupposes the presence in the country while being a citizen of a nation is rather a characteristic of a person who remains even in absentia. The concept of denizenship often refers to members of the country who are already considered members because of their status as permanent residents. Kymlicka and Norman (2000) correctly point out that citizenship within the framework of democratic theories is not limited to the formal status of a person and the resulting full membership in a community. If one follows Isin's (2008) view in the context of democratic theories, democratic citizenship can be divided into three areas: In addition to formal status, the concept can also cover political acts and habitus (see also the editors' introduction). Political act refers to the use of political privileges, which are provided by the residence in the territorial area or by the formal status. Habitus is defined according to Bourdieu (2002: 27) »as a system of dispositions, that is of permanent manners of being, seeing, acting and thinking, or a system of long-lasting (rather than permanent) schemes or schemata or structures of perception, conception and action«.

The focus on habitus underlines the compatibility to the concept of political culture. Theories of political culture research share the view that functioning democratic systems are bound to cultural conditions and cannot be based solely on the presence and effect of democratic institutions (Fuchs 2002). A persistent system is assumed if there is a congruent relationship between political culture and political structure. According to this paradigmatic assumption, the political system needs a suitable socio-psychological substructure, i.e. a democratic habitus (Almond/Verba 1963). Thus, the stability of a political system is largely dependent on the political support of its citizens (Easton 1965, 1975).

Political culture is understood as »the particular distribution of patterns of orientation towards political objects among the members of the nation« (Almond/Verba 1963). Therefore, citizens of a certain community and their dominant attitudes, norms and value orientations towards the political system are at the centre of attention (Pickel/Pickel 2006). Dimensions of orientation can be affective (emotion), cognitive (knowledge) and evaluative (rating). The political system is divided into three objects: the political community, the political regime, and the political authorities. This study is located between the poles of the community and the regime. While the independent variable focusses on a community level (in more detail below), the dependent variable focuses on the regime and three types of orientation towards the regime.

There is controversy as to how citizens' attitudes towards democracy can be conceptualised and empirically measured. For a long time, there has been a tradition of asking citizens in representative polls whether »democracy« is their preferred political system (for an exception see: Klingemann 1999). This procedure has been increasingly because several studies show that advocacy of democracy does not necessarily mean acceptance of democratic norms – such as freedom, equality, and the rule of law (Lauth 2004; also Cho 2015; Welzel/Alvarez 2014). This scepticism is also based on empirical evidence related to the rhetoric of contemporary populists and autocrats: They no longer openly campaign against democracy. Rather, it has become their approach to adopt the concept of democracy and to reinterpret it in an authoritarian way.

Vladimir Putin's »sovereign« democracy is one of the best-known examples. Victor Orban's »illiberal« democracy since 2014 shows that this trend is present in Europe as well (Puddington 2017).

The simplified question of the advocacy of democracy is likely to be a matter of lip service (Inglehart 2003: 51). Political culture research needs a normative point of reference when it comes to conceiving democratic value orientation. Otherwise, there is a risk of producing empirical artefacts and encouraging problematic social diagnoses. In the short term, the advocacy of a democratic political system is a necessary, but not sufficient, condition for the genuine support of democracy. The normative point of reference chosen to validate the democratic self-location of individuals is the liberal-democratic basic order of a political system.

Analyses of democratic values increasingly focus on citizens' understanding of democracy and resulted in four notions like types of democratic concepts (Pickel 2017; Welzel/Kirsch 2017). The liberal and social notations are compatible with democratic theory (Rawls 1971; Dahl 1972; Held 2006). The remaining two notations are the authoritarian and populist notation. Liberal Democracy is the dominant form, the opposite of which is an authoritarian democracy. In concepts of the understanding of democracy, authoritarian and liberal notations are used as subtypes of a democratic understanding of democracy (Welzel/Alvarez 2014). There are, however, many arguments against this perception. These primarily include the underlying normative point of reference, the lack of a link to democratic theories, and finally the empirical argument of an authoritarian redefinition of democracy. Therefore, we submit the liberal notation to correction by »subtracting« the authoritarian content.[2]

The last argument refers to the need for political support (Easton 1965, 1975). Unconditional political trust or satisfaction with the regime is not desirable if democratic ideas may be unfulfilled by the regime: »[T]he tensions between ideals and reality are essentially healthy for the future of democratic governance, since this indicates the emergence of more ›critical citizens‹, or ›dissatisfied democrats‹« (Norris 2011). Critical citizens, although they consider the existing structures of a representative government to be upgradeable, are strongly oriented towards democratic values. Democratic values combine

---

2   Populist and social notations can also be included in liberal notation, but this will not
     be discussed empirically. While a social adds another dimension to the liberal nota-
     tion, namely the outcome dimension, populism is a challenging form, but not a non-
     democratic one as the authoritarian notation (Welzel/Alvarez 2014).

»people's democratic desires with (1) a more liberal understanding of what democracy means and (2) a more critical assessment of how democratic their society actually is« (Welzel/Alvarez 2014). Based on these considerations, this paper focuses on a critical-liberal desire for democracy by members of the nation. *This type of democratic value orientation consists of three elements: 1) the advocacy of a democracy, 2a) the internalisation of the democratic meta-norms of liberal democracy, and 2b) a strict rejection of authoritarian systems of order (Norris 2011; Pickel/Pickel 2006; Lauth 2004), as well as 3) a critical satisfaction with the system in the sense of critical citizens.*

The present conception of democratic citizenship is best suited to cover the area of habitus. Given the fact that the political act is not considered, the formal status is irrelevant for the theoretical development of democratic citizens. People classified as democratic citizens can (but do not have to) have formal citizenship, and thus benefit from equal rights or are politically active in order to change the situation.[3] In this theoretical conceptualisation, denizens are classified as members of the nation. Consequently, everybody is a member of the nation by residence within the territorial borders. Democratic citizenship, in contrast, is nothing more than a democratic habitus that is empirically manifested in liberal-democratic regime support.

The democratic quality of a society only becomes noticeable through plurality. Migration stands for a visible form of this plurality. The normative-theoretical position states that democratic societies function based on the mutual recognition of their members as free and equal citizens (Habermaas 1998), which includes supposed others such as migrants, homosexuals or women. Socio-psychological research concentrates on the dynamics of intergroup relationships. For many studies on prejudice, discrimination, and ingroup or exclusion dynamics, the social categorisation process of the theory of social identity serves as a starting point (Tajfel/Turner 1979). Prejudice can be understood as »an antipathy based on faulty and inflexible generalisation. It may be felt or expressed. It may be directed toward a group as a whole, or toward an individual because he is a member of the group« (Allport 1954: 9). Every construction of an ingroup goes along with the identification of an outgroup. The democratic challenge is to avoid discriminatory processes and define more inclusive belongings.

---

3   Regarding the editors‹ introduction, the understanding developed here can ideally be assigned to the area of a democratic resident.

According to political culture research, one indicator – the identification with the national political community – provides information about the cohesion of a society (Pickel/Pickel 2018) and thus contributes to the stability of a democratic system (Mummendey et al. 2001: 159). In contrast, prejudice research suggests that a higher national identification can (but does not necessarily) lead to a degradation of other national, ethnic or cultural groups (Hopkins 2001; Pehrson et al. 2009). How can external boundaries be overcome if they are important for collective identities, and if »the others« are already members of the political community as denizens? It is important to consider whether national identification and related kinds of belonging favour a shift away from democratic value orientation (Helbing 2009).

Nations are imaginary communities that manifest themselves in individuals in affective attitudes to collective symbols, language, history, and traditions (Anderson 1991; Brubaker 1992). The »we«-feeling delimits the political culture of a nation, region or municipality (Elkins/Simeon 1979; Werz/Koschkar 2016). Any construction of boundaries is an imagination that includes some people and excludes others. National identity defines the boundaries of the political community (Yuval-Davis 2011: 26). Strong identification with the nation is called nationalism (Mummendey et al. 2001: 160)[4]. Thus, national identification is accompanied by a determination of »we« and »them« and is oriented towards so-called social locations. »Request of belonging that relate to social locations – origin, ›race‹, place of birth – would be the most racialised and the least permeable« (Yuval-Davis 2011: 30). This creates a tension between national identification and democratic value orientation (Pehrson et al. 2009). It is assumed that nationalist individuals tend to prefer exclusive rather than inclusive group identities (Gat 2012; Hjerm 1998; Welzel/Inglehart 2008). The differentiation refers to the permeability that is set as a benchmark for »the others« in the sense of belonging. In other words, it means that an exclusive understanding is based on characteristics that cannot be fulfilled by migrants and can therefore be classified as ethnocentric, e.g., ancestry and place of birth. In contrast to

---

4   The distinction between nationalism and patriotism is often introduced in debates on national identity (van der Zwet 2015). Patriotism, in comparison, is claimed to have a more inclusive sense of belonging; the conceptualisation shows a certain similarity to the framework of the presented democratic orientation. National identity cannot be used to measure patriotism, because »[p]atriotism is not necessarily directed toward a nation-state (Kelman 1997: 166).

that, inclusive group identities generally tend to focus on respect for political institutions as well as on speaking the national language and are traits that can be acquired (Helbing 2009).

> **H1**: The more individuals tend towards nationalism, the lower their support for democratic value orientation.

> **H2a**: The more individuals tend to have an inclusive sense of belonging, the stronger their support for democratic value orientation.
> **H2b**: The more individuals tend to have an exclusive sense of belonging, the lower their support for democratic value orientation.

Recognizing that the so-called »others«, through their residence within national territorial borders, are part of the political entity, they must be considered. Political communities are characterised as »that aspect of a political system that consists of its members seen as a group of persons bound together by a political division of labour« (Easton 1965: 177). This willingness is closely related to interpersonal trust, which Putnam calls social capital (Putnam 1993:36). However, interpersonal trust has different nuances.

> »In-group trust is limited to people with whom one has some familiarity, be it on the basis of kinship, acquaintance, or neighbourhood. Out-group trust relates to people whom one does not know or who differ by origin, like national or religious origin-two of the most powerful sources of collective identity formation« (Gat 2012, quoted from: (Welzel/Delhey 2015).

It is argued that ingroup-trust is a necessary but not sufficient condition for outgroup-trust. Therefore, only in the context of the consideration of outgroup-trust, the relevance of trust for democratic value orientation becomes apparent.

> **H3**: The more individuals tend to trust outgroups, the stronger their support for democratic value orientation.

Various studies show that identification with the we-group does not automatically lead to a negative perception of outgroups. Furthermore, there might be different effects for different groups. For example, when differentiating between different religious groups, Islam or Muslims are often perceived as more threatening in comparison to other religions Pickel 2018). The Integrated Threat Theory (Stephan/Stephan 2006) postulates prominently that threat perceptions themselves play a decisive role in the genesis of prejudice. At its core, the Integrated Threat Theory assumes that so-called realistic and symbolic threat perceptions can favour prejudice against outgroups. A realistic perception of threat is based on the perception that the »others« endanger the physical and material well-being of one's own group. For symbolic threat perceptions, outgroups are perceived as a danger to one's own cultural and moral concepts and value orientation (Stephan/Stephan 1985). These perceptions of threats represent resentments towards migrants. It should be examined whether these perceptions of threats also favour a renunciation of democracy.

H4: Individuals who have a tendency towards resentments of immigrants also tend to have lower support for democratic value orientation.

The previous considerations result from exclusion mechanisms to presumably »others«. Studies on group-related enmity assume a syndrome because enmity towards ethnic groups goes along with enmity towards other groups (Zick et al. 2008). Migrants and especially Muslims are often considered to be opponents of gay rights and gender equality. Sometimes this is also used as a pretext to legitimise one's own antipathy towards Muslims. This is one characteristic of the self-serving bias of prejudice and racism. Yet, anti-pluralism ideologies can also be directed internally against social groups instead of ethnic groups. In that case, the resentments are also directed against homosexuals and gender equality (Takács/Szalma 2011). These two explanatory factors are also taken into consideration as alternative explanatory approaches, which are also based on an ideology of inequality. It is assumed that by an ideology of unequal value, citizens are likely to turn away from democratic value orientation.

H5: Individuals who tend to hold anti-gay attitudes also tend to have lower support for democratic value orientation.

H6: Individuals who tend to hold anti-gender-equality attitudes also tend to show lower support for democratic value orientation.

3. Research design: Data, operationalisation and methodological approach

The empirical analysis is based on the European Value Study (EVS 2019). The survey displays the tension between nationalism and democratic value orientations for the following 20 EU member states: Austria, Bulgaria, Croatia, the Czech Republic, Denmark, the UK, Estonia, Finland, France, Germany, Hungary, Italy, Lithuania, the Netherlands, Poland, Romania, Slovakia, Slovenia, Spain, and Sweden. All surveys were conducted between June 29, 2017, and January 30, 2019. They cover a sample of 37.277 respondents (EVS 2019). Even if not all EU countries can be observed, at least the presented theoretical concept can be tested empirically with the data set. The concept argues that democratic orientation depends on questions of identification, trust, and belonging. According to political culture research, it is of course also possible that orientation towards the regime influence orientation towards the political community and thus identification, trust and belonging, but this is usually conceptualised as a feedback effect later on (Pickel/Pickel 2006: 144).

Before I describe the operationalisation of the previously latent constructs, I would like to point out that all scales were normalised to a range between 0 and 1. Different decimals are shown depending on the scale level (e.g. 4 and 5 scales). However, the minimum of the scale was 0, the maximum 1. Using normalisation as a method presents several advantages: For example, it permits to compare non-standardised regression coefficients (Welzel 2013: 64).

The analysis focuses on democratic value orientation as the dependent variable of this analysis. Starting with democratic citizenship, the critical liberal support of democracy was theoretically identified. To investigate the desire for democracy, the EVS contains the following question: »*How important is it for you to live in a country that is governed democratically?*« (0=not at all important; 1=very important). However, this question does not measure the citizens' commitment to democracy reliably. An additional way to capture democratic value orientation is the measurement of the liberal understanding of democracy by including items on the characteristics, norms, and values of democracy. Three items provide information about a liberal understanding of democracy: 1) »*characteristic for democracy is that people choose their leaders in free elections*«, 2) »*civil rights protect people from state oppression*«, and 3) »*women have the same rights*« (all: 0=it is against democracy; 1=an essential characteristic of democracy). These items form the so-called *Liberal Understanding of Democracy Index* (liberal notation).

Second, the EVS also allows investigating the so-called authoritarian notation. This is covered by the three other items, namely 1) »*characteristic for democracy is that religious authorities ultimately interpret the law*«, 2) »*the army takes over when government is incompetent*«, and 3) »*people obey their rules*«(all: 0=it is against democracy; 1=an essential characteristic of democracy). These three statements constitute another index that stands for an authoritarian understanding of democracy. After calculating the scores for each notation, the scores of the authoritarian notation were subtracted from the scores of the liberal notation. The resulting scale provides more reliable information on the support for liberal democracy.

Finally, the analysis focuses on the discussion of critical support for liberal democracy. For this purpose, the Liberal Democracy Index (Vdem) was integrated into the dataset as another variable. Within this index, each country was evaluated externally by a group of experts, resulting in a rating between 0 and 1 for its quality of democracy (Coppedge et al. 2019: 40). The citizens' assessment of »*how democratically is this country being governed today*« (0=not at all democratic; 1=completely democratic) was subtracted from the value of the expert opinion on the question »*to what extent is the ideal of liberal democracy achieved*«(0=low; 1=high). Starting from the theoretical assumption of a critical-liberal desire for democracy, the three scales were summarised multiplicatively. This procedure corresponds to the *weakest link approach*. Individual support for democratic value orientation is thus determined by its weakest pillar (Welzel 2013:63).

The central independent variables of the empirical analysis are national identity as well as inclusive and exclusive ideas of belonging since nationalism leads to a distinction between »us« and »them«. Several survey items capture aspects of nationalism, such as »*how proud are you to be a [Country] citizen*« (0=not at all proud; 1=very proud). Moreover, it is crucial to measure how inclusive or exclusive belonging to the nation is understood (»*Please indicate how important this is to be truly [Nationality]*«). The following two questions record inclusive ideas of belonging: »*To respect [Country]'s political institutions and laws*«; and »*To be able to speak [the national language]*«. Another two items (»*To have been born in [Country]*«; and »*To have [country]'s ancestry*«) record exclusive ideas of belonging (all: 0=not at all important; 1=very important). The respective two questions were combined in an additive index.

Trust is an important indicator when it comes to the willingness to engage politically or socially with persons from »outgroups« (Putnam 1993). Based on theoretical considerations on the different ranges of interpersonal trust, the variable »trust in supposed outgroups« was introduced into the analy-sis (Welzel/Delhey 2015). For this purpose, the following items were utilised: »*How far do you trust people you meet for the first time*«, »*people of another religion*«, and »*people of another nationality*« (all: 0=do not trust at all; 1=trust completely). The three items were combined to form an additive index.

The Integrated Threat Theory (e.g. Stephan/Stephan 2006) attributes a de-cisive role in the threat experience of individuals for the genesis of prejudice and exclusion mechanisms. The subjective assessment that »*immigrants take away jobs from nationals*«, »*immigrants increase crime problems*«, »*immigrants are a strain on the welfare system*«(0=immigrants do not or are not...; 1=immigrants make or are...) and of »*How would you evaluate the impact of [the immigrants] on the development of [your country]?*« (0=very good; 1=very bad) were combined to form an additive index of resentment towards migrants.

Conforming to the argument that marginalisation of groups weakens de-mocracy, two other social groups were identified, namely homosexuals and women. Both groups are part of ingroups. However, they are both socially marginalised. To measure anti-gay attitudes, respondents were asked whe-ther they »*don't like homosexual as neighbours*« (0=not mentioned; 1=mentio-ned), whether they consider »*homosexual couples as good parents as other couples*« (0=disagree strongly; 1=agree strongly), and whether they »*justify homosexuali-ty*« (0=always; 1=never). An additive index was also created from these items.

The second marginalisation category refers to gender equality. To track anti-gender-equality attitudes, the following six items were combined into an index: »*women really want home and children*«, »*family life suffers when a woman has a full-time job*«, »*a man's job is to earn money and a woman's job is to look after home and family*«, »*men make better political leaders than women*«, »*university education is more important for a boy than for a girl*«, and »*men make better business executives than women*« (0=disagree strongly; 1=agree strongly).

Socio-structural characteristics also seem to have an influence on demo-cratic orientation in addition to identity, trust and a sense of belonging. Com-mon features in the context of research on intergroup relations or prejudice research and on democratic support are age, gender, income and/or educati-on and formal citizenship or migration background (Cho 2015; Pehrson et al. 2009). The gender of respondents is determined by the variable *gender* (1=male; 0=female). Formal citizenship is determined by the variable *citizenship* (0=not a formal citizenship; 1=formal citizenship). The formal education level is in-cluded in the analysis by using *education* (0=less than primary; 1=doctoral or equivalent). The variable *income* (0=1st decile; 1=10th decile) is available for recording income. The *Age* (1=oldest respondent; 0=youngest respondent) of the respondents was considered as last control variable in the analysis.

In the empirical part of this paper, the mean values for the items above are presented. They provide a first impression of the social climate in the countries included in the analysis. In a second step, I approach the bivariate relationship between nationalism and democratic value orientation with grouped box plots. In order to analyse the robustness of the presumed tension between nationalism, ideas of belonging and democratic value orientation, I present the results of several OLS regressions by country. These include the alternative explanatory factors of socio-psychological prejudice research 8kleinbaum et al. 2013).

4.   Empirical evidence: What impacts the democratic value orientation of EU citizens?

Before moving to the inferential statistical analysis, descriptive statistics will provide an overview of the social climate in the selected EU countries and the EU as a whole. Table 1 shows a broad consensus regarding the importance of living in a democracy: 92.7 % of EU citizens prefer to live in a democracy.

However, as expected, the level of satisfaction with democracy in one's own country is lower (67.1 %). It also reveals that a liberal notation of democracy seems to be well-established. Nearly 90 % of the respondents believe both that democracies are characterised by the choice of leaders through free elections and that women and men enjoy the same rights. 82.8 % of EU citizens also regard the protection of people against state repression as a characteristic of democratic systems. However, authoritarian notations are also classified as democratic. Almost one in four persons (23.3 %) believes that an army takeover in case of government failure is democratic. Likewise, 36.9 % assume that people should obey their rulers. The religious authorities (14.6 %) are rated much lower as a characteristic of democracy. Looking at nationalism and an exclusive sense of belonging, the results show that the majority of citizens are proud to be a citizen of their country (87.5 %). Furthermore, more than half of the respondents find that ancestry is decisive for true membership. 60.1 % of the EU population believes that it is necessary to be born in the country for being a true national.

Table 1 does not specify the differences across countries. The visualisation using box plots (figure 1) depicts the dispersion in addition to mean values

Table 1: Distribution of democratic value orientation and nationalism

Desire for Democracy	
How important is it for you to live in a country that is governed democratically?	92.7
Liberal understanding of Democracy	
how essential you think it is as a characteristic of democracy: people choose their leaders in free elections	88.5
how essential you think it is as a characteristic of democracy: civil rights protect people from state oppression	82.8
how essential you think it is as a characteristic of democracy: women have the same rights as men	89.9
Authoritarian understanding of Democracy	
how essential you think it is as a characteristic of democracy: religious authorities ultimately interpret the laws	14.6
how essential you think it is as a characteristic of democracy: the army takes over when government is incompetent	23.3
how essential you think it is as a characteristic of democracy: people obey their rulers	36.9
Rating of Democracy	
And how democratically is this country being governed today?	67.1
Nationalism	
How proud are you to be a countries' citizen?	87.5
Excluding belonging	
How important do you think [for being a truly NATIONALTIY] is: to have been born in country?	60.1
How important do you think [for being a truly NATIONALTIY] is: to have countries' ancestry?	52.1

Source: EVS 2019, own calculation and illustration, Agreement rate in % of.

of the critical-liberal desire for democracy, differentiated according to nationalist attitudes. Figure 1 plots the degree of democratic value orientation between the extremes of identifying and not identifying with the nation. In this way, the tension between nationalism and democracy is depicted.

Figure 1: Critical-liberal desire for democracy and nationalism among EU member states

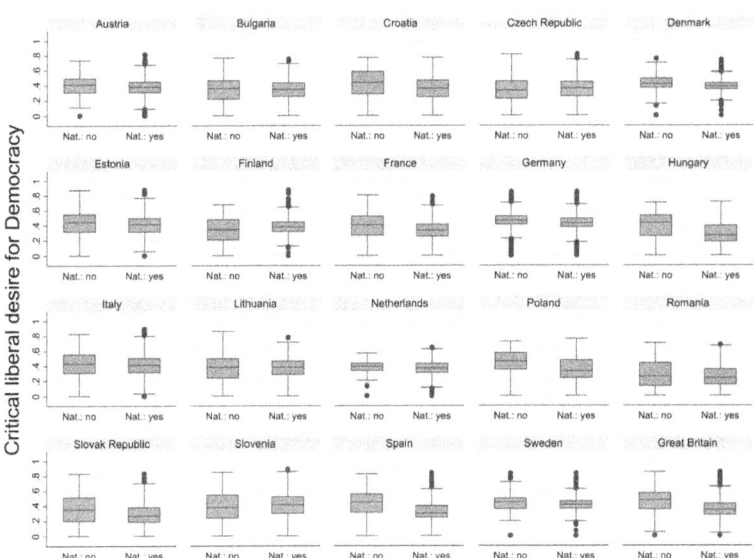

Source: EVS 2019, own calculation and illustration.

In most countries, there is a discrepancy between the democratic value orientation of individuals who tend towards nationalist attitudes and individuals who do not identify with the nation. As Figure 1 illustrates, the mean value of democratic value orientation of people not identifying with the nation is higher compared to those who do identify with the nation (H1). The differences are especially pronounced in Croatia, France, Hungary, Poland, Slovakia, Spain and the United Kingdom; whereas they are smaller in Denmark, Estonia, Germany, Romania, and Sweden. The observation displays that the phenomenon is not concentrated in particular EU member states. However, in several countries (such as Austria, Bulgaria, the Czech Republic, Italy, Lithuania, and the Netherlands) it is also visible that there are no major differences between the two groups in terms of their democratic value orientation. This leads to the conclusion that nationalism is not a sufficient condition for the absence of democratic value orientation, but in most cases does not contribute to democratic value orientation. Slovenia and Finland are exceptions to this observation, although the differences between the groups are not high. In Finland, in particular, a considerable minority does not tend towards nationalism, with 95.6 % in favour.

OLS regressions have been calculated for all 20 EU member states, some of which we shall inspect in more detail. Figure 2 shows the plotted regression coefficients of the inferential statistical analyses. The vertical line reflects the zero value, i.e. items in the positive range have a supportive effect on a person's democratic value orientation. On the one hand, negative effects of nationalism, exclusive feelings of belonging and discriminatory attitudes towards immigrants, homosexuals, and gender equality were assumed. On the other hand, trust in foreign groups and a tendency towards an inclusive sense of belonging are expected to positively affect democratic value orientation.

While taking the tensions between nationalism and democratic value orientation into account, the different parts of the analysis illustrate that a differentiated reflection is necessary. In most countries, the following can be observed: the more people tend to nationalist attitudes (in 12 out of 20 countries) or to exclusive ideas of belonging (in 13 out of 20 countries), the less they support democratic value orientation (H1 and H2a). National identification does not go together with the support for democratic values in any of the observed states. The same applies – with the exception of Hungary – to an exclusive sense of belonging. Bivariate analyses at the country level also demonstrate that if this exclusionary socio-psychological characteristic is widespread in society, anti-democratic values are also much more widespread here.

A significant effect of the control variable *formal citizenship* accompanies the exceptional observation of a positive effect of an exclusive sense of belonging on democratic value orientation in Hungary. This control variable is significant in none of the other cases. In other words, people who have formal citizenship are less inclined towards democracy than people who do not. The Hungarian observation suggests that historical developments and national discourse have some explanatory power as well. In Hungary, this is particularly true for the inclusive discourse of national minorities abroad. At the same time, nationalist narratives of an irredentist threat persist. This threat is defined »as the threat of territorial claims by neighbouring countries« (Pirro 2014: 607), and refers to a linguistically and ethnically related nationalism. In the case of inclusive belonging which refers to a democratic value orientation (H2b), Lithuania, Slovenia, and Slovakia stand out.

Figure 2a: OLS-Regression for 20 EU-countries

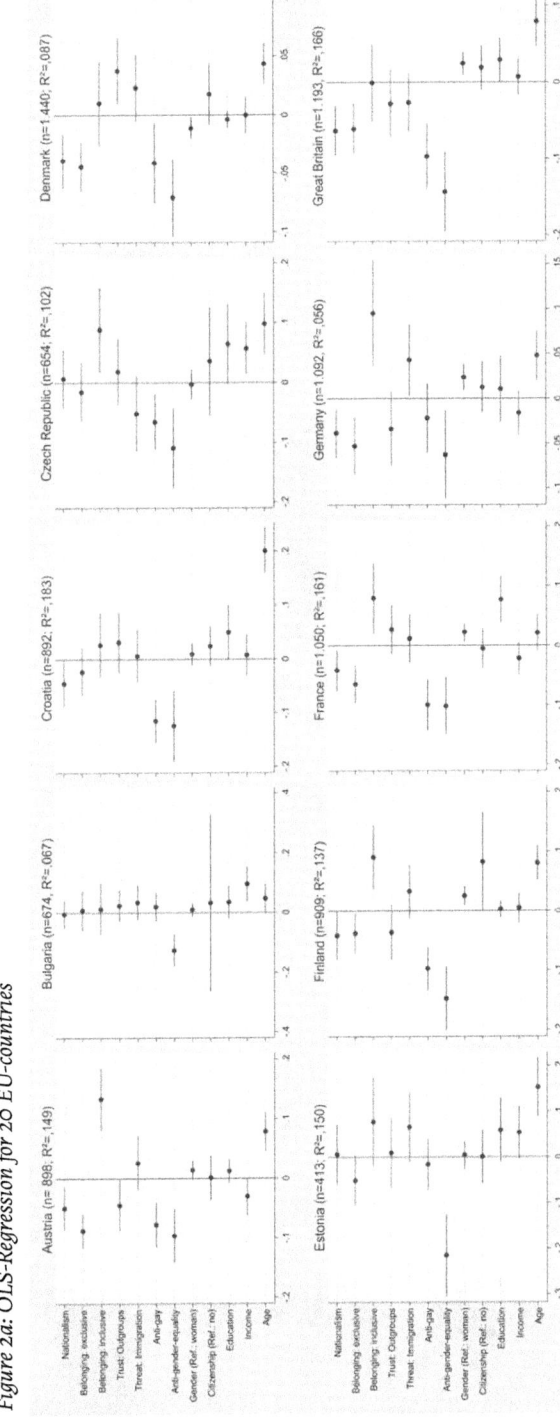

Figure 2b: OLS-Regression for 20 EU-countries

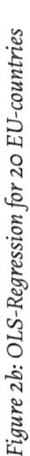

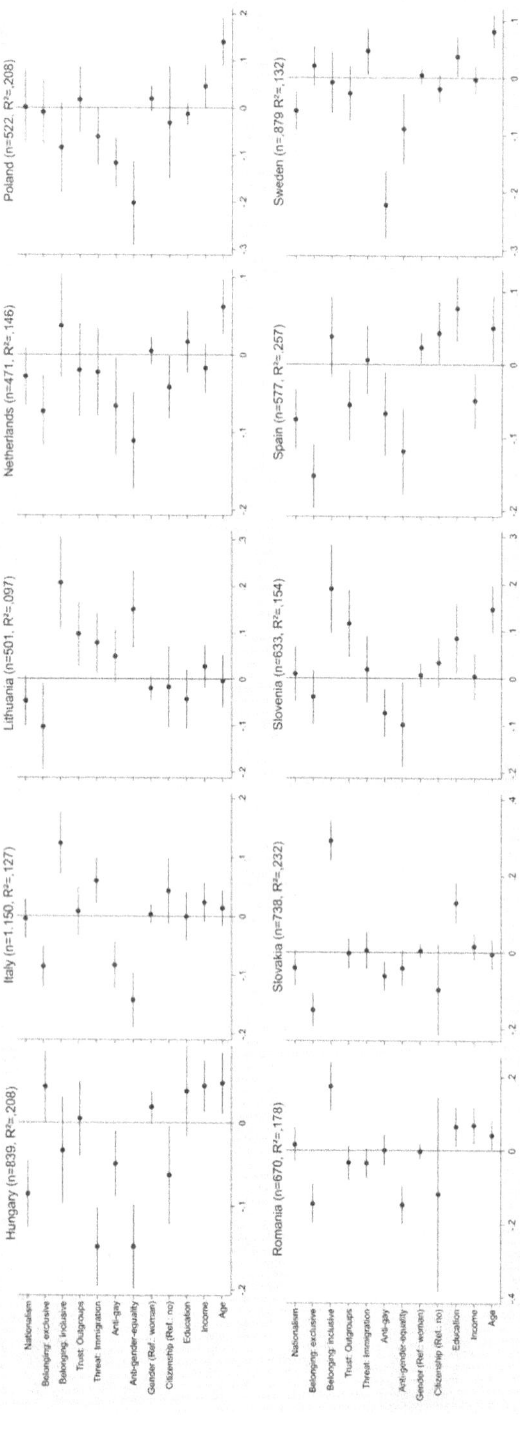

Source: EVS 2019, own illustration.

Trust in outgroups does not seem to be of great empirical importance. Only Italians, Lithuanians, and Swedes, who show a larger radius of trust, have a greater tendency towards democratic value orientation (H3). A significant effect is only observed in Austria. This result follows similar patterns as the findings for Germany, Italy, Lithuania, and Sweden regarding resentment towards immigrants. In general, only Hungary and Poland confirm the hypothesis that discriminatory attitudes towards migrants lead to anti-democratic value orientations (H4). Anti-democratic discourses on immigrants are a popular argumentation pattern containing gender equality problems as well as anti-gay attitudes, which are often attributed, for example, to Islam and Muslims (Schmitz-Vardar/Leonhardt 2019; also: Heyne 2019). However, these socially undesirable attitudes are only assigned to immigrant outgroups; this discourse does not reflect on discriminatory exclusion mechanisms of the ingroup.

This observation of trust in outgroups and resentment towards immigration is consistent with Hypotheses 5 and 6. Here, it was assumed that discriminatory attitudes towards homosexuals or women favour anti-democratic attitudes. Both relationships work in the expected direction. It is particularly striking that the effect of anti-gender-equality attitudes can be observed more frequently than anti-gay attitudes. Despite anti-gender-equality attitudes, people in Lithuania tend towards democratic value orientation. In Lithuania and Slovakia, agreement on gender equality is very high compared to the other countries under consideration. Accordingly, it can be assumed that the variable does not play a decisive role in the social climate.

Regarding the control variables, it has already been noted that formal citizenship does not seem to play a role in most cases. Also the other variables education, income, and gender rarely have a significant effect. Gender has no significant effect in 14 cases. Only in Denmark do men tend to support democratic values less than women. In Finland, France, Germany, Great Britain, and Spain the observation is the opposite. The control variable *age* is an exception to this. Older people tend share to democratic value orientation (in 15 countries). The income difference is only significantly relevant in five cases. The directions also differ: While people with higher income in Bulgaria, the Czech Republic, Hungary, and Romania tend to have democratic value orientations, the opposite is the case in Spain.

Overall, the model derived from theory only provides limited information on democratic value orientation in Bulgaria. Only the dimension of gender-equality-attitudes is relevant. All other variables are not empirically significant in this case. The model fits best in Denmark, where nationalism, an exclusive sense of belonging and anti-gay and anti-gender-equality attitudes are not compatible with democratic value orientation. Austria, Lithuania and Germany, for example, illustrate that not every theoretical assumption has empirical evidence without further context-sensitive information 8heyne 2019). Above all, the assessment of the social climate to the perceived others is important.

5.   Conclusion: Can nationalists be democratic citizens?

The nation is an »imaginary political community« to which people have an emotional attachment. This basis of collective identity serves, however, as a demarcation of presumed others at the same time. The difficulty in this context is that nations consist of plural societies. This plurality is often associated with immigration (Buonfino 2004). Therefore, the question of the boundaries of national communities arises anew because the imaginary others are part of the political entity. The guidelines of the EU do not only serve as internal self-assurance but also as external maxims for action (Schneider 2015: 313). This leads to the following question: How do including and excluding ideas of identity, trust, and belonging affect the democratic value orientation of EU citizens?

Several studies demonstrate a tension between nationalism and democracy (such as Helbing 2009). Nationalism has a Janus-faced character: On the one hand, it produces solidarity and trust as senses of belonging. For a functioning democracy, these characteristics are elementary. On the other hand, nationalism provides arguments for excluding so-called »others«. The theoretical basis for an empirical approach is political culture research (Fuchs 2002; Pickel/Pickel 2006), including socio-psychological explanatory approaches regarding the emergence of group-related prejudice (instead of many Adorno et al. 1950; Allport 1954). Political cultural research assumes that democracies are dependent on cultural anchoring in society. Following the normative-theoretical premise that democracies depend on the mutual recognition of their members as free and equal citizens (Habermas 1998), exclusive sources of national affiliation and resentment towards marginalised groups point to a lack of social support for democratic standards (Groß et al. 2012).

The findings of the empirical analysis show that the dimensions of democratic value orientation differ. This is in line with empirical observations that distinguish between desire for democracy and support for democracy (Norris 1999). The consideration of an affective bond is not sufficient as the concept of democracy allows for many different associations. Therefore, basic support is usually high – leading to a lack of variable variance to record effects – and the »democratic content« of this support remains unknown. Even within the EU, a democratic habitus is not a norm. Democratic value orientation are rarer, especially in Hungary, Slovakia, and Romania. Particularly in Slovakia and Romania, the proportion of people with an exclusive sense of belonging is also high. The three cases – just as the associated discussion of the effect of exclusive mechanisms of group identity – show very well that the context can play a decisive role when it comes to perceptions and attitudes at the individual level. However, ideas of community do not arise in a vacuum. In fact, they are always context-sensitive, which should not be neglected when conducting macro or multi-level analyses. The OLS regressions, which were determined separately for each country, show that above all, discriminatory attitudes towards women and homosexuals are a good predictor for explaining anti-democratic value orientation. This meets the expectation because these two mechanisms specifically concern ingroup dynamics.

These findings – that people tend to democratic value orientation despite having low trust in outgroups or antipathies towards immigrants – are counterintuitive and require empirical clarification. The anti-pluralism discourse fuels tensions between group-based hostility and democratic citizenship, whereas public discourse often links discriminatory statements to democratic values. Hostile positions to these values are often attributed to people of other religions, nationalities or to immigrants. Therefore, it is assumed that one need not be tolerant towards these groups. Regarding the question of whether nationalists can be democrats, it should be noted that nationalism is a necessary but not a sufficient condition for an anti-democratic habitus. This means that, as a rule, not every tendency towards nationalism goes hand in hand with an anti-democratic attitude. Still, it is never conducive to the critical-liberal advocacy of democracy.

References

Adorno, Theodor W./Frenkel-Brunswik, Else/Levinson, Daniel J. (ed.) (1950): The Authoritarian Personality. Studies in Prejudice, New York: Harper & Brothers.

Allport, Gordon W. (1954): The Nature of Prejudice. Oxford, England: Addison-Wesley.

Almond, Gabriel A./Verba, Sidney (1963): The Civic Culture. Political Attitudes and Democracy in Five Nations. Princeton, New Jersey: Princeton University Press.

Anderson, Benedict (1991): Imagined Communities. Reflections on the Origin and Spread of Nationalism, London/New York: Verso.

Bourdieu, Pierre (2002): Habitus. In: Emma Rooksby, Habitus: A Sense of Place, London: Routledge, 43-51.

Brubaker, Rogers (1992): Citizenship and Nationhood in France and Germany, Cambridge/London: Harvard University Press.

Buonfino, Alessandra (2004): Between Unity and Plurality: The Politicization and Securitization of the Discourse of Immigration in Europe. New Political Science 26 (1): 23-49. https://doi:10.1080/0739314042000185111

Cho, Youngho (2015): How Well are Global Citizenries Informed about Democracy? Ascertaining the Breadth and Distribution of Their Democratic Enlightenment and its Sources. Political Studies 63: 240-258. https://doi:10.1111/1467-9248.12088

Coppedge, Michael/Gerring, John/Knutsen, Carl Henrik (eds.) (2019): V-Dem Country-Year Dataset 2019.

Dahl, Robert A. (1972): Polyarchy. Participation and Opposition, New Haven: Yale University Press.

Easton, David (1965): A Systems Analysis of Political Life, New York/London/Sydney: John Wiley & Sons, Inc.

Easton, David (1975): A Re-assessment of the Concept of Political Support. British Journal of Political Science: 435-457. https://doi:10.1017/S0007123400008309

Eger, Maureen A./Valdez, Sarah (2015): Neo-nationalism in Western Europe. European Sociological Review 31: 115-130. https://doi:10.1093/esr/jcu087

Elkins, David J./Simeon, Richard E. B. (1979): A Cause in Search of Its Effect, or What Does Political Culture Explain? Comparative Politics 11: 127-145. https://doi:10.2307/421752

EVS (2019): European Values Study 2017: Integrated Dataset (EVS 2017). GESIS Data Archive, Cologne. ZA7500 Data file Version 2.0.0, https://doi:10.423 2/1.13314

Foroutan, Naika (2019): The Post-migrant Paradigm. In: Jan-Jonathan Bock/Sharon Macdonald (eds.) Refugees welcome? Difference and diversity in a changing Germany, New York/Oxford: Berghahn Books, 142-167.

Fuchs, Dieter (2002): Das Konzept der politischen Kultur: Die Fortsetzung einer Kontroverse in konstruktiver Absicht. In: Dieter Fuchs/Edeltraud Roller/Bernhard Weßels (eds.): Bürger und Demokratie in Ost und West. Studien zur politischen Kultur und zum politischen Prozess, Wiesbaden: VS Verlag, 27-49.

Fukuyama, Francis (2018): Why National Identity Matters. Journal of Democracy 29: 5-15. https://doi:10.1353/jod.2018.0058

Gat, Azar (2012): Nations. The Long History and Deep Roots of Political Ethnicity and Nationalism, Cambridge: Cambridge University Press.

Groß, Eva/Zick, Andreas/Krause, Daniela (2012): Von der Ungleichwertigkeit zur Ungleichheit: Gruppenbezogene Menschenfeindlichkeit. Aus Politik und Zeitgeschichte 62: 11-18.

Habermas, Jürgen (1998): The Inclusion of the Other. Studies in Political Theory, Cambridge: MIT Press.

Hammar, Tomas (1990): Democracy and the Nation State. Aliens, Denizens and Citizens in a World of International Migration, Aldershot: Avebury.

Helbing, Marc (2009): Nationalism and Democracy: Competing or Complementary Logics? Living Reviews in Democracy 1: 1-14.

Held, David (2006): Models of Democracy, Cambridge: Polity Press.

Heyne, Lea (2019): The Making of Democratic Citizens. How Regime-Specific Socialization Shapes Europeans' Expectations of Democracy. Swiss Political Science Review 25: 40-63. https://doi:10.1111/spsr.12338

Hjerm, Mikael (1998): National Identities, National Pride and Xenophobia. A Comparison of Four Western Countries. Acta Sociologica 41: 335-347. https://doi:10.1177/000169939804100403

Hopkins, Nick (2001): National Identity. Pride and Prejudice? The British Journal of Social Psychology 40: 183-186. https://doi:10.1348/014466601164795

Inglehart, Ronald (2003): How Solid is Mass Support for Democracy-And How Can We Measure It? APSC 36: 51-57. https://doi:10.1017/S10490965030016 89

Isin, Engin Fahri (2008): Theorizing Acts of Citizenship. In: Engin Fahri Isin/Greg Marc Nielsen (eds.): Acts of Citizenship, London: Palgrave Macmillan, 15-43.

Kelman, Herbert C. (1997): Nationalism, Patriotism and National Identity: Social-Psychological Dimensions. In: Daniel Bar-Tal/Ervon Staub (eds.): Patriotism in the Life of Individuals and Nations, Chicago: Nelson-Hall, 165-189.

Kleinbaum, David G./Kupper, Lawrence L./Nizam, Azhar/Rosenberg, Eli (2013): Applied Regression Analysis and Other Multivariable Methods, Boston: Cengage Learning, Inc.

Klingemann, Hans-Dieter (1999): Mapping Political Support in the 1990s. A Global Analysis. In: Pippa Norris: Critical Citizens. Global Support for Democratic Government, Oxford: Oxford University Press: 31-56.

Kymlicka, Will/Norman, Wayne J. (2000): Citizenship in Culturally Diverse Societies: Issues, Contexts, Concepts. In: Will Kymlicka/Wayne J. Norman (eds.): Citizenship in Diverse Societies, Oxford: Oxford University Press: 1-41.

Lauth, Hans-Joachim (2004): Demokratie und Demokratiemessung. Eine konzeptionelle Grundlegung für den interkulturellen Vergleich, Wiesbaden: VS Verlag.

Manent, Pierre (2013): Democracy Without Nations? The Fate of Self-Government in Europe, Wilmington: ISI Books.

Mummendey, Amélie/Klink, Andreas/Brown, Rupert (2001): Nationalism and Patriotism. National Identification and Out-Group Rejection. British Journal of Social Psychology 40: 159-172. https://doi:10.1348/014466601164740

Norris, Pippa (1999): Critical Citizens. Global Support for Democratic Government, Oxford: Oxford University Press.

Norris, Pippa (2011): Democratic Deficit. Critical Citizens Revisited, New York: Cambridge University Press.

Pehrson, Samuel/Vignoles, Vivian L./Brown, Rupert (2009): National Identification and Anti-Immigrant Prejudice. Individual and Contextual Effects Of National Definitions. Social Psychology Quarterly 72: 24-38. https://doi:10.1177/019027250907200104

Pickel, Gert (2018): Perceptions of Plurality. The Impact of the Refugee Crisis on the Interpretation of Religious Pluralization in Europe. In: Ulrich Schmiedel/Graeme Smith (eds.): Religion in the European Refugee Crisis, Cham: Palgrave Macmillan, 15-37.

Pickel, Gert/Pickel, Susanne (2018): Migration als Gefahr für die politische Kultur? Zeitschrift für Vergleichende Politikwissenschaft 12: 297-320. https://doi:10.1007/s12286-018-0380-2

Pickel, Susanne (2017): Unequal Democracies in Europe: Modes of Unequal Democracies in Europe: Modes of Participation, Understanding, and Perception of Democracy. In: Barbara Hahn/Kerstin Schmidt (eds.): Inequality in America. Interdisciplinary Perspectives, Heidelberg: Universitätsverlag Winter, 25-44.

Pickel, Susanne/Pickel, Gert (2006): Politische Kultur- und Demokratieforschung. Grundbegriffe, Theorien, Methoden. Eine Einführung, Wiesbaden: VS Verlag.

Pirro, Andrea L.P. (2014): Populist Radical Right Parties in Central and Eastern Europe: The Different Context and Issues of the Prophets of the Patria. Government and Opposition 49: 600-629. https://doi:10.1017/gov.2013.32

Puddington, Arch (2017): Breaking Down Democracy: Goals, Strategies, and Methods of Modern Authoritarians, Washington: Freedom House.

Putnam, Robert D. (1993): What makes Democracy work? National Civic Review 82: 101-107. https://doi:10.1002/ncr.4100820204

Rawls, John (1971): A theory of justice, Cambridge: Harvard University Press.

Schmitz-Vardar, Merve/Leonhardt, Christoph (2019): Die parlamentarische Sprache der Grenzziehung gegenüber Muslim*innen als Grenzen der Demokratie? Conference Paper: 2. DeZIM-Nachwuchstagung, 17.-19.07.2019, Universität Duisburg-Essen.

Schneider, Heinrich (2015): »Europäische Identität« – Ist das Thema abschiedsreif? Oder nötigen die Krisen zu einem neuen Begriffsverständnis? Integration 38: 306-336. https://doi:10.5771/0720-5120-2015-4-273

Stephan, Walter G./Stephan, Cookie White (1985): Intergroup Anxiety. Journal of Social Issues 41: 157-175. https://doi:10.1111/j.1540-4560.1985.tb01134.x

Tajfel, Henry/Turner, John (1979): An Integrative Theory of Intergroup Conflict. In: William G. Austin/Stephen Worchel (eds.): The social psychology of intergroup relations, Monterey: Brooks/Cole, 33-48.

Takács, Judit/Szalma, Ivett (2011): Homophobia and Same-Sex Partnership Legislation in Europe. In Equality, Diversity and Inclusion 30: 356-378. https://doi:10.1108/02610151111150627

Turner, Bryan S. (2016): We are All Denizens now. On the Erosion of Citizenship. Citizenship Studies 20: 679-692. https://doi:10.1080/13621025.2016.1191432.

van der Zwet, Arno (2015): Operationalising National Identity. The Cases of the Scottish National Party and Frisian National Party. Nations and Nationalism 21: 62-82. https://doi:10.1111/nana.12091

Welzel, Christian (2013): Freedom Rising. Human Empowerment and the Quest for Emancipation, New York: Cambridge University Press.

Welzel, Christian/Alvarez, Alejandro Moreno (2014): Enlightening People: The Spark of Emancipative Values. In: Russell J. Dalton/Christian Welzel (eds.): The Civic Culture Transformed. From Allegiant to Assertive Citizens, New York: Cambridge University Press: 59-88.

Welzel, Christian/Delhey, Jan (2015): Generalizing Trust. Journal of Cross-Cultural Psychology 46: 875-896. https://doi:10.1177/0022022115588366

Welzel, Christian/Inglehart, Ronald (2008): The Role of Ordinary People in Democratization. Journal of Democracy 19: 126-140. https://doi:10.1353/jod.2008.0009

Welzel, Christian/Kirsch, Helen (2017): Democracy Misunderstood: Authoritarian Notions of Democracy around the World. World Values Research 9: 1-29. https://doi:10.13140/RG.2.2.34471.96165

Werz, Nikolaus/Koschkar, Martin (2016): Einleitung: Regionale politische Kultur im Vergleich. In: Nikolaus Werz, Martin Koschkar (eds.): Regionale politische Kultur in Deutschland. Fallbeispiele und vergleichende Aspekte, Wiesbaden: Springer VS, 1-20.

Yuval-Davis, Nira (2011): Belonging and the Politics of Belonging. In: Janice McLaughlin/Peter Phillimore/Diane Richardson (eds.): Contesting Recognition. Culture, Identity and Citizenship, London: Palgrave Macmillan Limited, 20-35.

Zick, Andreas/Wolf, Carina/Küpper, Beate (eds.) (2008): The Syndrome of Group-Focused Enmity. The Interrelation of Prejudices Tested with Multiple Cross-Sectional and Panel Data. Journal of Social Issues 64: 363-383. https://doi:10.1111/j.1540-4560.2008.00566.x

About the authors

Markus Bayer works as a senior researcher at the Bonn International Center for Conversion (BICC). He holds a Ph. D. in Political Science from the University of Duisburg-Essen. He is specialised in the fields of resistance studies, democratic transitions, peace and conflict studies, arms control and militarization. E-Mail: markus.bayer@bicc.de.

Kathrin Behrens is a research assistant and doctoral student at the Institute for the Social Science at the Heinrich-Heine-University Düsseldorf, Germany. Her research interests are sociology of constitutions, of religion and of national identity. E-Mail: kathrin.behrens@hhu.de.

Roula Nezi is Lecturer (Assistant Professor) in political science at the University of Surrey, UK. Her research follows two broad themes: the effect of policy change on political attitudes, and the impact of economic factors on political outcomes. Her research has been published in the British Journal of Political Science, Party Politics, the Journal of European Social Policy and Electoral Studies among others. E-Mail: s.nezi@surrey.ac.uk.

Lea Rzadtki is currently a PhD student in the doctoral program »Democracy under Stress« at Leuphana University in Lüneburg. From 2014-2016 she has done an Erasmus Mundus master program in European Studies. Her research focus is on social movements and political activism. For her doctoral research, she has been working on migrant rights activism in Hamburg. She is particularly interested in the intersections between academia and activism – which she understands as spaces with the potential to question and transform power structures. E-Mail: rzadtki@leuphana.de.

Thorsten Schlee is a postdoctoral political scientist currently leading the Migration and Social Policy research Group and a project examining the changing role of migrant's organizations co-producing social security at the Institute for Work, Skills and Training (IAQ) at the University of Duisburg-Essen. His research focuses lie on constructivist state theories to grasp the nexus and the contradictions between migration control and social policy. E-Mail: thorsten.schlee@uni-due.de.

Merve Schmitz-Vardar is a doctoral researcher and lecturer at the Institute for Political Science at the University of Duisburg-Essen, Germany. Her expertise lies in comparative politics. Her main areas of interest are research of political culture in immigration societies, democratic value orientation, the discourse of migration and integration, and methods of empirical social research. E-Mail: merve.schmitz-vardar@uni-due.de.

Oliver Schwarz is a postdoctoral researcher and lecturer at the Institute for Political Science at the University of Duisburg-Essen, Germany. His expertise lies in the field of European integration. His main areas of interest are EU enlargement in Southeastern Europe, Europeanisation processes and the role of the EU as a global actor for security and peace. E-Mail: oliver.schwarz@uni-due.de.

Toralf Stark is a postdoctoral researcher and lecturer at the Chair of Comparative Political Science at the Institute of Political Science at the University of Duisburg-Essen. His research preferences include democracy research, research on political culture and political attitudes, participation research and research on political systems. E-Mail: toralf.stark@uni-due.de.

Christian Tischmeyer works at the Willy Brandt School of Public Policy at the University of Erfurt, Germany. His research interest revolves around political economies in the context of (neo)liberalism and the consequent political culture. E-Mail: christian.tischmeyer@uni-erfurt.de.

Aukje van Loon is Postdoctoral research Associate at the Chair of International Politics, Ruhr University Bochum (RUB), Germany. Research concentrates on European financial and trade governance. She is author of Domestic Politics in European Trade Policy: Ideas, Interests and Variation in Governmental Trade Positions (forthcoming) and co-editor of Global Power Europe Vol.1-2. Articles appeared in Politics and Governance, Journal of Contemporary European Studies, European Politics and Society. E-Mail: aukje.van-loon@rub.de.

Carsten Wegscheider is a PhD fellow at the Department of Political Science at the University of Salzburg. His main area of research is comparative politics with an interest in democratization, political parties as well as political sociology and psychology. In his doctoral studies, he works on citizens' discontent with liberal democracy and support for radical populist parties from a comparative European perspective. His research has been published in Politics and Governance. E-Mail: carsten.wegscheider@sbg.ac.at.

Feyza Yildirim-Sungur is a researcher at the Foundation for Migration Studies in Ankara and a PhD student at the University of Duisburg-Essen. Her specialization lies in the area of German-Turkish relations, particularly the political participation of the Turkish Diaspora living in Germany. Until she migrated to Turkey, Yildirim-Sungur was active in different political and civil society organizations Germany. E-Mail: f.feyzayildirim@gmail.com.

Social Sciences

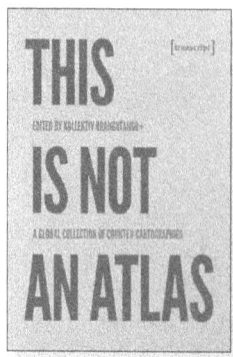

kollektiv orangotango+ (ed.)
This Is Not an Atlas
A Global Collection of Counter-Cartographies

2018, 352 p., hardcover, col. ill.
34,99 € (DE), 978-3-8376-4519-4
E-Book: free available, ISBN 978-3-8394-4519-8

Gabriele Dietze, Julia Roth (eds.)
Right-Wing Populism and Gender
European Perspectives and Beyond

April 2020, 286 p., pb., ill.
35,00 € (DE), 978-3-8376-4980-2
E-Book: 34,99 € (DE), ISBN 978-3-8394-4980-6

Mozilla Foundation
Internet Health Report 2019
2019, 118 p., pb., ill.
19,99 € (DE), 978-3-8376-4946-8
E-Book: free available, ISBN 978-3-8394-4946-2

**All print, e-book and open access versions of the titles in our list
are available in our online shop www.transcript-publishing.com**

Social Sciences

James Martin
Psychopolitics of Speech
Uncivil Discourse and the Excess of Desire

2019, 186 p., hardcover
79,99 € (DE), 978-3-8376-3919-3
E-Book:
PDF: 79,99 € (DE), ISBN 978-3-8394-3919-7

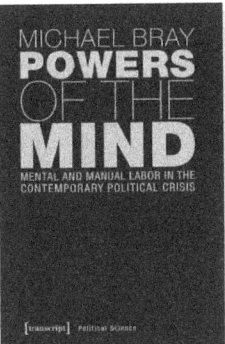

Michael Bray
Powers of the Mind
Mental and Manual Labor

in the Contemporary Political Crisis

2019, 208 p., hardcover
99,99 € (DE), 978-3-8376-4147-9
E-Book:
PDF: 99,99 € (DE), ISBN 978-3-8394-4147-3

Dorothee Brantz, Avi Sharma (eds.)
Urban Resilience in a Global Context
Actors, Narratives, and Temporalities

October 2020, 224 p., pb.
30,00 € (DE), 978-3-8376-5018-1
E-Book: available as free open access publication
PDF: ISBN 978-3-8394-5018-5

**All print, e-book and open access versions of the titles in our list
are available in our online shop www.transcript-publishing.com**

CPSIA information can be obtained
at www.ICGtesting.com
Printed in the USA
JSHW031453030421
13257JS00001B/25